Photoshop® Elements 9 FOR DUMMIES®

by Barbara Obermeier and Ted Padova

WILEY

Wiley Publishing, Inc.

Photoshop® Elements 9 For Dummies®

Published by
Wiley Publishing, Inc.
111 River Street
Hoboken, NJ 07030-5774

www.wiley.com

Copyright © 2010 by Wiley Publishing, Inc., Indianapolis, Indiana

Published by Wiley Publishing, Inc., Indianapolis, Indiana

Published simultaneously in Canada

For general information on our other products and services, please contact our Customer Care Department within the U.S. at 877-762-2974, outside the U.S. at 317-572-3993, or fax 317-572-4002.

For technical support, please visit www.wiley.com/techsupport.

Wiley also publishes its books in a variety of electronic formats. Some content that appears in print may not be available in electronic books.

Library of Congress Control Number: 2010933480

ISBN: 978-0-470-87872-9

Manufactured in the United States of America   MAR 1 9 2011

10 9 8 7 6 5 4 3 2 1

About the Authors

Barbara Obermeier is the principal of Obermeier Design, a graphic design studio in Ventura, California. She is the author of *Photoshop CS5 All-in-One For Dummies* and has contributed as author or coauthor on over two dozen books on Photoshop, Photoshop Elements, Illustrator, and PowerPoint. She is currently a faculty member in the School of Design at Brooks Institute.

Ted Padova is the former chief executive officer and managing partner of The Image Source Digital Imaging and Photo Finishing Centers of Ventura and Thousand Oaks, California. He has been involved in digital imaging since founding a service bureau in 1990. He retired from his company in 2005 and now spends his time writing and speaking on Acrobat, PDF forms, and LiveCycle Designer forms.

Ted has written more than 35 computer books and is the world's leading author on Adobe Acrobat. He has written books on Adobe Acrobat, Adobe Photoshop, Adobe Photoshop Elements, Adobe Reader, Microsoft PowerPoint, and Adobe Illustrator. Recent books published by John Wiley and Sons include *Adobe Acrobat PDF Bible* (versions 4, 5, 6, 7, 8, and 9), *Acrobat and LiveCycle Designer Forms Bible, Adobe Creative Suite Bible* (versions CS, CS2, CS3, CS4, and CS5), *Color Correction for Digital Photographers Only, Color Management for Digital Photographers For Dummies, Microsoft PowerPoint 2007 For Dummies Just the Steps, Creating Adobe Acrobat PDF Forms, Teach Yourself Visually Acrobat 5,* and *Adobe Acrobat 6.0 Complete Course.* He also co-authored *Adobe Illustrator Master Class — Illustrator Illuminated* and wrote Adobe Reader Revealed for Peachpit/Adobe Press.

Authors' Acknowledgments

We would like to thank our excellent project editor, Jean Nelson, who kept us and this book on track; Bob Woerner, our great Executive Editor; Andy Cummings, Dummies Royalty; Dennis Cohen, technical editing wizard, who made what we wrote sound better; and all the dedicated production staff at Wiley. Finally, a big thank you to Gary Sadamori and the team at Tyco Electroncis (www.tycoelectronics.com) and Elo Touch Systems (www.elotouch.com) for the use of their fabulous touch screen monitor.

Barbara Obermeier: A special thanks to Ted Padova, my co-author, and friend, who always reminds me there is still a 1 in 53 million chance that we can win the lottery.

Ted Padova: This is my 11th collaboration with Barbara, and it's always a marvelous experience to work with her. I'm indebted to Barbara and her husband Gary for all their support and assistance in helping me do my part in this book. Also, a special thanks to Malou Pelletier, Grace Curtis, Christine Plett, and Irene Windley for all their special modeling assistance.

Publisher's Acknowledgments

We're proud of this book; please send us your comments at http://dummies.custhelp.com. For other comments, please contact our Customer Care Department within the U.S. at 877-762-2974, outside the U.S. at 317-572-3993, or fax 317-572-4002.

Some of the people who helped bring this book to market include the following:

Acquisitions and Editorial

Project Editor: Jean Nelson

Executive Editor: Bob Woerner

Copy Editor: Virginia Sanders

Technical Editor: Dennis Cohen

Editorial Manager: Kevin Kirschner

Editorial Assistant: Amanda Graham

Sr. Editorial Assistant: Cherie Case

Cartoons: Rich Tennant (www.the5thwave.com)

Composition Services

Project Coordinator: Patrick Redmond

Layout and Graphics: Joyce Haughey, Kelly Kijovsky

Proofreader: Sossity R. Smith

Indexer: Cheryl Duksta

Special Help
Tonya Cupp

Publishing and Editorial for Technology Dummies

Richard Swadley, Vice President and Executive Group Publisher

Andy Cummings, Vice President and Publisher

Mary Bednarek, Executive Acquisitions Director

Mary C. Corder, Editorial Director

Publishing for Consumer Dummies

Diane Graves Steele, Vice President and Publisher

Composition Services

Debbie Stailey, Director of Composition Services

Contents at a Glance

Table of Contents

Introduction

*P*hotoshop Elements is now in its 9th version. The product has matured as a tool for both professional and amateur photographers who want to edit, improve, manage, manipulate, and organize photos and other media. Considering the power of the program and impressive features, Elements remains one of the best values for your money among computer software applications.

A wave of new hardware devices has hit the shelves this year (no doubt, with more to come in the next few years). The handhelds and iDevices provide their users many different alternatives for showing off photos, and Photoshop Elements 9 is up to the task of tossing your images into the cloud and displaying them on the latest gadgets. From touch screen support to iPhone connectivity, Photoshop Elements stays current with the times.

Why should you buy Photoshop Elements (and, ultimately, this book)? The range of people who can benefit from using Elements is wide and includes a vast audience. From beginning image editors to intermediate users to more advanced amateurs and professionals, Elements has something for everyone. We'll even stick our necks out a little and suggest that many Photoshop users can benefit greatly by adding Elements to their software tool cabinets. Why? Because Elements offers some wonderful creation and sharing tools that Photoshop hasn't yet dreamed of supporting. For example, in Photoshop Elements 9, you can create postcards, greeting cards, and photo albums with just a few mouse clicks. You can place orders with online service centers that professionally print your photo creations.

To set your frame of mind to thinking in Photoshop Elements terms, don't think of the program as a scaled-down version of Adobe Photoshop; those days are gone. Consider the following:

- **If you're a digital photographer** and you shoot your pictures in JPEG or Camera Raw format, Elements has the tools for you to open, edit, and massage your pictures into professional images.

- **If you worry about color profile embedding,** Elements can handle the task for you, as we explain in Chapter 4, where we talk about Camera Raw, and in Chapter 14, where we talk about color profiling and printing. For the professional, Photoshop Elements has almost everything you need to create final images for color printing and commercial printing.

- **If you're interested in displaying photos on online services or handheld devices,** you're in the right spot. We cover everything from copying and pasting Facebook images to connecting to an iPhone or iPad. Look over Chapters 4, 5, and 16 to find out more.

✔ **If you're a beginner or an intermediate user,** you'll find that some of the Photoshop Elements quick-fix operations are a breeze to use for enhancing your images, as we explain in Chapters 9 and 10.

✔ **If you like to print homemade greeting cards and photo albums —** whether you're a beginner, an intermediate user, or a professional user — Elements provides you with easy-to-follow steps to package your creations, as we discuss in Chapters 15 and 16. In addition, the wonderful sharing services available are your gateway to keeping family, friends, and clients connected to your photos, as we explain in Chapter 16.

About This Book

This book is an effort to provide, in about 400 pages, as much of a comprehensive view of a wildly feature-rich program as we can. Additionally, this book is written for a cross-platform audience. If you're a Macintosh user, you'll find all you need to work on Elements 9 for the Macintosh including the new support for the Organizer on the Mac.

There's a lot to Elements, and we try to offer you as much as possible within a limited amount of space. We begged for more pages, but alas, our publisher wants to get this book in your hands in full color and with an attractive price tag. Therefore, even though we may skip over a few little things, all you need to know about using Photoshop Elements for designing images for print, sharing, Web hosting, versatile packaging, e-mailing, and more is covered in the pages ahead. If you still crave more, take a look at our *Adobe Photoshop Elements 9 All-in-One For Dummies* (Wiley Publishing), where you can find more comprehensive coverage of Photoshop Elements 9.

As we said, Photoshop Elements has something for just about everyone. Hence, we know that our audience is large and that not everyone will use every tool, command, or method described in this book. Therefore, we added a lot of cross-references in the text, in case you want to jump around. You can go to just about any chapter and start reading; and, if some concept needs more explanation, we point you in the right direction for getting some background when it's necessary.

Conventions Used in This Book

Throughout this book, we point you to menus where commands are accessed frequently. A couple of things to remember are the references for where to go when we detail steps in a procedure. For accessing a menu command, you may see a sentence like this one:

Choose File➪Get Photos➪From Files and Folders.

When you see commands like this one, we're asking you to click the File menu to open the drop-down menu, click the menu command labeled Get Photos, and then choose the command From Files and Folders from the submenu that appears.

Another convention we use refers to context menus. A *context menu* jumps up at your cursor position and shows you a menu similar to the menu you select at the top of the Elements workspace. To open a context menu, right-click the mouse (Control-click on the Mac if you don't have a two-button mouse).

A third item relates to using keystrokes on your keyboard. When we mention that some keys need to be pressed on your keyboard, the text is described like this:

Press Alt+Shift+Ctrl+S (Option+Shift+⌘+S on the Macintosh).

In this case, you hold down the Alt key on Windows or the Option key on the Macintosh, the Shift key, and the Control key on Windows or the ⌘ key on the Macintosh, and then press the S key. Then, release all the keys at the same time.

How This Book Is Organized

This book is divided into logical parts where related features are nested together in chapters within six different parts of the book.

Part 1: Getting Started

If you just bought a digital camera and you're new to image editing in a program such as Photoshop Elements, you're probably tempted to jump into fixing and editing your pictures. The essentials usually aren't the most exciting part of any program or book. That's true with this book, too: The more mundane issues related to understanding some basics are assembled in the first three chapters. Although some bits of information aren't as exciting as in many other chapters, you must understand them before you start editing images. Be sure to review the first three chapters before you dive into the other chapters.

In Part I, we talk about the tools, menus, commands, preferences, workspaces, and features that help you move around easily in the program. The more you pick up in the preliminary chapters, the more easily you can adapt to the Elements way of working.

Part II: Getting Organized

In Part II, we talk about getting photos in Elements, organizing your files, searching for files, and grouping your photos, and we give you much more information related to the Photoshop Elements Organizer. The *Organizer* is your central workplace for both Windows and Macintosh users, and knowing a great deal about using the Organizer window helps you move around much faster in the program.

Part III: Selecting and Correcting Photos

Part III relates to creating and manipulating selections. There's a lot to making selections in photos, but after you figure it out (by reading Chapter 7), you can cut out a figure in a picture and drop it into another picture, drop different backgrounds into pictures, or isolate an area that needs some brightness and contrast adjustment. In Chapter 8, we talk about layers and how to create and manage them in Elements. In many other chapters, we refer you to Chapter 8 because you need to work with layers for many other tasks you do in Elements.

In Chapter 9, we talk about fixing image flaws and problems. That picture you took with your digital camera may be underexposed or overexposed, or it may need some work to remove dust and scratches. Maybe it needs a little sharpening, or another imperfection requires editing. All the know-how and how-tos are in this chapter.

In Chapter 10, we cover how to correct color problems, brightness, and contrast. We show you ways to quickly fix photos, as well as some methods for custom image corrections.

Part IV: Exploring Your Inner Artist

This part is designed to bring out the artist in you. Considering the easy application of Elements filter effects, you can turn a photo image into a drawing or apply a huge number of different effects to change the look of your image.

In Chapter 12, we talk about drawing and painting so that you can let your artistic expression run wild. We follow up in Chapter 13 by talking about adding text to photos so that you can create your own layouts, posters, cards, and more.

Part V: Printing, Creating, and Sharing

You may find yourself printing fewer photos than ever with all the online opportunities and the display devices available to you. However, when it comes time to print a photo, we provide you information on how to produce good color on your desktop color printer in Chapter 14.

If screen viewing is of interest to you, we cover a number of different options for viewing your pictures onscreen in Chapter 15. For slide shows, Web-hosted images, animated images, photo viewing on your TV, and even creating movie files, this chapter shows you the many ways you can view your Elements images onscreen.

We wrap up this part with Chapter 16, in which we describe how to make creations and share files by using various online services. You have a number of different options for making creations to share or print.

Part VI: The Part of Tens

The last part of the book contains the Part of Tens chapters. We offer ten tips for composing better images and give you ten more project ideas to try with Elements.

Icons Used in This Book

In the margins throughout this book, you see icons indicating that something important is stated in the respective text.

This icon informs you that the item discussed is a new feature in Photoshop Elements 9.

A Tip tells you about an alternative method for a procedure, by giving you a shortcut, a workaround, or some other type of helpful information related to working on tasks in the section being discussed.

Pay particular attention when you see the Warning icon. This icon indicates possible side-effects you might encounter when performing certain operations in Elements.

This icon is a heads-up for something you may want to commit to memory. Usually, it tells you about a shortcut for a repetitive task, where remembering a procedure can save you time.

Elements is a computer program, after all. No matter how hard we try to simplify our explanation of features, we can't entirely avoid the technical information. If we think that a topic is on the technical side, we use this icon to alert you that we're moving into a complex subject. You won't see many of these icons in the book because we try our best to give you the details in nontechnical terms.

Where to Go from Here

As we say earlier in this Introduction, the first part of this book serves as a foundation for all the other chapters. Try to spend a little time reading through the three chapters in Part I. After that, feel free to jump around and pay special attention to the cross-referenced chapters, in case you get stuck on a concept.

When you need a little extra help, refer to Chapter 1, where we talk about using the online help documents available in Elements.

If you have questions, comments, suggestions, or complaints, go to

```
http://support.wiley.com
```

We hope you have much success and enjoyment in using Adobe Photoshop Elements 9, and it's our sincere wish that the pages ahead provide you with an informative and helpful view of the program.

Part I
Getting Started

The 5th Wave — By Rich Tennant

"Try putting a person in the photo with the product you're trying to sell. We generated a lot of interest in our eBay listing once Leo started modeling my hats and scarves."

In this part . . .

*H*ere you have it: a computer book specifically designed to help you get the most out
of a computer software program — and not just
any software program, but a powerful one with
many complicated features. You probably want to
jump in and perform some spiffy editing operations to get that prize photo looking the best you
can. Inasmuch as we try to accommodate you in
setting forth a how-to book in a nonlinear fashion,
where you can freely move around and read about
the techniques you want to use without having to
read each chapter in order, you have to understand a few basics for editing your photos.

In this first part of the book, we talk about essentials to help you fully understand all the parts
ahead. We first talk about your Photoshop
Elements working environment and describe the
many tools and features you can use for all your
Elements sessions. We also cover the very important task of getting color set for optimum viewing
on your computer monitor and explain what you
need to know about color as it relates to photo
images. Part I contains some important information that you should plan to carefully review and
understand before going too far into all the
Elements features. Don't pass up this part. Turn
the page and start getting acquainted with the
Adobe Photoshop Elements basics.

Getting to Know the Work Area

*W*hen you first launch Photoshop Elements, you arrive at a Welcome screen. The Welcome screen offers to open different editing modes and to help you start special Elements tasks.

When it comes to editing a photograph, you find quite a collection of tools, panels, buttons, and options in the Photoshop Elements Edit mode. Just a quick glance at the Elements workspace when you enter Edit Full mode shows you some of the power that Elements offers with just a click of your mouse button. With all the possibilities, navigating the Elements workspaces and engaging in an editing session can be intimidating. To ease your introduction to the many options for editing your pictures, we break them down for you in this chapter.

Elements has several work areas, and we start off by introducing you to the Welcome screen. Then, we move on to the mode you'll likely use frequently: Edit Full mode. In this mode, you can be creative with all the tools and features Photoshop Elements is known for, such as filters, drawing tools, layers, and more. We then introduce other work areas and tools you may not be as familiar with: Edit Quick mode for making common corrections to photos; Creation mode for collecting your photos into creations, such as calendars; and the Project Bin for navigating among all your open images.

Before you start working in Elements, you may find it helpful to know how to undo edits so that you can start over easily and find additional sources of help within Elements. We also explain one of the handiest ways to select tools and enter common commands: keyboard shortcuts.

Elements also has the *Organizer* (now available to both Windows and Macintosh users), a powerful tool for acquiring your images and keeping them organized. The Organizer includes features that help you view and search for images, too. We introduce the Organizer in Part II.

Launching Photoshop Elements 9

A great place to start in Elements is a central navigation area, where you can choose what mode and activity you want to engage in. Well, that's exactly what Adobe provides you when you open Photoshop Elements. It's like the command center on the Starship Enterprise, except you won't find Spock asking the computer any questions. The Welcome screen is easy to navigate and intuitive, as you can see in Figure 1-1.

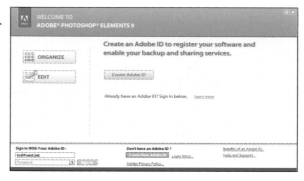

Figure 1-1: The Photoshop Elements Welcome screen (Windows) appears when you launch Elements.

Here's what you find on the Welcome screen:

✓ **Organize:** Click the Organize button to open the Organizer, where you can manage your collections of pictures stored on your hard drive. We cover using the Organizer and many of its great features in Part II.

✔ **Edit:** If you need to edit a photo, click the Edit button to access options for using either the Quick Fix mode to do some quick editing tasks or Edit Full mode, in which you can do the extraordinary editing jobs.

✔ **Learn More (Windows):** Click the Learn More button to get help information from Adobe's Web site.

If you know what you want to do in Elements, go ahead and click the appropriate button. But if you enter one mode and then decide you want to do something in another mode, Elements provides you the freedom to easily change modes from within the different workspaces.

You can always return to the Welcome screen after you enter any editing mode. At the top of the Elements window in all modes, a house icon appears, as shown in Figure 1-2. Click this icon to open the Welcome screen again.

Figure 1-2: Click the house icon on the menu bar in any editing mode to reopen the Welcome screen.

Getting Around in Edit Full Mode

Edit Full mode offers bundles of tools that you can use to edit your images, from correction tools for fixing color and clarity to filters, layers, and more for changing existing photos or creating entirely original images from scratch. But all these tools also make Edit Full mode complex.

Figure 1-3 shows Elements in Edit Full mode, highlighting all the tools and features we discuss in the following sections.

Jumping to Edit Full mode

You can move into Edit Full mode in a couple of ways:

✔ **From the initial Welcome screen:** Click Edit and open a photo. Your Elements window appears in Edit Full mode, as shown in Figure 1-3.

✔ **From the Organizer:** Click a photo and choose Edit Photos from the Fix drop-down menu. The selected file opens in Edit Full mode.

You can also open a contextual menu on a photo in the Organizer (right-click to make this menu appear) and choose Edit with Photoshop Elements from the menu.

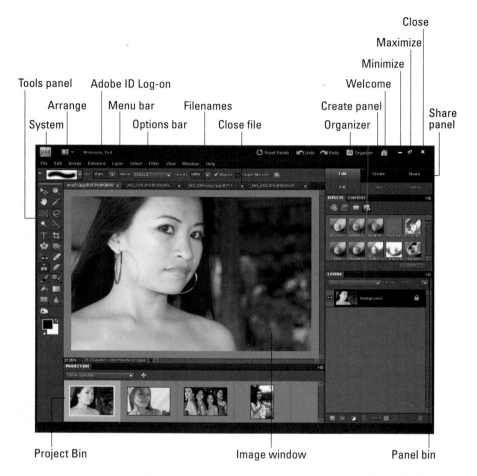

Close
Maximize
Minimize
Welcome
Tools panel   Adobe ID Log-on
Create panel
Arrange   Menu bar   Filenames   Share panel
System   Options bar   Close file   Organizer

Project Bin   Image window   Panel bin

Figure 1-3: The Photoshop Elements workspace appears when you open a file in Edit Full mode.

Examining the image window

Not surprisingly, the image window's tools and features are most useful when an image is open in the window. To get an image into the image window (as shown in Figure 1-3), follow these steps:

1. Choose File➪Open.

The standard Open dialog box appears. It works like any ordinary Open dialog box you find in other applications.

2. **Move around your hard drive by using methods you know to open folders and then select a picture.**

   If you haven't yet downloaded digital camera images or acquired scanned photos and want an image to experiment with, you can use an image found in your Pictures folder that was installed with your operating system.

   Elements installs some nice sample images with the application installation. Look in the Photoshop Elements 9\Tutorials folder to find some photos to play with.

3. **After selecting a picture, click Open.**

   The photo opens in a new image window in Elements.

You can open as many image windows in Elements as your computer memory can handle. When each new file is opened, a thumbnail image is added to the Project Bin at the bottom of the screen. (Refer to Figure 1-3.)

Notice in Figure 1-3 that filenames appear as tabs above the image window. To bring a photo forward, click the filename. To close a photo, click the X adjacent to the filename.

Here's a quick look at important items in the image window, as shown in Figure 1-4:

- ✔ **Filename:** Appears above the image window for each file open in the Editor.

- ✔ **Close button:** Click the X to the right of the filename to close the file. (On the Macintosh, click the far-left button.)

- ✔ **Scroll bars:** Become active when you zoom in on an image. You can click the scroll arrows, move the scroll bar, or grab the Hand tool in the Tools panel and drag within the window to move the image.

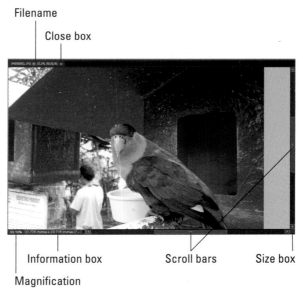

Filename

Close box

Information box   Scroll bars   Size box

Magnification

Figure 1-4: The image window displays an open file within the Elements workspace.

✔ **Magnification box:** Shows you at a glance how much you've zoomed in or out.

✔ **Information box:** Shows you a readout for a particular tidbit of information. You can choose what information you want to see in this area by selecting one of the options from the pop-up menu, which we discuss in more detail later in this section.

When you're working on an image in Elements, you always want to know the physical image size, the image resolution, and the color mode. (These terms are explained in more detail in Chapters 3 and 4.) Regardless of which menu option you select from the status bar, you can get a quick glimpse at these essential stats by clicking the Information box, which displays a pop-up menu like the one shown in Figure 1-5.

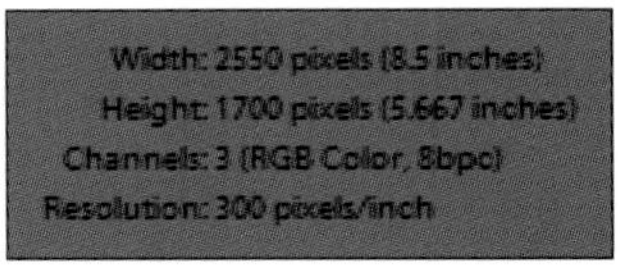

Width: 2550 pixels (8.5 inches)
Height: 1700 pixels (5.667 inches)
Channels: 3 (RGB Color, 8bpc)
Resolution: 300 pixels/inch

Figure 1-5: Click the readout on the status bar, and a pop-up menu shows you important information about your file.

✔ **Size box:** Enables you to resize the window. If you move the cursor to the box, a diagonal line with two opposing arrows appears. When the cursor changes, drag in or out to size the window smaller or larger, respectively.

You can also resize the window by dragging any corner in or out (Windows).

When you're familiar with the overall image window, we want to introduce you to the Information box's pop-up menu, which enables you to choose the type of information you want to view in the Information box. Click the right-pointing arrow to open the menu, as shown in Figure 1-6.

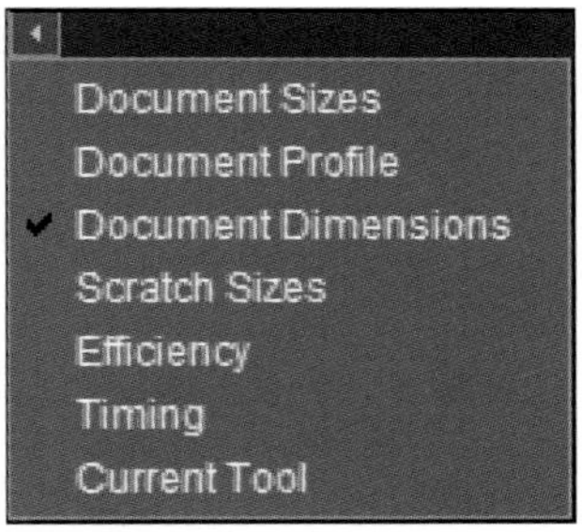

Here's the lowdown on the options you find on the pop-up menu:

Document Sizes
Document Profile
✔ Document Dimensions
Scratch Sizes
Efficiency
Timing
Current Tool

Figure 1-6: From the pop-up menu on the status bar, choose commands that provide information about your file.

✔ **Document Sizes:** Shows you the saved file size.

✔ **Document Profile:** Shows you the color profile used with the file. Understanding color profiles is important when printing files. Look to Chapters 2 and 14 for more information on using color profiles.

✔ **Document Dimensions:** When selected (as shown in Figure 1-6), this option shows you the physical size in your default unit of measure, such as inches.

- ✓ **Scratch Sizes:** Displays the amount of memory on your hard drive that's consumed by all documents open in Elements. For example, 20M/200M indicates that the open documents consume 20 megabytes and that a total of 200 megabytes are available for Elements to edit your images. When you add more content to a file, such as new layers, the first figure grows while the second figure remains static.

- ✓ **Efficiency:** Indicates how many operations you're performing in RAM, as opposed to using your scratch disk (space on your hard drive). When the number is 100%, you're working in RAM. When the number drops below 100%, you're using the scratch disk. If you continually work below 100%, it's a good indication that you need to buy more RAM to increase your efficiency.

- ✓ **Timing:** Indicates the time it took to complete the last operation.

- ✓ **Current Tool:** Shows the name of the tool selected from the Tools panel.

Why is this information important? Suppose you have a great photo you want to add to your Facebook account and you examine the photo to find the physical size of 8 x 10 inches at 72 pixels per inch (ppi). You also find the saved file size over 5 MB. At a quick glance, you know you want to resize the photo to perhaps a 4 x 6 inch size and 72 ppi. Changing the resolution dramatically reduces the file size. We cover file sizes and changing the physical dimensions of your photos in Chapter 3. For now, realize that the pop-up menu shows you information that can be helpful when preparing files for print and display.

Don't worry about trying to understand all these terms. The important thing to know is that you can visit the pop-up menu and change the items at will during your editing sessions.

Moving through the menu bar

Like just about every program you launch, Elements supports drop-down menus. The menus are logically constructed and identified to provide commands for working with your pictures (including many commands that you don't find supported in tools and on panels). A quick glimpse at the menu names gives you a hint of what might be contained in a given menu list.

Here are the 10 different menus (11 on a Mac):

- ✓ **Photoshop Elements (Mac only):** On the Macintosh, you find the Photoshop Elements menu preceding the File menu. This menu provides you the Quit command used to exit Elements, and it provides access to Edit Full Preferences, as we explain in Chapter 2.

- ✓ **File:** Just as you might suspect, the File menu contains commands for working with your picture as a file. You find commands on the menu for saving, opening, processing, importing, exporting, and printing. We cover saving files in Chapter 3 and printing or exporting for other output in Part V.

✔ **Edit:** The old-fashioned Copy, Cut, and Paste commands are located on this menu. Additionally, you have some important application settings commands on the menu, including Preferences (Windows), which we cover in more detail in Chapter 2.

✔ **Image:** You use the Image menu most often when you want to effect changes to the entire image, such as changing a color mode or cropping, rotating, and resizing the image. For details about sizing and color modes, check out Chapter 3. For more about cropping and rotating images, flip to Chapter 9.

✔ **Enhance:** Just the name of this menu should tell you what commands to expect here. This is where you go to change the appearance of an image, such as changing its brightness and contrast, adjusting its color and lighting, and doing some other smart fix-up work to improve its appearance. On the Enhance➪Adjust Color submenu, you find a number of commands that offer you a variety of color adjustments. Look to Chapter 10 for some detail on correcting color. In Chapters 9 and 10, you can find out how to use correction tools so that your images look their best.

✔ **Layer:** As we describe in great detail in Chapter 8 (a whole chapter just about layers), most kinds of editing you do in Elements are best handled by using layers. Elements neatly tucks away most of the relevant commands associated with working in layers right in this menu.

✔ **Select:** Of just about equal importance to layers are selections. Whereas the Image menu contains commands that are applied to the entire image, you can edit isolated areas of an image by using the commands on the Select menu. To isolate an area, you need to create a selection, as we explain in Chapter 7. This menu contains commands to help you with many essential tasks related to working with selections.

✔ **Filter:** The Filter menu is where you find some professional photographic darkroom techniques, or you can completely leave the world of photography and explore the world of a fine artist. With tons of different filter commands, you can create some extraordinary effects. Find out all about filters in Chapter 11.

✔ **View:** Zooming in and out of images, turning on a grid, exposing horizontal and vertical rulers, adding annotations, and checking out the print sizes of your pictures are handled on the View menu. Chapter 5 unearths secrets of the Zoom tool, rulers, and more.

✔ **Window:** Elements supports a number of different panels, as we explain in the section "Playing with panels," later in this chapter. Elements has so many panels that keeping them all open at one time is impractical. Thanks to the Window menu, you can easily view and hide panels, reopen the Welcome window, tile and cascade open windows, and bring inactive windows to the foreground.

> ✏ **Help:** We hope that you get all the help you need right here in this book; but just in case we miss something (or your neighbor has borrowed it, fine book that it is), you have some interactive help right at your mouse-tip on the Help menu. The menu also offers links to the Adobe Web site for more information and a little assistance, courtesy of the tutorials accessible from this menu. (Find a little more detail about accessing help in the section "Getting a Helping Hand," later in this chapter.)

Uncovering the contextual menus

Contextual menus are common to many programs, and Photoshop Elements is no exception. They're those little menus that appear when you right-click or Control-click on a Mac with a one-button mouse, offering commands and tools related to whatever area or tool you right-clicked.

The contextual menus are your solution when you may be in doubt about where to find a command on a menu. You just right-click an item, and a short-cut menu opens. Before you become familiar with Photoshop Elements and struggle to find a menu command, always try to first open a contextual menu and look for the command you want on that menu.

Because contextual menus provide commands respective to the tool you're using or the object or location you're clicking, the menu commands change according to the tool or feature you're using and where you click at the moment you open a contextual menu. For example, in Figure 1-7, you can see the contextual menu that appears after we create a selection marquee and right-click that marquee in the image window. Notice that the commands are all related to selections.

In Figure 1-7, notice the Transform Selection command. Photoshop Elements 9 enables you to modify selections using this command, as we explain in Chapter 7.

Using the Tools panel

Elements provides a good number of panels for different purposes. The one that you'll find you use most is the Tools panel. In panel hierarchy terms, you typically first click a tool on the Tools panel and then use another panel for additional tool options or use the Options bar (which we describe

| Deselect |
| Select Inverse |
| Feather... |
| Refine Edge... |
| Layer via Copy |
| Layer via Cut |
| New Layer... |
| Free Transform |
| Transform Selection |
| Fill Selection... |
| Stroke (Outline) Selection... |
| Last Filter |

Figure 1-7: A contextual menu for selections.

in the section "Selecting tool options from the Options bar," later in the chapter) for fine-tuning your tool instruments. More often than not, clicking a tool on the Tools panel is your first step in most editing operations.

By default, the Tools panel opens as a single row of tools down the left side of the Elements window. You can change the view to a double row of tools by clicking the right-pointing double chevron. Doing so shows all tools when you're working on smaller computer monitors.

You can easily access tools in Elements by pressing shortcut keys on your keyboard. For a quick glance at the Tools panel and the keystrokes needed to access the tools, look over Figure 1-8.

Notice on the Tools panel that several tools appear with a tiny arrowhead pointing right and downward in the lower-right corner of the tool. Whenever you see this arrowhead, remember that more tools are nested within that tool group. Click a tool with an arrowhead and hold down the mouse button, or for a faster response from Elements, just right-click a tool. The fly-out toolbar that opens, as shown in Figure 1-9, offers you more tool selections within that group.

To select tools within a tool group by using keystrokes, hold down the Shift key and strike the respective key (as shown in Figure 1-9) to access the tool. Keep the Shift key down and repeatedly press the shortcut key to step through all tools in a given group.

Whether you have to press the Shift key to select tools is controlled by a preference setting. To change the default setting so that you don't have to press Shift, choose Edit⇨Preferences⇨General (Adobe Photoshop Elements 9⇨Preferences⇨General) or press Ctrl+K (⌘+K on the Mac).

The shortcuts work for you at all times except when you're typing text with the cursor active inside a text block. Be certain to click the Tools panel to select a tool when you finish editing some text.

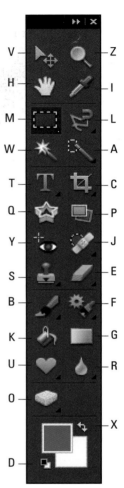

Figure 1-8: You access tools by clicking the tool on the Tools panel or typing a keyboard shortcut.

The tools are varied, and you may find that you don't use all the tools in the Tools panel in your workflow. Rather than describe the tool functions here, we address the tools in the rest of this book as they pertain to the respective Elements tasks.

Figure 1-9: Click and hold the mouse button on a tool that has a tiny arrowhead to open a pop-up toolbar.

Selecting tool options from the Options bar

When you click a tool on the Tools panel, the Options bar offers you choices specific to the selected tool. Figure 1-10 shows the options available when you select the Brush tool.

Figure 1-10: The Options bar provides attribute choices for a tool selected on the Tools panel.

Playing with panels

Elements provides you with a bunch of panels that contain settings and options used to refine the tools you select on the Tools panel and tasks you perform to edit images. Assume for a moment that you want to let your creative juices loose and create a Picasso-esque painting — something that you can do easily in Photoshop Elements.

First, click the Brush tool and then click a color on the Color Swatches panel. On a new canvas, begin to paint. When you want to change color, click again on the Color Swatches panel on a different color. This kind of interactivity between the Tools panel and another panel is something you frequently use in Elements.

You can access panels from either the Panels Bin or the Window menu. Many options on panels are intuitive. To become familiar with various panel options, just poke around a little.

You can drag panels away from the Panel Bin and scatter them all over the Elements workspace. If you remove panels and want to return to all panels docked in the Panel Bin, click Reset Panels at the top of the Editor window.

By default, you find the panel buttons for Edit Full (while in Edit Full mode), Create, and Share with the panels expanded, as shown in Figure 1-11.

You can use these panels as we explain in the following list:

Figure 1-11: The default view shows panels expanded.

- ✔ **Edit Full:** Gain quick access to editing tasks. From a drop-down menu, you can toggle editing modes. While you're in Edit Full mode, you see the button appearing as Edit Full. Open the drop-down menu and you find Edit Quick and Edit Guided. You can change editing modes by choosing one of the menu commands. If you change to Edit Quick, the tab name likewise changes to Edit Quick.

- ✔ **Create:** Click this button to access options to create photo books, photo collages, and slide shows and also to order prints and greeting cards. Click More Options on the Create panel to access additional creation options.

- ✔ **Share:** Click this button to access options that offer many different ways to share your photos with others. On the Share panel, you find options for creating an online album, sending photos via e-mail attachments, using photo and writing CDs and DVDs of photo collections and slide shows. Clicking More Options on the Share panel offers additional options for sharing photos.

 There are differences between creation and sharing options available on Windows versus the Macintosh. Windows users have more creation and sharing options than Macintosh users. For a complete list of what's available for each platform, see Chapter 15.

 Choose Window➪Panel Bin (see Figure 1-12) to remove the Panel Bin check mark, and the Panel Bin temporarily hides providing more editing space.

 When the Panel Bin is hidden, choose Window➪Panel Bin again to display the panels.

Figure 1-12: When you click panel names, the panels collapse, providing you more space to work in the image window.

Juggling all your interface options

With all the settings you can use for any given tool, trying to find the option for the edit you want to make can become downright frustrating. To help simplify the process of using tools and selecting options for the tools, here's what you might do in your normal workflow:

1. **Select a tool on the Tools panel.**

   Obviously, you need to know what task you want to perform, so selecting the proper tool to complete the task is important to know upfront.

2. **Take a quick look at the Options bar.**

   Before moving to other options, be certain that you look over the choices on the Options bar. If you want to use a tool such as the Brush tool or the Clone Stamp tool, perhaps you want to make a decision about what size brush tip you want to use. This choice is specific to the selected tool and therefore appears as an Options bar choice.

3. **Open a panel for more options.**

   If you want to use the Brush tool to apply some color to an image, for example, after you select the Brush tip on the Options bar, open the Color Swatches panel and select a color.

4. **Open a drop-down menu.**

   Not all tools support a drop-down menu on the Options bar. When you see a down-pointing arrow on a tool, click the arrow to open a menu on which you can find more options for that tool.

5. **Get some help.**

   When you hover your cursor over a tool, you see that tool described in blue text. Click the blue text, and your default Web browser opens, displaying a page on Adobe's Web site where help information and tips explain how to use the respective tool. You also find blue text on the More menu. The blue text alerts you to help information that can be shown in your Web browser.

Changing Workspaces

When you're in Edit Full mode, which we discuss in preceding sections, you can apply any kind of edits to a picture, improve the picture's appearance, and apply all that Elements offers you. This mode is the richest editor in Elements, in terms of accessing all features. Because Elements has so many different kinds of editing opportunities, the program offers you other workspace views, tailored to the kinds of tasks people typically want to perform.

Using Edit Quick mode

Edit Quick mode is designed to provide you with just those tools that you need to prepare a picture for its intended destination, whether it's printing, onscreen viewing, or one of the other organizing items. Use this mode to make your pictures look good. You don't find tools for adding text, painting with brushes, or applying gradients in Edit Quick mode. Rather, what you find is a completely different set of panels for balancing contrast and brightness, lighting, and sharpening, for example. This mode is like having a digital darkroom on your desktop, where you take care of perfecting an image like you would in analog photography darkrooms.

To enter Edit Quick mode while you're in Edit Full mode, click the Edit Full button to open the drop-down menu and choose Edit Quick; the view changes, as shown in Figure 1-13.

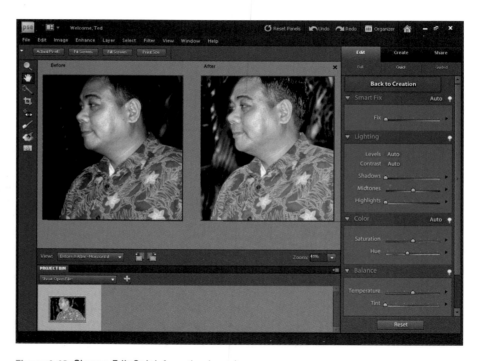

Figure 1-13: Choose Edit Quick from the drop-down menu.

Here are several differences between Edit Full mode and Edit Quick mode:

- **Completely different sets of panels are docked in the Panels Bin.** All the panels in Edit Quick mode are related to adjusting brightness controls, and they're designed to improve the overall appearance of your pictures. In addition, all the Windows menu commands for accessing panels are grayed out. While you work in Edit Quick mode, Elements insists on limiting your use of panels to just the ones docked in the Panels Bin. Moreover, you can't undock panels from the Panels Bin by dragging them out, as you can in other modes.

- **The Tools panel shrinks.** Edit Quick mode offers only these tools on the Tools panel:

  - Zoom

  - Hand

  - Magic Selection Brush

  - Crop

  - Red Eye Removal

  - Whiten Teeth

  - Make Dull Skies Blue

  - Black and White — High Contrast

  None of the other Elements tools are accessible while you work in this mode.

- **Multiple viewing options are available.** Notice in Figure 1-13 that you see two views of the same image. The Before view on the left displays the unedited image. The After view shows you the results of changes you make with panel options and menu commands. You select different viewing modes from menu choices on the View drop-down menu below the image window.

If you want to return to Edit Full mode, open the drop-down menu where you see Edit Quick, and choose Edit Full.

Using creation tools

To organize your pictures for display in a variety of different ways, begin by clicking the Create button. The panels in the Panels Bin change to support different creation options. Click one of the listed options for making a new creation or click the More Options button to select from additional options. In Figure 1-14, we clicked the Create button to open the creation options.

As you can see in Figure 1-14, the Panels Bin changed to reflect options available for many different creation tasks.

We cover each option available in the various creation panels in greater detail in Chapter 15.

Using Options Menus

Each panel in the Panel Bin and the Project Bin contains an Options menu. Click the icon in the top-right corner in a panel and you find menu commands related to the respective panel. As you travel through Elements 9 in this book, we make reference to various menu selections you need to make to perform different editing tasks. For now, realize that when we refer to a panel's Options menu, you open the menu by clicking the top-right icon, as shown in Figure 1-15.

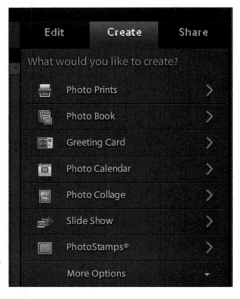

Figure 1-14: Click Create and then choose an option for the type of creation you want to edit.

Using the Project Bin

The Project Bin displays thumbnail views of all your open images. Regardless of whether you work in Edit Full or Edit Quick mode, you can immediately see a small image of all the pictures you have open at one time, as shown in Figure 1-16. You can also see thumbnail views of all the different views you create for a single picture. Find out all the details in the following sections.

If you want to rearrange the thumbnails in the Project Bin, click and drag horizontally to reorganize the order of the thumbnails.

Figure 1-15: Click the icon in the top-right corner of a panel to open the Options menu.

Creating different views of an image

What? Different views of the same picture, you say? Yes, indeed. You might create a new view when you want to zoom in on an area for some precise editing and then want to switch back to a wider view. Here's how you do it:

1. **Double-click a thumbnail image in the Project Bin.**

   You must have a photo open in Edit Full mode. The photo you double-click in the Project Bin appears in the image window as the active document.

2. **Choose View⇨New Window for *<filename>*.**

   Note that *<filename>* is the name of the file in the image window.

3. **Zoom to the new view.**

   A new view appears for the active document, and you see another thumbnail image added to the Project Bin.

   To zoom quickly, click the Zoom tool and click a few times on the picture in the image window to zoom in to the photo.

4. **Toggle views of the same image.**

   Double-click the original thumbnail to see the opening view; double-click the other thumbnail to see the zoomed view.

Figure 1-16: All open pictures and new views are displayed as thumbnails in the Project Bin.

Hiding the Project Bin

The Project Bin takes up a lot of room at the bottom of the image window, and you're not likely to want it open all the time while editing pictures. You can temporarily hide the Project Bin when you want more room in your Elements workspace for editing photos.

In Elements 9, the Project Bin behaves very similarly to other panels in the Panels Bin. Click the left-pointing chevrons to collapse the bin (Windows) or double-click the title bar (Mac). When collapsed, the bin appears as a panel button. You can drag the button off to the right side of the screen in the Panel Bin area. To reopen the bin, click the right-pointing chevrons (Windows) or double-click the title bar (Mac).

Using Bin Actions

A nice feature in Elements is the Bin Actions menu at the top of the Project Bin (Windows) or the Options menu on the far top right side of the bin (Macintosh). Click Bin Actions (Windows) or open the Options menu (Macintosh) to start a new creation, share photos, print all the files open in the Bin, and save the Bin files as an album.

To the left of the Bin Actions menu, you can find another feature for viewing files in Elements. The Show Open Files (shown by default) is another drop-down menu that offers two options: the default option to show open files and another choice to show files from the Organizer. Choose Show Files from Organizer to add the files in your Organizer to the Project Bin.

Retracing Your Steps

Ever since the Apple Macintosh brought a window-like interface to the masses, the Undo command has been one of the most frequently used menu commands in every program developed. You make a change to your document, and if you don't like it, you simply choose Edit➪Undo or press the keyboard short-cut Ctrl+Z (⌘+Z on the Macintosh).

In Elements, your options to undo your work provide you much more than reverting to the last view, as we explain in the following sections.

Using the Undo History panel

Elements takes the Undo command to new levels by offering you a panel on which all (well, almost all) your changes in an editing session are recorded and available for undoing at any step in an editing sequence.

Each edit you make is recorded on the Undo History panel. To open the panel, choose Window➪Undo History. Make changes to your document, and each step is recorded on the panel, as you see in Figure 1-17.

Figure 1-17: The Undo History panel.

If Elements slows down and you're moving along at a snail's pace, choose Edit⇨Clear⇨Undo History or choose Clear Undo History from the panel's Options menu. Elements flushes all the recorded history and frees up some precious memory that often enables you to work faster. You can also use Edit⇨Clear Clipboard or Edit⇨Clear⇨All to eliminate Clipboard data from memory.

We said *almost all* steps are recorded because the number of steps the History panel can record is controlled by a preference setting that tops out at 1,000 steps. If you choose Edit⇨Preferences (Windows) or Photoshop Elements⇨Preferences (Mac) and look at the Performance preferences, as we explain in more depth in Chapter 2, the number of *history states* (times you can go back in history and undo) defaults to 50. You can change the number to the maximum 1,000, if you like. But realize that the more history states you record, the more memory Elements requires.

When you want to undo multiple edits, open the Undo History panel and click any item listed on the panel. Elements takes you to that last edit while scrubbing all edits that follow the selected item. If you want to bring back the edits, just click again on any step appearing grayed out on the panel to redo up to that level.

All your steps are listed on the Undo History panel as long as you remain in Elements and don't close the file. When the file is closed, all history information is lost.

Reverting to the last save

While you work away in Elements, always plan on saving your work regularly. Each time you save in an editing session, the Undo History panel preserves the list of edits you made before the save and up to the maximum number of history states defined in the General preferences.

If you save, then perform more edits, and then want to return to the last saved version of your document, Elements provides you with a quick, efficient way to do so. If you choose Edit⇨Revert, Elements eliminates your new edits and takes you back to the last time you saved your file.

When you choose Revert, *Revert* appears in the Undo History panel. You can eliminate the Revert command from the Undo History panel by right-clicking Revert on the Undo History panel and choosing Delete from the context menu that appears. This command returns you to the edits made after the last save.

Getting a Helping Hand

You can reach for this book whenever you want some details about accomplishing a task while working in Elements. However, for those little annoying moments, and just in case some coffee stains blot out a few pages in this book, you may want to look for an alternative feature description from another source.

Rather than accumulate a library of Elements books, all you need to do is look within Elements to find valuable help information quickly and easily. If you're stuck on understanding a feature, ample help documents are only a mouse click away and can help you overcome some frustrating moments.

Using Help

Your first stop in exploring the helpful information Elements provides is on the Help menu. On this menu, you can find several menu commands that offer information:

- **Photoshop Elements Help:** Choose Help⇨Photoshop Elements Help or press the F1 key (Windows) or the Help key (Macintosh) to open the Elements Help file. You can type a search topic and press Enter to open a list of items that provide helpful information about the searched words.

  For quick access to the Help document, type the text you want to search into the text box on the right side of the menu bar in Edit Full or Edit Quick mode.

- **Key Concepts:** While you read this book, if we use a term that you don't completely understand, open the Photoshop Elements Key Concepts. A Web page opens in your default Web browser and provides many Web pages with definitions of terms and concepts.

- **Support:** This menu command launches your default Web browser and takes you to the Adobe Web site, where you can find information about Elements, problems reported by users, and some work-around methods for getting a job done. You can find additional Web-assisted help information by clicking Photoshop Elements Online and Online Learning Resources. The vast collection of Web pages on Adobe's Web site offers you assistance, tips and techniques, and solutions to many problems that come with editing images. Be sure to spend some time browsing these Web pages.

- **Video Tutorials:** Choose Help⇨Video Tutorials to open a Web page where videos for common tasks are hosted on Adobe's Web site.

- **Forum:** Choose Help⇨Forum to explore user comments and questions with answers to many common problems.

Using ToolTips

While you move your cursor around tools and panels, pause a moment before clicking the mouse. A slight delay in your actions produces a ToolTip. Elements provides this sort of dynamic help when you pause the cursor before moving to another location.

Getting Ready to Edit

*A*lthough not as exciting as firing up Elements and working on your precious pictures, customizing Elements for your personal work habits and properly setting up color management is critical to everything else you do in the program. This chapter explains how to take charge of Elements and customize your work environment by adjusting preference settings and setting up a color management system. If you're new to Elements or image editing in general, you might not know just how you want to set up certain features right away. However, you can always refer to this chapter when you review and update settings and options later, after you become familiar with other features in Elements.

PhotoDisc

Controlling the Editing Environment

Opening Elements for the first time is like moving into a new office. Before you begin work, you need to organize the office. At minimum, you need to set up the desk and computer before you can do anything. In Elements terms, the office organization consists of specifying Preferences settings. *Preferences* are settings that provide a means to customize your work in Elements and to fine-tune the program according to your personal work habits.

What we offer in the following sections is a brief description of the preference options available to you. When you need some detail regarding one preference option or another, look at the help documents we discuss in Chapter 1. If you use the help documents as a reference, you won't need to memorize the vast number of settings Elements provides.

There are two Preferences dialog boxes. One Preferences dialog box is available in the Edit Full mode workspace, and the other is available in the Organizer workspace. This section covers the Preferences dialog box that you open when in Edit Full mode; it's common to both Windows and the Macintosh.

Launching and navigating Preferences

Preferences, which you can access in Edit Full mode, are all contained in a dialog box that's organized into nine panes. By default, when you open the Preferences dialog box, you first see the General pane. To open the Preferences dialog box, choose Edit➪Preferences➪General. (Or choose Photoshop Elements➪Preferences➪General on a Macintosh.) Alternatively, press Ctrl+K (⌘+K on a Macintosh). Using either method opens the Preferences dialog box to the General pane, as shown in Figure 2-1.

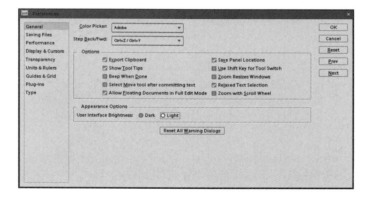

Figure 2-1: The General pane in the Preferences dialog box.

In Figure 2-1, you see items on both the left and right sides of the dialog box that are common to all preferences panes. Here's a quick introduction to what these items are and how they work:

✓ **Panes list:** Elements lists all the different panes in the Preferences dialog box along the left side of the dialog box. Click an item in the list to make the respective pane open on the right side of the dialog box. (In earlier versions of Elements, you had a drop-down menu from which you selected the different panes.)

✔ **OK:** Click OK to accept any changes made in any pane and dismiss the Preferences dialog box.

✔ **Cancel:** Click Cancel to return to the same settings as when you opened a pane and to dismiss the dialog box. If you hold down the Alt (Option on Mac) key, the Cancel button changes to Reset, and clicking that button performs the same action as clicking the Reset button.

✔ **Prev:** Switch to the previous pane.

✔ **Next:** Switch to the next pane. You can also press Ctrl+(1 through 9 keys) to jump to another pane. Or press ⌘+(1 through 9 keys) on a Macintosh.

Checking out all the preferences panes

The settings in the Preferences dialog box are organized into different panes that reflect key categories of preferences. The following list briefly describes the types of settings you can adjust in each of the preferences panes:

✔ **General preferences**, as the name implies, apply to overall general settings you adjust for your editing environment.

✔ **Saving Files preferences** relate to options available for saving files. You can choose to add extensions to filenames, save files with layers or flatten layers when you're saving a file (as we explain in Chapter 8), save files with image previews that appear when you're viewing files as icons on your desktop, and save with some compatibility options.

✔ **Performance preferences** is the pane where you find history states (explained in Chapter 1) and memory settings, such as scratch disk settings. (See the sidebar "What's a scratch disk?" in this chapter for more on scratch disks.)

What's a scratch disk?

Assume that you have 100 megabytes (MB) of free RAM (your internal computer memory) and you want to work on a picture that consumes 200MB of hard drive space. Elements needs to load all 200MB of the file into RAM. Therefore, an auxiliary source of RAM is needed in order for you to work on the image; Elements uses your hard drive. When a hard drive is used as an extension of RAM, this source is a *scratch disk*.

If you have more than one hard drive connected to your computer, you can instruct Elements to use all hard drives, and you can select the order of the hard drives that Elements uses for your extension of RAM. All disks and media sources appear in a list as 1, 2, 3, 4, and so on.

Warning: Don't use USB 1.1 external hard drives or other drives that have connections slower than USB 2 or FireWire. Using slower drives slows Elements' performance.

- ↙ **Display & Cursors preferences** offer options for how certain tool cursors are displayed and how you view the Crop tool when you're cropping images.

- ↙ **Transparency preferences** require an understanding of how Elements represents transparency. Imagine painting a portrait on a piece of clear acetate. The area you paint is opaque, and the area surrounding the portrait is transparent. To display transparency in Elements, you need some method to represent transparent areas. (Chapter 7 has more details.) Open the Transparency preferences and make choices for how transparency is displayed in your 2-D Elements environment.

- ↙ **Units & Rulers preferences** let you specify settings for ruler units, column guides, and document preset resolutions.

- ↙ **Grid preferences (Windows) or Guides & Grid (Macintosh)** offer options for gridline color, divisions, and subdivisions. A *grid* shows you nonprinting horizontal and vertical lines. You use a grid to align objects, type, and other elements. You can snap items to the gridlines to make aligning objects much easier. Guidelines can be dragged from the ruler and positioned between guidelines.

- ↙ **Plug-Ins preferences** include options for selecting an additional Plug-Ins folder for storing third-party utilities to work with Elements.

- ↙ **Type preferences** provide options for setting text attributes. You have options for using different quote marks, showing Asian characters, showing font names in English, and previewing font sizes.

Controlling the Organizing Environment

A whole different set of Preferences appears when you open the Organizer and choose Edit⇨Preferences or press Ctrl+K (Adobe Elements 9 Organizer⇨ Preferences or ⌘+K on the Mac). Initially, you may be confused because the dialog box that opens when you work in the Organizer is also named Preferences. However, a quick glance at the dialog box shows you a different set of choices. In the following sections, you can find a brief introduction to the Organizer and discover all the different organization preferences that Elements has to offer.

When you open the Edit Full or Edit Quick mode and press Ctrl+K (⌘+K on Mac) to open the Preferences dialog box, pressing Ctrl (⌘)+K+0 (zero) opens the Organizer Preferences. After you make a preference adjustment in the Organizer Preferences and click OK — or you click Cancel or press the Esc key to dismiss the dialog box — you're returned to the Editing mode's Preferences dialog box.

Understanding the Photoshop Elements Organizer

We cover all you need to know about the wonderful Adobe Photoshop Elements Organizer environment in Chapter 6, so we don't describe in this chapter all that the Organizer offers you. Just be aware that when you're setting the Organizer preferences, you're setting preferences for the Organizer only. To take a quick peek at the Organizer, click the Organizer button at the top of the Elements window while in Edit Full or Edit Quick mode.

Navigating Organizer preferences

You can open the Organizer Preferences dialog box after opening the Organizer. You can use a keyboard shortcut to open the Organizer Preferences dialog box. Press Ctrl(⌘)+0 (zero) to open the Organizer from within a Preferences dialog box in either editor to gain access to the Organizer Preferences dialog box. Alternatively, you can choose Edit⇨ Preferences (Windows) or Adobe Elements 9 Organizer⇨Preferences (Macintosh) or press Ctrl+K (⌘+K on the Macintosh) in the Organizer window to open the Preferences dialog box, shown in Figure 2-2.

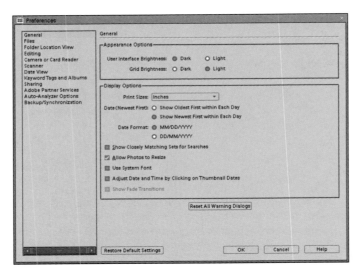

Figure 2-2: Choose Edit⇨Preferences and select a submenu item to open the Organizer Preferences dialog box shown here.

The Organizer Preferences dialog box uses the same metaphor to toggle through a number of panes that the Edit Preferences dialog box uses. Click the names in the list on the left side of the dialog box to open the respective panes on the right. At the bottom of the dialog box, you find items that are common to all panes in the Preferences dialog box. These include

- ✔ **Restore Default Settings:** Click Restore Default Settings to change all panes to their original defaults.

- ✔ **OK:** Click OK to accept new changes.

- ✔ **Cancel:** If you click Cancel in any pane, any changes you made aren't registered.

- ✔ **Help:** Click Help to open the Help window and find information about Organize & Share preferences.

Setting preferences in all the panes

With the Organizer Preferences dialog box open, here's a quick overview of what you find there:

- ✔ **General:** These items affect a miscellaneous group of settings that are applied to files when you're using the Create tool. Chapter 16 explains this tool in detail. You also find settings for changing the Interface Brightness from Dark to Light.

- ✔ **Files:** Here you find options for managing file data, connecting to missing files, setting prompts to back up your data, saving catalogs, choosing file and folder locations for saved files, rotating images, burning CD/DVDs (Windows-only), and handling preview sizes.

- ✔ **Folder Location View:** These are options for showing files and folders in groups and selected folders.

- ✔ **Editing:** You can enable another application that provides some editing features not found in Elements to edit an image based on its file type. One good example for adding another editor is when you're editing video clips. If you have Adobe Premiere Elements, you can add Premiere Elements as another editor. If you don't have Premiere Elements installed, you can use another editor, such as Windows Movie Maker (Windows) or iMovie (Macintosh).

- ✔ **Camera or Card Reader:** Here you can determine how to handle acquiring images from digital cameras and media storage cards. Your computer may have a built-in card reader in which you can insert a media card, such as CompactFlash or Smart Media, or a USB card reader that supports a media card. In other cases, you may have a cable that connects from your camera to a USB port on your computer. Use these preferences with media cards, camera connections, and download options.

- ✔ **Scanner (Windows):** If you scan images with a scanner connected to your computer, the Scanner preferences hold all the options you may want to set.

- ✔ **Date View:** View files that you can add to the pane or from selections for a variety of holiday dates.

- **Keyword Tags and Albums:** These preferences help you find and sort your images, as we explain in much more detail in Chapters 5 and 6. Tag preferences offer options for sorting tags and icon views for tags.

- **Sharing:** The options on this preferences pane relate to sharing files via e-mail. Options are available for setting an e-mail client and adding captions to e-mailed files.

- **Adobe Partner Services:** These preferences offer choices for handling program updates and online service orders. You can choose to check for program updates automatically or manually, choose options for printing and sharing images, and specify how you want to update creations, accounts, and more.

- **Media-Analysis options:** Media-Analysis performs automatic analysis of media in a catalog — things like analyzing photos with people in the images. You can turn off Media-Analysis in this pane.

- **Backup/Synchronization:** You have a choice here to sign in with your Adobe ID account. Once signed in, you can back up photos to your library on Photoshop.com.

Customizing Presets

Part of the fun of image editing is choosing brush tips, swatch colors, gradient colors, and patterns to create the look you want. To get you started, Elements provides you with a number of preset libraries that you can load and use at your will. For example, you can load a Brushes library to acquire different brush tips you use with the Brush tool. But you're likely to want to customize the preset libraries at least a little bit, too.

You can change libraries individually in respective panels where the items are used. For example, you can change color swatch libraries on the Color Swatches panel or brush tips libraries from Options bar choices. Another way you can change libraries is to use the Preset Manager dialog box, as shown in Figure 2-3.

We cover using the presets in Chapter 12, which is where you can find out how to use the many different presets that Elements provides.

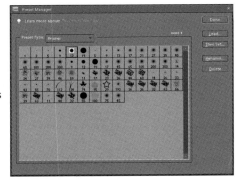

Figure 2-3: The Preset Manager dialog box provides a central area where you can change libraries.

The important thing to note here is that you can change the presets according to your editing needs.

To open the Preset Manager dialog box, choose Edit➪Preset Manager. The options you have available include

- ✔ **Learn More About: The Preset Manager:** Click the blue Preset Manager hyperlinked text to open the Help document and find out more about managing presets.

- ✔ **Preset Type:** Open the drop-down menu to choose from Brushes, Swatches, Gradients, and Patterns.

- ✔ **More:** The More drop-down menu lists different viewing options. You can view the library items as text lists or as thumbnail views.

- ✔ **Done:** Any changes you make in the Preset Manager are recorded and saved when you click Done.

- ✔ **Load:** Click this button to open another library. Elements provides you with several libraries for each preset type from which to choose.

- ✔ **Save Set:** You can save any changes you make in the Preset Manager as a new library. If you make a change, use this option so that you don't disturb the original presets.

- ✔ **Rename:** Each item in a library has a unique name. If you want to rename an item, click the thumbnail in the Preview pane, click Rename, and type a new name in the dialog box that appears.

- ✔ **Delete:** Click an item in the Preview window and click Delete to remove the item from the library.

Getting Familiar with Color

We could spend a whole lot of time and many pages in this book delving into the complex world of color theory and definitions. You wouldn't likely read it, and we're not so inclined to reduce this book from a real page-turner to something that's likely to sedate you. Rather, in the following sections, we offer some fundamental principles to make your work in Elements easier when you're editing color images.

Introducing color channels

Your first level of understanding color is to understand what RGB is and how it comes about. *RGB* stands for *red, green,* and *blue.* These are the primary colors in the computer world. Forget about what you know about primary colors in an analog world; computers see primary colors as RGB.

RGB color is divided into *color channels*. Although you can't see the individual channels in Elements, you still need to understand just a little about color channels.

When you see a color *pixel* (a tiny square), the color is represented as different levels of gray in each channel. This may sound confusing at first, but stay with us for just a minute. When you have a color channel, such as the red channel, and you let all light pass through the channel, you end up with a bright red. If you screen that light a little with a gray filter, you let less light pass through, thereby diluting the red color. This is how channels work. Individually, they all use different levels of gray that permit up to 256 levels of light to pass through them. When you change the intensity of light in the different channels, you ultimately change the color.

Each channel can have up to 256 levels of gray that mask out light. The total number of possibilities for creating color in an RGB model is achieved by multiplying the values for each channel ($256 \times 256 \times 256$). The result is more than 16.7 million; that's the total number of colors a computer monitor can display in RGB color.

This is all well and good as far as theory goes, but what does that mean in practicality? Actually, you see some of this information in Elements tools and dialog boxes. As an experiment, open a file in Elements and choose Enhance⇨Adjust Lighting⇨Levels; the dialog box shown in Figure 2-4 opens.

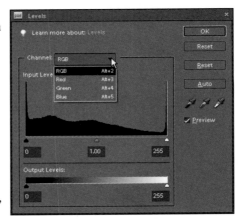

Notice that the Channel drop-down menu shows you Red, Green, and Blue as individual channels, as well as a composite RGB selection. Furthermore, the Output Levels area shows you values ranging from 0 on the left to 255 on the right. Considering that 0 is a number, you have a total of 256 different levels of gray.

Figure 2-4: Choose Enhance⇨Adjust Lighting⇨ Levels to open the Levels dialog box shown here.

What's important is that you know that your work in color is related to RGB images that comprise three different channels. There are 256 levels of gray that can let through or hold back light and change brightness values and color. See Chapters 9 and 10 for more on using tools, such as levels, to adjust color in this way.

Understanding bit depth

Another important item to understand about channels is bit depth. A *bit* holds one of two values; one value is for black, the other for white. When you have 256 levels of gray, you're working with an 8-bit-per-channel image — 8 bits with two possible values each is 2^8, or 256, possible levels of gray. Multiply 8 bits per channel times 3 channels (the red, green, and blue channels), and you get 24 bits, which is the common bit depth of images you print on your desktop printer.

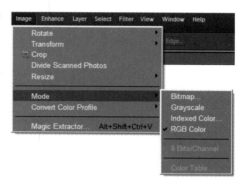

Now, take a look at the Image⇨Mode menu. You should see a menu selection that says 8 Bits/Channel. When you open an image in Elements, if this menu command is grayed out as shown in Figure 2-5, you're working with a 24-bit image, or an image of 8 bits per channel.

What does it mean when you can select the 8 Bits/Channel menu command? You can be certain that your image isn't an 8-bit-per-channel image. You may be able to select this command because some digital cameras and most low-end, consumer-grade scanners can capture images at higher bit depths. You can scan

Figure 2-5: When you can choose 8 Bits/Channel, your image bit depth is higher than 8 bits per channel.

a photo on a scanner at 16 bits per channel. When you do, you end up with many more levels of gray. When you take a picture with a quality digital camera, you can capture 16-bit-per-channel images, and you end up with a file containing more than 4,000 levels of gray. That's a lot!

Now, here's the catch. All files need to be reduced to 8 bits per channel before you print them because that's all the information any printer uses. In addition, many tools, commands, and panel options work only with 8-bit-per-channel images. So, you ask, "What's the benefit of acquiring images at higher bit depths than I can print them?"

If you attempt to adjust brightness and contrast, or other image enhancements, in an 8-bit-per-channel image, you often destroy some data. You can cause some noticeable image degradation if you move adjustment sliders too far while working with 8-bit-per-channel images. When you edit your 16-bit and 32-bit images, you don't destroy data — you simply inform Elements which 256 of the total available levels of gray you want to use. The result is an image with more continuous gray tones than you can achieve in 8-bit-per-channel images. (The following section explains how you change an image's bit depth.)

To clarify the advantages of working with 16-bit images, take a look at the effects of adjusting photos in 8-bit versus 16-bit modes. In Chapters 9 and 10 we talk about using the Enhance menu commands and, more specifically, using the Levels dialog box to adjust image brightness. Before you jump to those chapters, take a look at the results you get when adjusting a photo using Levels on an 8-bit image and the same adjustment on a 16-bit image.

Take a look at Figure 2-6. This image is flat and needs a contrast boost. The first edit you need to make in Elements is a Levels adjustment. When you choose Enhance➪Adjust Lighting➪Levels or just press Ctrl+L (⌘+L on the Mac), the Levels dialog box opens.

Figure 2-6: An image that needs a contrast adjustment.

Notice in the Levels dialog box that the histogram shows no data on the far left side of the histogram in Figure 2-7.

An image with a good tonal range has data across the histogram and appears like a bell shaped graph. To make a Levels adjustment, you simply move the slider below the histogram to the right (in this image) until it appears at the beginning of the data in the graph, as you see in Figure 2-8.

If you make a similar adjustment, click OK, then reopen the Levels dialog box, you see the histogram appearing similar to what's shown in Figure 2-9. Notice that the histogram now has gaps along the graph. These gaps indicate that no data are contained in the areas where you see the white lines. In essence, you have experienced data loss.

To contrast this adjustment on an 8-bit image with the same adjustment applied to a 16-bit image, look at Figure 2-10. After making the same Levels adjustment and reopening the Levels dialog box you find a much different result. Notice the histogram displays a solid tonal range with no gaps in the graph.

The bottom line in regard to making contrast adjustments in Elements is that you're always best served by making your edits for brightness and contrast as well as for color correction on 16-bit images compared to 8-bit images.

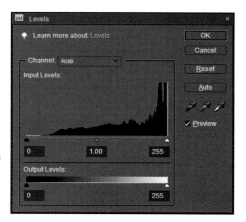

Figure 2-7: No data appear on the far left side of the histogram.

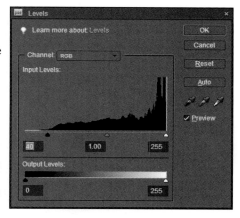

Figure 2-8: Move the left slider to the right to the point where you see the first data in the histogram.

Converting 8-bit images to 16-bit images

If you don't have a digital camera capable of capturing 16-bit images, are you limited to only working in 8-bit mode? Quite simply, the answer is no. You can convert any image taken in 8-bit mode with a digital camera or a scanner to a full 16-bit image.

Follow these steps to make the conversion from 8-bit to 16-bit mode:

1. **Open Elements in Edit Full mode.**

2. **Choose File➪Open As. In the Open As dialog box choose Camera Raw from the Open As drop-down menu.**

3. **Click Open Copy in the Camera Raw converter.**

   Don't make any adjustments in the Camera Raw converter, shown in Figure 2-11. As yet, the photo is not a true 16-bit image.

4. **Choose Image➪Resize➪Image Size to open the Image Size dialog box (shown in Figure 2-12).**

5. **Select the the check boxes for Constrain Proportions and Resample Image. Choose Percent from the Width drop down-menu and type 71 in the text box.**

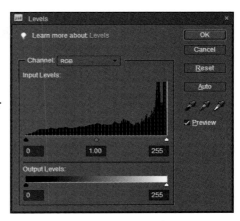

Figure 2-9: After making a Levels adjustment and reopening the Levels dialog box, you see the histogram appearing with data loss.

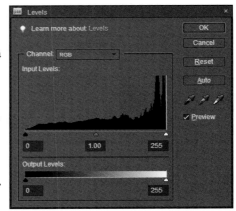

Figure 2-10: When adjusting contrast on 16-bit images, you retain a smooth tonal transition.

Figure 2-11: The Camera Raw converter.

Both the Width and Height are sized when the Constrain Proportions check boxes are selected as shown in Figure 2-12.

6. **Click OK.**

You now have a true 16-bit image.

The reason we resampled the image to 71 percent is that we needed to downsample the image 50 percent. By setting the value to 71 you get one half the number of pixels in the resultant image. Don't worry about the math, just believe us that the end result will be a true 16-bt image. You can compare adjusting Levels on an image before and after following these steps and examine the histograms to see the results.

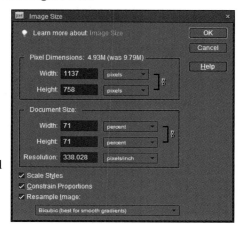

Figure 2-12: Resample the image to 71 percent.

Getting Color Right

In Elements, when it comes to color, the challenge isn't understanding color theory or definitions, but rather matching the RGB color you see on your computer monitor as closely as possible to your output. *Output* can be a printout from a color printer or a screen view on a Web page.

We say match "as closely as possible" because you can't expect to achieve an exact match. You have far too many printer and monitor variables to deal with. However, if you properly manage color, you can get a very close match.

To match color between your monitor and your output, you need to first calibrate your monitor and then choose a color workspace profile. In the following sections, you can find all the details.

Color the easy way

This section is complex and requires some serious study to follow the descriptions in the upcoming sections. If you're interested in sharing photos only onscreen (that is, on Web pages, Flickr, Facebook, Twitter, and so on) and you plan to leave the printing to others, you don't need to bother with color correction and going through a maze of steps to get the color perfected.

The only consideration you need to make is your overall monitor brightness. If your monitor displays images darker or lighter than other computers viewing your images, then you need to follow the upcoming sections and understand how to adjust your overall monitor brightness.

If, on the other hand, you adjust brightness and contrast to get a snappy good-looking photo, upload it to Facebook, and the rest of the world sees a reasonable representation of the photo, then skip all the technical stuff following this section. Your monitor is fine, and you're ready to go.

Calibrating your monitor

Your monitor needs to be calibrated to adjust the gamma and brightness, correct any color tints or colorcasts, and generally get your monitor to display, as precisely as possible, accurate colors on your output. You can choose among a few tools to adjust monitor brightness. These tools range from a low-cost hardware device that sells for less than $100 to expensive calibration equipment of $3,000 or more — or you can skip the hardware and use tools provided by Mac OS X or Windows.

Gamma is the brightness of midlevel tones in an image. In technical terms, it's a parameter that describes the shape of the transfer function for one or more stages in an imaging pipeline.

We skip the high-end costly devices and software utilities that don't do you any good and suggest that you make, at the very least, one valuable purchase for creating a monitor profile: a hardware profiling system. On the low end, some affordable devices go a long way in helping you adjust your monitor brightness and color balance, with prices ranging from $60 to $100 U.S. The best way to find a device that works for you is to search the Internet to find hardware descriptions, dealers, and costs. You'll find items such as the ColorVision Spyder2express and Pantone Huey Monitor Color Correction, to name just a few.

On LCD monitors, you need to adjust the hardware controls to bring your monitor into a match for overall brightness with your photo prints. Be certain to run many test prints and match your prints against your monitor view to make the two as similar as possible.

You have a lot to focus on to calibrate monitors and get color right on your monitor and your output. We talk more about color output in Chapter 14. For a good resource for color correction and printing using Photoshop Elements, we recommend that you look at *Color Management for Digital Photographers For Dummies,* by Ted Padova and Don Mason (Wiley).

Choosing a color workspace

After you adjust your monitor color by using a hardware profiling system, your next step is to choose your color workspace. In Elements, you have a choice between two workspace colors: either sRGB or Adobe RGB (1998). You access your color workspace settings by choosing Edit➪Color Settings. The Color Settings dialog box opens, as shown in Figure 2-13.

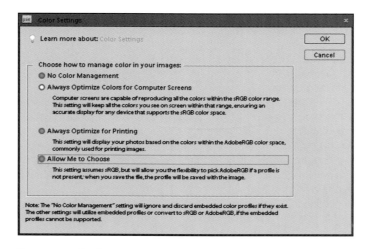

Figure 2-13: The Color Settings dialog box.

The options you have in the Color Settings dialog box include

- **No Color Management:** This choice turns off all color management. Don't choose this option for any work you do in Elements. When using No Color Management, you need to work with files that have color profiles embedded in the photos. Most likely you won't use these types of photos. For information related to when you might use the No Color Management option, see Chapter 14.

- **Always Optimize Colors for Computer Screens:** Selecting this radio button sets your workspace to sRGB. sRGB color is used quite often for viewing images on your monitor. But this workspace often results in the best choice for color printing, too. Many color printers can output all the colors you can see in the sRGB workspace. In addition, many photo services, such as the Kodak EasyShare services we talk about in Chapter 16, prefer this workspace color.

- **Always Optimize for Printing:** Selecting this option sets your color workspace to Adobe RGB (1998). The color in this workspace has more available colors than you can see on your monitor. If you choose this workspace, be certain that your printer is capable of using all the colors in this color space.

- **Allow Me to Choose:** When you choose this option, Elements prompts you for a profile assignment when you open images that contain no profile. This setting is handy if you work back and forth between screen and print images.

Understanding how profiles work

You probably created a monitor color profile when you calibrated your monitor. You probably also selected a color profile when you opened the Color Settings dialog box and selected your workspace color. When you start your computer, your monitor color profile kicks in and adjusts your overall monitor brightness and corrects for any colorcasts. When you open a photo in Elements, color is automatically converted from your monitor color space to your workspace color.

At print time, you use another color profile to output your photos to your desktop color printer. Color is then converted from your workspace color to your printer's color space. In Chapter 14, we show you how to use color profiles for printing. For now, just realize that each of these color profiles, and using them properly, determines whether you can get good color output.

3

Working with Resolutions, Color Modes, and File Formats

*W*hen you open a picture in Photoshop Elements, you're looking at a huge mass of pixels. These *pixels* are tiny, colored squares, and the number of pixels in a picture determines the picture's *resolution*. This relationship between pixels and resolution, which is important for you to understand in all your Elements work, relates to creating selections (as we explain in Chapter 7), printing files (Chapter 14), and sharing files (Chapter 16).

Color modes are also represented as collections of pixels. Color modes are important when you're using tools, and printing and sharing files.

This chapter explains some essential points about resolution, color modes, and the file formats you use to save your Elements images. We talk about changing resolution by resizing images, converting color modes, and saving the results in different file formats.

The Ubiquitous Pixels

Files you open in Elements are composed of millions of tiny, square pixels. Each pixel has one, and only one, color value. The arrangement of the pixels of different shades and colors creates an illusion to your eyes when you're viewing an image onscreen. For example, you may have black and white pixels arranged in an order that creates the impression that you're looking at something gray — not at tiny black and white squares.

Just about everything you do in Elements has to do with changing pixels. You surround them with selection tools to select what appear to be objects in your image; you make pixels darker or lighter to change contrast and brightness; you change shades and tints of pixels for color correction; and you perform a host of other editing possibilities.

We also have another term to throw at you when talking about pixels and Elements files: Your pictures are *raster images*. When you have pixels, you have raster data. If you open a file in Elements that isn't made of pixels, Elements *rasterizes* the data. In other words, Elements converts other data to pixels if the document wasn't originally composed of pixels.

You can also have vector content in an Elements file. Text added with the Type Tool, for example, is a vector object. When you save an Elements file with the Text layer intact or save as a Photoshop PDF file, the vector data is maintained. We talk more about vector data in Chapter 13. For this chapter, you just need to focus on raster data.

To use most of the tools and commands in Elements, you must be working on a raster image file. If your data isn't rasterized, many tools and commands are unavailable.

Understanding resolution

The number of pixels in a file determines its image resolution. If you have 72 pixels across a 1-inch horizontal line, your image is 72 pixels per inch (ppi). If you have 300 pixels in 1 inch, your image resolution is 300 ppi.

Image resolution is critical to properly outputting files in these instances:

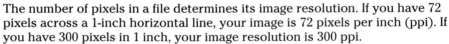

- **When you print images:** If the resolution is too low, the image prints poorly. If the image resolution is too high, you waste time processing all the data that needs to be sent to your printer.

- **When you show images onscreen:** Just like images have resolution inherent in their files, your computer monitor displays everything you see on it in a fixed resolution. Computer monitors display images at 72 ppi (or 85 or 96 ppi or higher). That's all you get. What's important to know is that you can always best view photos on your computer monitor at a 72-ppi image size in a 100-percent view.

As an example, take a look at Figure 3-1. You see an image reduced to 50 percent and then at different zoom sizes. When the size changes, the resolution display on your monitor changes. When the size is 100 percent, you see the image exactly as it will print. The 100-percent size represents the image displayed on your monitor at 72 ppi, regardless of the resolution of the file.

This relationship between the image resolution and viewing the image at different zoom levels is an important concept to grasp. If you grab an image off the Web and zoom in on it, you may see a view like the 800-percent view shown in Figure 3-1. If you acquire a digital camera image, you may need to zoom out to a 16-percent view to fit the entire image in the Image window.

The reason that these displays vary so much is all image resolution. That Web page image you grabbed off the Web might be a 2-inch-square image at 72 ppi, and that digital camera image might be a 10-x-15-inch image at 240 ppi. To fill the entire window with the Web image, you need to zoom in on the file. When you zoom in, the resolution is lowered. The more you zoom, the lower the resolution on your monitor.

When you zoom into or out of an image, you change the resolution as it appears on your monitor. No resolution changes are made to the file. The image resolution remains the same until you use one of the Elements tools to reduce or increase image resolution.

Understanding image dimensions

Image dimensions involve the physical size of your file. If the size is 4 x 5 inches, for example, the file can be any number of different resolution values. After the file is open in Elements, you can change the dimensions of an image, the resolution, or both.

When you change only the dimensions of an image (not the number of pixels it contains), an inverse relationship exists between the physical size of your image and the resolution. When image size is increased, resolution decreases. Conversely, when you raise resolution, you lower image size.

50%

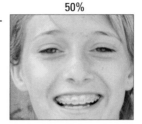

100%

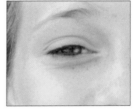

200%

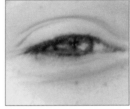

400%

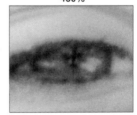

800%

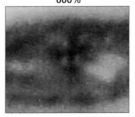

Figure 3-1: The same image is viewed at different zoom levels.

The Art of Resampling

In some cases, images are too large, and you need to reduce their resolution and physical size. In other cases, you might need a higher resolution to output your images at larger sizes. This method of sizing — changing the size, as well as the number of pixels — is *resampling* an image.

Specifically, reducing resolution is *downsampling,* and raising resolution is *upsampling.*

Use caution when you resample images; when you resample, you toss away pixels or manufacture new pixels. We discuss the sampling details in the section "Understanding the results of resampling," later in this chapter.

Changing image size and resolution

You can change an image's size and resolution in a couple different ways. One method is cropping images. You can use the Crop tool with or without resampling images. For more information on using the Crop tool, see Chapter 9. Another method is using the Image Size dialog box, which you use in many of your editing sessions in Elements.

To resize an image with the Image Size dialog box, follow these steps:

1. **Choose Image⇨Resize⇨Image Size.**

   Alternatively, you can use the keyboard shortcut Ctrl+Alt+I (⌘+Option+I on the Mac). The Image Size dialog box opens, as shown in Figure 3-2.

   The Pixel Dimensions area in the Image Size dialog box shows the file size (such as 2.00M). This number is the amount of space the image takes up on your hard drive. The width and height values are fixed unless you click the Resample Image check box at the bottom of the dialog box.

2. **In the Document Size area, you can redefine dimensions and resolution. The options are**

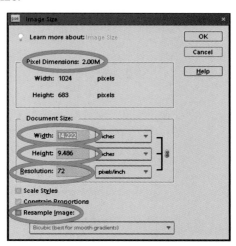

Figure 3-2: Choose Image⇨Resize⇨Image Size to open the Image Size dialog box shown here.

- *Width:* Type a value in the text box to resize the image's width and then press Tab to move out of the field to implement the change. From the drop-down menu to the right of the text box, you can choose a unit of measure: percent, inches, centimeters, millimeters, points, picas, or columns.

- *Height:* The Height options are the same as the Width options with the exception of no column setting. If you keep the sizing proportional, you typically edit either the Width or Height text box, but not both. When you alter either width or height, the resolution changes inversely.

- *Resolution:* Edit the text box to change resolution, and press the Tab key to change the value. When resolution is edited, the Width and Height values are changed inversely (if the Constrain Proportions check box is selected).

3. **If you're okay with resampling your image to get the desired size, select the Resample Image check box.**

   With this check box selected, you can change dimensions and pixels at the same time, which results in reducing or increasing the number of pixels. When the box is deselected, the values for dimensions are linked. Changing one value automatically changes the other values.

   Before you resample your image, however, be sure to check out the following section.

4. **If you select the Resample Image check box, you can choose a resampling method, as well as other resample options.**

   In the drop-down list, you find resampling-method choices. See Table 3-1 for details. The two check boxes above the Resample Image check box become active when you select the Resample Image box. Here's what they do:

   - *Scale Styles:* Elements has a Styles panel from which you can add a variety of different style effects to images. (See Chapter 11 for details.) When you apply a style, such as a frame border, the border appears at a defined width. When you select the Scale Styles box and then resize the image, the Styles effect is also resized. Leaving the check box deselected keeps the style at the same size while the image is resized.

   - *Constrain Proportions:* By default, this check box is selected, and you want to keep it that way unless you want to intentionally distort an image.

5. **When you're done selecting your options, click OK to resize your image.**

Table 3-1	Resampling Methods	
Method	*What It Does*	*Best Uses*
Nearest Neighbor	This method is fastest, and the results produce a smaller file size.	This method is best used when you have large areas of the same color.
Bilinear	This method produces a medium-quality image.	You might use this option with grayscale images and line art.
Bicubic	This method is the default and provides a good-quality image.	Unless you find better results by using any of the other methods, leave the default at Bicubic.
Bicubic Smoother	This method improves on the Bicubic method, but you notice a little softening of the edges.	If sharpness isn't critical and you find Bicubic isn't quite doing the job, try this method. This method tends to work best if you have to upsample an image.
Bicubic Sharper	This method produces good-quality images and sharpens the results.	Downsample high-resolution images that need to be output to screen resolutions and Web pages.

Understanding the results of resampling

As a general rule, reducing resolution is okay, but increasing resolution isn't. If you need a higher-resolution image and you can go back to the original source (such as rescanning the image or reshooting a picture), try (if you can) to create a new file that has the resolution you want, instead of resampling in Elements. In some cases, upsampled images can be severely degraded.

If you take a picture with a digital camera and want to add the picture to a Web page, the image needs to be sampled at 72 ppi. In most cases, you visit the Image Size dialog box, select the Resample Image check box, add a width or height value, and type **72** in the Resolution text box. What you end up with is an image that looks great on your Web page. In Figure 3-3, you can see an image that was downsampled in Elements from over 14 inches horizontal width.

WARNING!

If you start with an image that was originally sampled for a Web page and you want to print a large poster, you can forget about using Elements or any other image editor. Upsampling low-resolution images often turns them to mush, as you can see in Figure 3-4.

Figure 3-3: Downsampling images most often produces satisfactory results.

You might wonder whether upsampling can be used for any purpose. In some cases, yes, you can upsample with some satisfactory results. You can experience better results with higher resolutions of 300 ppi and more if the resample size isn't extraordinary. If all else fails, try applying a filter to a grainy, upsampled image to mask the problem. Chapter 11 has the details on filters.

Figure 3-4: Upsampling low-resolution images often produces severely degraded results.

Choosing a Resolution for Print or Onscreen

The importance of resolution in your Elements work is paramount to printing files. Good ol' 72-ppi images can be forgiving, and you can get many of your large files scrunched down to 72 ppi for Web sites and slide shows. With output to printing devices, it's another matter. There are many different printing output devices, and their resolution requirements vary.

For your own desktop printer, plan to print a variety of test images at different resolutions and on different papers. You can quickly determine the best file attributes by running tests. When you send files to service centers, ask the technicians what file attributes work best with their equipment.

For a starting point, look over the recommended resolutions for various output devices listed in Table 3-2.

Table 3-2	Resolutions and Printing	
Output Device	*Optimum*	*Acceptable Resolution*
Desktop Laser Printers	300 ppi	200 ppi
Desktop color inkjet printers	300 ppi	180 ppi
Large-format inkjet printers	150 ppi	120 ppi
Professional photo lab printers	300 ppi	200 ppi
Desktop laser printers (black and white)	170 ppi	100 ppi
Magazine quality — offset press	300 ppi	225 ppi
Screen images (Web, slide shows, video)	72 ppi	72 ppi

Go Ahead — Make My Mode!

Regardless of what output you prepare your files for, you need to consider color mode and file format. In Chapter 2, we talk about RGB (red, green, and blue) color mode. This color mode is what you use to prepare color files for printing on your desktop color printer or for preparing files for photo service centers.

You can also use color modes other than RGB. If you start with an RGB color image and want to convert to a different color mode, you have menu options for converting color. Photoshop Elements uses an *algorithm* (a mathematical formula) to convert pixels from one mode to another. In some cases, the conversion that's made via a menu command produces good results, and in other cases, you can use some different options for converting modes.

In the following sections, we introduce the modes that are available in Elements and explain how to convert from RGB to the mode of your choice: bitmap, grayscale, or indexed color.

Another mode you may have heard of is CMYK. Although CMYK mode isn't available in Photoshop Elements, you should be aware of what it is and the purposes of CMYK images. CMYK, commonly referred to as *process color,* contains percentages of cyan, magenta, yellow, and black colors. This mode is used for commercial printing. If you design a magazine cover in Elements and send the file to a print shop, the file is ultimately converted to CMYK. Also note that most desktop printers use different ink sets within the CMYK color space.

Converting to Bitmap mode

Bitmap mode is most commonly used in printing line art, such as black-and-white logos, illustrations, or black-and-white effects that you create from your RGB images. Also, you can scan your analog signature as a bitmap image and import it into other programs, such as the Microsoft Office programs. If you're creative, you can combine bitmap images with RGB color to produce many interesting effects.

The Elements Bitmap mode isn't the same as the Windows .bmp file format. In Elements, Bitmap mode is a color mode. A .bmp file can be an RGB color mode image, a Grayscale color mode image, or a Bitmap color mode image.

One important thing to keep in mind is that when you combine images into single documents, as we explain in Chapter 8, you need to convert bitmap files to grayscale or color if you want to merge the images with an RGB image. If you convert to grayscale, Elements takes care of converting grayscale to RGB mode.

As an example of an effect resulting from combining grayscale and color images, look over Figure 3-5. The original RGB image was converted to a bitmap and then saved as a different file. The bitmap was converted to grayscale and dropped on top of the RGB image. After adjusting the opacity, the result is a grainy effect with desaturated color.

You can acquire Bitmap mode images directly in Elements when you scan images that are black and white. Illustrated art, logos, your signature, or a copy of a fax might be the kind of files you scan directly in Bitmap mode. Additionally, you can convert your images to Bitmap mode.

Converting RGB color to bitmap is a two-step process. You need to first convert to grayscale and then convert from grayscale to bitmap. If you select the Bitmap menu command while in RGB color, Elements prompts you to convert to grayscale first.

Figure 3-5: You can create some interesting effects by combining the same image from a bitmap file and an RGB file.

To convert RGB mode to Bitmap mode, do the following:

1. **Open an image that you want to convert to Bitmap mode in either Edit Full or Edit Quick mode.**

2. **Choose Image⇨Mode⇨Bitmap.**

   If you start in RGB mode, Elements prompts you to convert to grayscale.

3. **Click OK, and the Bitmap dialog box opens.**

   The Bitmap dialog box provides options for selecting the output resolution and a conversion method.

4. **Select a resolution.**

   By default, the Bitmap dialog box, as shown in Figure 3-6, displays the current resolution. You can edit the text box and type a new resolution value or accept the default.

5. **From the Use drop-down menu, select from these settings:**

   • *50% Threshold*

   • *Pattern Dither*

   • *Diffusion Dither*

   Look over Figure 3-7 to see a comparison of the different methods used in converting RGB images to bitmaps.

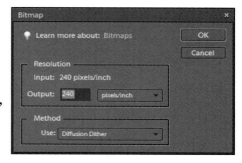

Figure 3-6: Type a resolution for your output and select the conversion method from the Use drop-down menu.

6. **Click OK to convert your image to Bitmap mode.**

Converting to Grayscale mode

Grayscale images have black and white pixels and any one of 256 levels of gray. By converting an RGB image to grayscale, you can make it look like a black-and-white photo.

You can convert an image to grayscale in one of three ways, but remember that one of these methods isn't as good as the others. We recommend that you avoid converting to grayscale by choosing Image⇨Mode⇨Grayscale. When Elements performs this conversion, it removes all the color from the pixels, so you lose some precious data during the conversion and can't regain the color after conversion. If you were to convert an image to grayscale, save the file, and delete the original from your hard drive or memory card, the color image would be lost forever. You could save a secondary file, but this method can add a little confusion and require some more space on your hard drive.

Figure 3-7: An original RGB image converted to bitmap by using 50% Threshold, Pattern Dither, and Diffusion Dither.

You don't *have* to give up your color data, though. As an alternative to using the menu command for converting images to grayscale, follow these steps:

1. **Open an RGB image in Elements.**

2. **Duplicate a layer.**

   The default Panels Bin contains the Layers panel. In this panel, you find a pop-up menu when you click the icon in the upper-right corner. From the menu commands, choose Duplicate Layer. (For more information on working with layers, see Chapter 8.)

   You can also duplicate a layer by dragging the layer name to the New Layer icon at the bottom of the Layer panel.

3. **Choose Enhance⇨Adjust Color⇨Adjust Hue/Saturation to open the Hue/Saturation dialog box, shown in Figure 3-8.**

   Alternatively, you can press Ctrl+U (⌘+U on the Macintosh).

4. **Drag the Saturation slider to the far left to desaturate the image and click OK.**

   All color disappears, but the brightness values of all the pixels remain unaffected. (For more information on using the Hue/Saturation dialog box and the other Adjust Color commands, see Chapter 10.)

5. **Turn off the color layer by clicking the eye icon in the Layers panel.**

   In the Layers panel, you see two layers, as shown in Figure 3-9. You don't need to turn off the color layer to print the file in grayscale, but turning it off can help you remember which color layer you used the last time you printed or exported the file.

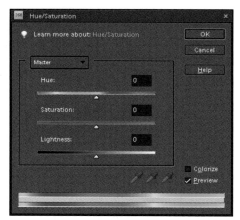

Figure 3-8: Open the Hue/Saturation dialog box and move the Saturation slider to the far left to eliminate color.

Following the preceding steps provides you with a file that contains both RGB and grayscale. If you want to print the color layer, you can turn off the grayscale layer. If you need to exchange files with graphic designers, you can send the layered file, and then the design professional can use both the color image and the grayscale image.

The other advantage of converting RGB color to grayscale by using the Hue/Saturation dialog box is that you don't disturb any changes in the brightness values of the pixels.

Figure 3-9: The Layers panel shows the grayscale and color layers. You can turn layers on or off by clicking the eye icon.

Moving the Saturation slider to desaturate the image affects only the color. The luminance and lightness values remain the same.

A menu command was introduced in Photoshop Elements 5 for converting color images to grayscale. Choose Enhance⇨Convert to Black and White in either Edit Full mode or Edit Quick mode, and you see the Convert to Black and White dialog box, as shown in Figure 3-10.

Figure 3-10: The Convert to Black and White dialog box.

This dialog box contains many controls for adjusting brightness and contrast in images that you convert to grayscale. You can select from some preset options in the Select a Style list. You move the sliders in the Adjustment Intensity area and view a dynamic preview in the After thumbnail area.

If you want to keep your original RGB image in the same file as the grayscale version, duplicate the background by choosing Duplicate Layer from the Layers panel's More menu. Click the background and choose Enhance⇨ Convert to Black and White. The conversion is applied only to the background, leaving the Background copy layer in your original color mode.

Converting to Indexed Color mode

Indexed Color is a mode you use occasionally with Web graphics, such as saving in GIF format or PNG-8. When saving indexed color images, you can, at times, create smaller file sizes than RGB that are ideal for using in Web site designs.

RGB images in 24-bit color (8 bits per channel) are capable of rendering colors from a palette of 16.7 million colors, as we explain in Chapter 2. An indexed color image is an 8-bit image with only a single channel. The total number of colors you get with indexed color can be no more than 256. When you convert RGB images to indexed color, you can choose to *dither* the color, which displays the image with a dithered effect much like you see with bit-mapped images. This dithering effect makes the file appear as though it has more than 256 colors, and the transition between colors appears smoother than if no dithering was applied.

On occasion, indexed color images have an advantage over RGB images when hosting the images on Web servers: The fewer colors in a file, the smaller the file size. When you prepare images for Web hosting, you can choose to use indexed color or RGB color. Whether you choose one over the other really depends on how well the image appears on your monitor. If you have some photos that you want to show on Web pages, you should use RGB images and save them in a format appropriate for Web hosting, as we explain in the section "Saving files for the Web," later in this chapter.

If you have files composed of artwork, such as logos, illustrations, and drawings, you may find that the appearance of index colors is no different from the same images as RGB. If that's the case, you can keep the index color image and use it for your Web pages.

To convert RGB images to indexed color, choose Image➪Mode➪Indexed Color; the Indexed Color dialog box opens. A number of different options are available to you, and fortunately, you can preview the results while you make choices. Get in and poke around, and you can see the options applied in the image window.

Saving Files with Purpose

Photoshop Elements files can be saved in a variety of different formats. Some format types require you to convert a color mode before the format can be used. Therefore, a relationship exists between file formats and saving files. Additionally, bit depths in images also relate to the kinds of file formats you can use when saving files.

Before you go too far in Elements, become familiar with file formats and the conversions that you need to make in order to save in one format or another. If you do nothing to an image in terms of converting modes or changing bit depth, you can save a file after editing in the same format in which the file was opened. In many circumstances, you open an image and prepare it for some form of output, which requires more thought about the kind of file format you use when saving the file.

Using the Save/Save As dialog box

In most any program, the Save (or Save As) dialog box is a familiar place where you make choices about the file to be saved. With Save As, you can save a duplicate copy of your image or a modified copy and retain the original file.

To use the Save (or Save As) dialog box, choose File➪Save for files to be saved the first time, or choose File➪Save As for any file, and a dialog box then opens.

The standard navigational tools you find in any Save dialog box appear in the Elements Save/Save As dialog box. Here are some standard options you find in the Elements Save/Save As dialog box:

- **Filename:** This item is common to all Save dialog boxes (Windows) or Save As (Macintosh). Type a name for your file in the text box.

- **Format:** From the drop-down menu, you select file formats. We explain the formats supported by Elements in the section "Understanding file formats," later in this chapter.

A few options make the Photoshop Elements Save/Save As dialog box different from other Save dialog boxes that you might be accustomed to using. The Save Options area in the Save As dialog box provides these choices:

- **Include in the Organizer:** If you want the file added to the Organizer, select this check box. (For more information about using the Organizer, see Chapter 6.)

- **Save in Version Set with Original:** You can edit images and save a version of your image, but only in Edit Quick mode. When you save the file from Edit Quick mode, this check box is active. Select the box to save a version of the original, which appears in the Organizer.

- **Layers:** If your file has layers, clicking this check box preserves the layers.

- **As a copy:** Use this option to save a copy without overwriting the original file.

- **Color:** Select the box for ICC (International Color Consortium) Profile. Depending on which profile you're using, the option appears for sRGB or Adobe RGB (1998). When the check box is selected, the profile is embedded in the image. See Chapter 2 for more information on profiles.

- **Thumbnail (Windows only):** If you save a file with a thumbnail, you can see a miniature representation of your image when viewing it in folders or on the desktop. If you select Ask When Saving in the Saving Files preferences, the check box can be enabled or disabled. If you select an option for Never Save or Always Save in the Preferences dialog box, this box is enabled or disabled (and grayed out) for you. You need to return to the Preferences dialog box if you want to change the option.

- **Use Lower Case Extension (Windows only):** File extensions give you a clue to which file format was used when a file was saved. Elements automatically adds the extension to the filename for you. Your choices are to use uppercase or lowercase letters for the extension name. Select the check box for Use Lower Case Extension for lowercase or deselect the check box if you want to use uppercase characters in the filename.

Saving files for the Web

You save files for Web hosting in a different dialog box than when you're saving files for other output. Choose File➪Save for Web, and the Save for Web dialog box opens. We explain all you need to know about how to use the Save for Web dialog box in Chapter 15.

Understanding file formats

When you save files in Elements, you need to pick a file format in the Format drop-down menu found in both the Save and Save As dialog boxes.

When you choose from the different format options, keep the following information in mind:

- ✔ File formats are especially important when you exchange files with other users. Each format has a purpose, and other programs can accept or reject files depending on the format you choose.

- ✔ Whether you can select one format or another when you save a file depends on the color mode, the bit depth, and whether layers are present. If a format isn't present in the Format drop-down menu when you attempt to save a file, return to one of the edit modes and perform some kind of edit, such as changing a color mode or flattening layers, in order to save the file in your chosen format.

For a glimpse at all the file formats available to you, open a standard RGB color image in Edit Full mode, choose File➪Save As, and click the down arrow to open the Format drop-down menu. As you can see in Figure 3-11, you have many format options.

In the following sections, we explain most of the file formats supported by Elements and the purpose for each format.

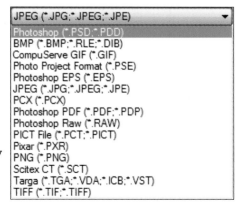

Figure 3-11: Open the Format drop-down menu in either the Save or Save As dialog box to make the formats supported by Elements appear.

Photoshop (*.PSD, *.PDD)

This format is the native file format for both Photoshop and Photoshop Elements. The format supports saving all color modes and bit depths, and you can preserve layers. Use this format when you want to save in a native format or exchange files with Photoshop users. Also use it for saving files that you need to return to for more editing. When you save layers, any text you add to layers can be edited when you return to the file. (See Chapter 13 for more information on adding text to an image.)

Alias PIX (Macintosh)

This format was introduced by Wavefront Technologies to import geometric data from ASCII files.

BMP (*.BMP, *.RLE, *.DIB)

The term *bitmap* can be a little confusing. You have both a file format type that's bitmap and a color mode that's also bitmap. Don't confuse the two. The bitmap *format* supports saving in all color modes and in all bit depths. The Bitmap *color mode,* which we cover in the section "Converting to Bitmap mode," earlier in this chapter, is 1-bit black-and-white only.

Use the bitmap format when you want to add images to system resources, such as wallpaper for your desktop. Bitmap is also used with many different programs. If you can't import images in other program documents, try to save them as BMP files.

CompuServe GIF (*.GIF)

Barb was a college coed, and Ted had a mustache and wore a green leisure suit, when CompuServe was the host for our e-mail accounts. We exchanged files and mail on 300-baud modems. Later, in 1987, CompuServe developed GIF (Graphics Interchange Format) to exchange files between mainframe computers and the ever-growing number of users working on Osborne, Kaypro, Apple, and Radio Shack TRS-80 computers.

GIF is now a popular format for hosting Web graphics. GIF images can be indexed color or animated images, and they support the smallest file sizes. Use this format when you need fewer than 256 colors and want to create animation in your images.

Photo Project Format (*.PSE)

Use this option when you create a project and want to save the file as a project. See Chapter 16 for more on creating projects in Elements.

Photoshop EPS (*.EPS)

Photoshop EPS (Encapsulated PostScript) files are sometimes used by graphic artists when they're designing jobs for commercial printing. The more popular format for creative professionals is TIFF, but Photoshop EPS has some advantages not found in other formats.

Depending on the color mode of your image, you have different options when you're using the Photoshop EPS file format. Select the format in the Save/Save As dialog box and click Save. If you're working on a bitmap image (1 bit), the EPS Options dialog box, as shown in Figure 3-12, opens. It offers an option to save transparency wherever white appears in your document.

Figure 3-12: When you're working on 1-bit bitmap images, this dialog box offers an option to save transparency where white appears in the document.

Notice the Transparent Whites check box. You might have a circular logo for which you want the area around the circle to appear transparent. If you import the graphical image in another program, you can see the black in the image, and all the white area is transparent and shows any background through what was white in the original bitmap image. If you save a file in a higher bit depth, the EPS Options dialog box doesn't provide an option for making whites transparent.

IFF (Macintosh)

A generic file format introduced by Electronic Arts to ease transfer of data between software produced by different companies.

JPEG (*.JPG, *.JPEG, *.JPE)

JPEG (Joint Photographic Experts Group) is perhaps the most common file format now in use. JPEG files are used with e-mail attachments and by many photo labs for printing files, and they can be viewed in JPEG viewers and directly in Web browsers. Just about every program capable of importing images supports the JPEG format. Creative professionals wouldn't dream of using the JPEG format in design layouts, but everyone else uses the format for all kinds of documents.

You need to exercise some caution when you're using the JPEG format. JPEG files are compressed to reduce file size. You can scrunch an image of several megabytes into a few hundred kilobytes. When you save a file with JPEG compression, you experience data loss. You might not see this on your monitor, or it might not appear noticeably on photo prints if you're using low compression while preserving higher quality. However, when you save with maximum compression, more pixels are tossed away, and you definitely notice image degradation.

When you save, open, and resave images in JPEG format, each new save degrades an image more. If you need to submit JPEG images to photo labs for printing your pictures, keep saving in the Photoshop PSD file format until you're ready to save the final image. Save in JPEG format when you want to save the final file for printing, and use a low compression with high quality.

When you select JPEG for the format and click Save, the JPEG Options dialog box opens, as shown in Figure 3-13. You choose the amount of compression by typing a value in the Quality text box or by moving the slider below the Quality text box. The acceptable ranges are from 0 to 12 — 0 is the lowest quality and results in the highest compression, and 12 is the highest quality that results in the lowest amount of compression.

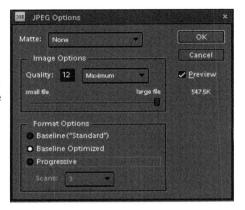

Notice that you also have choices in the Format Options area of the JPEG Options dialog box. The Progressive option creates a progressive JPEG file commonly used with Web browsers. This file type shows progressive

Figure 3-13: When saving in JPEG format, choose the amount of compression you want to apply to the saved image.

quality while the file downloads from a Web site. The image first appears in a low-quality view and shows higher-resolution views until the image appears at full resolution when it's completely downloaded in your browser window.

PCX (*.PCX)

PCX is a native PC format first used with PC Paintbrush. Most programs now support newer file formats, and you're not likely to need to save in PCX format. If you have legacy files from years ago, you can open PCX files in Elements, edit them, and save them in a newer format.

Photoshop PDF (*.PDF, *.PDP)

Adobe PDF (Portable Document Format) is designed to maintain document integrity and exchange files between computers. PDF is one of the most popular formats and can be viewed in the free Adobe Reader program available for installation on your Elements CD installer or by downloading it from the Adobe Web site.

PDF is all over the place in Elements. When you jump into Organize mode and create slide presentations, cards, and calendars, for example, you can export your documents as PDF files. When you save in Photoshop PDF format, you can preserve layers and text. Text is recognizable in Adobe Reader (or other Acrobat viewers) and can be searched by using the Reader's Find and Search tools.

PDF files can be printed, hosted on Web sites, and exchanged with users of Windows, Macintosh, Unix, and Linux. All in all, this format is well suited for all the files you create in Elements that contain text, layers, and transparency, and for when you want to exchange files with users who don't have Elements or Photoshop.

Photoshop Raw (*.RAW)

This format is used to exchange files between Windows and Mac users and mainframe computers. Unless you prepare files to be viewed on mainframes, don't bother saving in this format.

PICT File (*.PCT, *.PICT)

PICT (Picture) format is Apple's answer to PCX on Windows. This format originated with the 1984 introduction of the Macintosh and the MacDraw program. PICT files were helpful in the past for creating slides and video files on the Macintosh and for printing your images on film recorders that don't use PostScript. The format is rarely used today.

PICT Resource (Macintosh)

PICT images are stored as a Macintosh resource type. Apple Computer ended support for PICT and PICT Resource in 2009. The format is essentially not used with images today but is available for opening legacy files.

Pixar (*.PXR)

This format is used for exchanging files with Pixar workstations.

PNG (*.PNG)

PNG (Portable Network Graphics) is another format used with Web pages. PNG supports all color modes, 24-bit images, and transparency. Some older browsers, however, may need a plug-in to see PNG files on Web pages. One disadvantage of using PNG is that color profiles can't be embedded in the images, like they can with JPEG. An advantage however, is that PNG uses lossless compression, resulting in images without degradation.

Scitex CT (*.SCT)

The Scitex Continuous Tone (CT) format is used by Scitex workstations in commercial printing environments.

Targa (*.TGA, *.VDA, *.ICB, *.VST)

Targa is a format for describing bitmap images and is capable of representing bitmaps from black and white, indexed color, and RGB color. It's used for applications that can read Targa files, such as Truevision's hardware.

TIFF (*.TIF, *.TIFF)

TIFF (Tagged Image File Format) is the most common format used by graphic designers. TIFF is generally used for importing images in professional layout programs, such as Adobe InDesign and Adobe PageMaker, and when commercial photo labs and print shops use equipment that supports downloading TIFF files directly to their devices. (***Note:*** Direct downloads are used in lieu of opening a Print dialog box.)

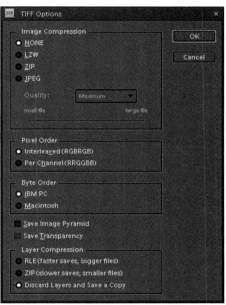

Inasmuch as creative professionals have used TIFF for so long, a better choice for designers using a program such as Adobe InDesign is saving in the native Photoshop PSD file format. This requires a creative professional to save only one file in native format without bothering to save both native and TIFF formats.

TIFF, along with Photoshop PSD and Photoshop PDF, supports saving layered files and works in all color modes. When you save in TIFF format, you can also compress files in several different compression schemes, and compression with TIFF files doesn't lose data unless you choose a JPEG compression.

When you select TIFF for the format and click Save in the Save/Save As dialog box, the TIFF Options dialog box opens, as shown in Figure 3-14.

Figure 3-14: Choose TIFF from the Format drop-down menu and click Save to open the TIFF Options dialog box.

In the Image Compression area, you have these choices:

- ✔ **NONE:** Selecting this option results in no compression. You use this option when sending files to creative professionals for creating layouts in programs such as Adobe InDesign. None of the compression schemes in the following bullets is recommended for printing files to commercial printing devices.

- ✔ **LZW:** This lossless compression scheme results in much lower file sizes without destroying data.

- ✔ **ZIP:** ZIP is also a lossless compression scheme. You can favor ZIP compression over LZW when you have large areas of the same color in an image.

- ✔ **JPEG:** JPEG is lossy and results in the smallest file sizes. Use JPEG here the same as when you apply JPEG compression with files saved in the JPEG format.

File formats at a glance

We've been working with Photoshop, which saves in the same formats listed in this section, since 1989. Yet we have never used all the formats available in Photoshop Elements. At most, you'll use maybe three or four of these formats.

You don't need to remember all the formats and what they do. Just pick the ones you use in your workflow, mark Table 3-3 for reference, and check it from time to time until you have a complete understanding of how files need to be prepared in order to save them in your desired formats. If you happen to receive a file from another user in one of the formats you don't use, come back to the description in this chapter when you need some detail on what the format is used for.

Table 3-3	File Format Attributes Supported by Photoshop Elements			
Format	*Color Modes Supported*	*Embed Profiles* Supported*	*Bit Depth Supported***	*Layers Supported*
Photoshop PSD, PDD	Bitmap, RGB, Index, Grayscale	Yes	1, 8, 24, H	Yes
BMP	Bitmap, RGB, Index, Grayscale	No	1, 8, 24, H	No
CompuServe GIF***	Bitmap, RGB, Index, Grayscale	No	1, 8	No
Photoshop EPS	Bitmap, RGB, Index, Grayscale	Yes	1, 8, 24	No
JPEG	RGB, Grayscale	Yes	8, 24	No
PCX	Bitmap, RGB, Index, Grayscale	No	1, 8, 24	No
Photoshop PDF	Bitmap, RGB, Index, Grayscale	Yes	1, 8, 24, H	Yes
Photoshop RAW	RGB, Index, Grayscale	No	8, 24, H	No
PICT File	Bitmap, RGB, Index, Grayscale	Yes	1, 8, 24	No
Pixar	RGB, Grayscale	No	8, 24	No
PNG	Bitmap, RGB, Index, Grayscale	No	1, 8, 24, H	No

Format	Color Modes Supported	Embed Profiles* Supported	Bit Depth Supported**	Layers Supported
Photoshop Multiple Page Document	Bitmap, RGB, Index	No	1, 8, 24, H	No
Scitex CT	RGB, Grayscale	No	8, 24	No
Targa	RGB, Index, Grayscale	No	8, 24	No
TIFF	Bitmap, RGB, Index, Grayscale	Yes	8, 24, H	Yes

* Embedding profiles is limited to embedding either sRGB IEC61966-2.1 or AdobeRGB (1998).

** The letter H in Column 4 represents higher-bit modes, such as 16- and 32-bit images, which you might acquire from scanners and digital cameras. See Chapter 2 for more information on higher-bit images.

*** CompuServe GIF doesn't support saving layers, although it supports saving layers as frames. You use the frames when creating an animated GIF file used for Web pages.

Audio and video formats supported in Elements

In addition to the image formats listed in Table 3-3, Elements supports audio and video files. The support is limited to adding and viewing audio and video files in the Organizer and printing the first frame in a video file. Other kinds of edits made to audio and video files require special software for audio and video editing.

Audio files can be imported in slide shows, as we explain in Chapter 15. The acceptable file formats for audio files are MP3, WAV, QuickTime, and WMA. If you have audio files in another format, you need to convert the file format. For these kinds of conversions, you can search the Internet for a shareware audio-conversion program.

Video files can also be imported in slide shows, as we discuss in Chapter 15. Elements supports the WMV (Windows) and Apple QuickTime (Macintosh) video formats. Like with audio files, if videos are saved in other formats (too numerous to mention), you need to convert the video format to a format acceptable by Elements. For video-conversion utilities, you can also find shareware programs to do the job. Search the Internet for a video converter.

Part II
Getting Organized

The 5th Wave   By Rich Tennant

"These are the parts of our life that aren't in the Photoshop Elements Organizer."

In this part . . .

The first thing you want to do after opening the Photoshop Elements program is to access your photos from a digital camera, hard drive, iPad, iPod, iPhone, or scanner. In this part, we talk about how to access your pictures and get them into Elements for editing. We talk about organizing your pictures by using many impressive organizing features in the program, as well as by searching for photos, labeling them, and then creating different versions of the same picture. New in Photoshop Elements 9 is the Organizer on the Macintosh. You can find all you need to know if you're a Mac user in working with this great tool. When it comes to organizing pictures, Elements is one of the best tools you can find to keep your precious photos neatly cataloged and accessible.

4

Getting Your Images

In This Chapter

▶ Acquiring photos from cameras and card readers

▶ Scanning photos and artwork

▶ Importing photos from CDs, DVDs, and other media

▶ Working with online services

▶ Acquiring photos from cellphones

▶ Creating new documents

▶ Working with Camera Raw files

You have many different ways to import a picture into Elements, where you can play with it, experiment on it, and edit it. If you have a digital camera, you're in the right place; we walk you through all kinds of different options for getting the shots you took with your camera into Elements.

If you have a digital scanner, you're in the right place, too! We talk about scanning photos, as well. If you have CDs, sources of files on the Internet, some massive collection of images written to a DVD, or even a picture or two that you took with your cellphone, you're still in the right place!

In Chapter 1, we flirt with opening files. If you followed the steps in those chapters for opening images, you should have a feel for using the Open tool and Open command. But there's more to acquiring images than just using the Open command, as you can find out in this chapter.

This chapter covers all you need to know about getting images into Elements from all kinds of sources and explains how to move around the workspaces to get your files into Elements.

Grabbing Images from Your Camera

Copying photos from your digital camera to your computer so that you can work with them in Elements is simple if you're familiar with your camera and the tools at your disposal. In the following sections, you find points to consider about choosing a resolution when you shoot your pictures, as well as how to use the Microsoft AutoPlay Wizard (Windows Vista/Windows 7) and Adobe Photoshop Elements 9.0 – Photo Downloader (Windows and Macintosh) after you hook up your camera to your computer.

Choosing a file format

When you work with digital photos in Elements, the file format of your images is an important point to consider. You choose this format on your camera before you take your pictures, and the format is carried over to your computer when you pull images off your camera.

The most common file formats that digital cameras offer are JPEG and Camera Raw. Some cameras offer other options, but these two formats are the most common. Low-cost point-and-shoot cameras offer you only the JPEG format, and the more expensive cameras, including the dSLR types, offer you both JPEG and Camera Raw:

- **JPEG:** Cameras that produce JPEG images process images with JPEG compression before saving them. It's as though your camera performs a darkroom method of film processing when the shot is taken.

  We describe the JPEG file format in Chapter 3.

- **Camera Raw:** This format provides you with an optimum image for editing in Elements. When a Camera Raw image is saved to a media source, all the information the sensor captured is saved with the file. These images are post-processed when you open them. (See the "A Basic Primer on Camera Raw" section, later in this chapter, to find out about opening Camera Raw images.) For example, you can open a Camera Raw image and, before the image opens in Elements, adjust temperature, exposure, and a bunch of other settings. You can return to the original Camera Raw file and change the temperature or exposure, for example, to open the file with different settings. Just like chemical temperature and development time affect analog film processing, similar options affect post-processing Camera Raw images. The difference between analog film and Camera Raw is that after your analog film is processed, you can't change the processing attributes. With Camera Raw, you can go back and post-process the image as many times as you want and change the processing attributes each time.

  Camera Raw also supports higher-bit-depth images than JPEG files do. For more understanding of higher bit-depth images, see Chapter 3.

If you have a choice between just JPEG and both JPEG and Camera Raw, always choose the latter. You have much more editing control over your images, and ultimately, you get better results.

Using the AutoPlay Wizard

Microsoft AutoPlay Wizard may launch automatically when your computer is connected to a media source. You can use the wizard to download images from your media source to your computer.

On the Macintosh, you have several options. If you have Adobe Bridge installed on your computer, the Bridge Downloader opens. You can also import photos in iPhoto and from there import photos directly into the Organizer. Your third option is to get the photos into the Organizer from a camera or card reader via a menu command. (See the section, "Getting Files from Storage Media," later in this chapter.) Finally, you can copy files from the mounted media on your desktop to a location on your hard drive by dragging from the media icon to a folder on your hard drive.

To copy images from a media source or when your camera is connected to your computer, follow these steps:

1. **Hook up the media to your computer.**

   Connect your camera or external media reader to your computer, or insert a media source into a port or drive on your computer. The methods available to you should be detailed in the user's guide that shipped with your camera.

   When you connect your media to your computer, a dialog box opens, providing options for how to handle the media. On the Mac, if you don't have applications installed such as Adobe Bridge, the Adobe Photo Downloader opens. The Adobe Photo Downloader provides options similar to the Windows AutoPlay Wizard shown in Figure 4.1.

Figure 4-1: Click the Open Folder to View Files option.

2. **In Windows, you see the AutoPlay Wizard, as shown in Figure 4-1.**

Here you have a few options. You can click Open Folder to View Files and follow the steps for copying files to your hard drive as we outline for you.

The other option you have is to click the Organize and Edit button. Clicking this button opens the Elements Organizer – Photo Downloader Wizard shown in Figure 4-2.

3. **Open the folder containing images on the media card.**

   You might find a folder listed as DCIM or another name when you open the media card in Windows. Double-click the folder name to open the folder.

4. **Select folders in Windows Explorer and drag them to a folder on your hard drive to copy them to your computer.**

   The images are copied to the target folder.

Figure 4-2: Click Organize and Edit and the Elements Organizer – Photo Downloader Wizard opens.

You can set preferences for AutoPlay by clicking the Set AutoPlay Defaults in Control Panel link in the AutoPlay dialog box. When you open the Control Panel preferences, you can choose from a number of options for handling media. If you want to prevent the AutoPlay Wizard from automatically opening, you can select Take No Actions from the media type drop-down menus. On the Mac, you make settings changes in the Image Capture application. Image Capture is an executable application residing in your Applications folder. You must have a camera or media card attached to your computer in order to make settings changes.

Using Adobe Photoshop Elements 9.0 – Photo Downloader

The Adobe Photoshop Elements 9.0 – Photo Downloader shown in Figure 4-2 is installed with your Elements program. Photo Downloader acquires images from digital cameras connected to your computer, from card readers, and from card reader ports on your computer.

To use the Adobe Photoshop 9.0 – Photo Downloader, follow these steps:

1. **Hook up the media to your computer.**

2. **Click the Organize and Edit option in the AutoPlay Wizard.**

3. **Click the Get Media button, and the photos are copied to your computer.**

   After the files are copied to your computer, the Photoshop Elements Organizer is automatically launched.

   Note that you have some options choices in the Elements Organizer – Photo Downloader Wizard for browsing a target location where you want to save your images, creating subfolders, renaming files, auto launching the Organizer (on by default), and choosing a disposition for the files after copying such as deleting or retaining them on the media card.

   You also have an advanced settings dialog box that you can open by clicking the Advanced Dialog button (in the lower-left corner in Figure 4-2, shown earlier). Poke around in this dialog box — the items are self explanatory.

 To simplify the process, stick with using one tool to acquire your digital camera images — either the Microsoft AutoPlay or the Adobe Photo Download Manager.

Resizing images from digital cameras

Depending on your camera and the camera settings you use, you may need to resize your images after you download them. Many cameras take pictures at 72 ppi, but the physical size of the image varies according to the resolution that the camera LCD is capable of acquiring. You'll frequently need to resize images taken with your digital camera. For more more information on resizing images, see Chapter 3.

Using a Scanner

Scanners connect through the same ports as cameras and card readers. Unless you have a SCSI *(Small Computer Systems Interface)* device, which is another type of connection port but almost nonexistent today, you use either USB or FireWire. Most low-end scanners sold now are USB devices.

Even the lowest-end scanners provide 16-bit scans that help you get a little more data in the shadows and highlights. Like with a digital camera, a scanner's price is normally in proportion with its quality.

Preparing before you scan

Just as you'd clean a lens on a digital camera and set various menu selections before clicking the shutter button, you should prepare a few things ahead of time before scanning:

✔ **Connect the scanner properly.** Make sure that you have all connections made to your computer according to the user manual that came with your scanner. If you just purchased a scanner, check for any lock bolts and remove them according to the instructions.

✔ **Clean the scanner platen.** Use a lint-free cloth and glass cleaner (applied to the cloth) to remove all dust and particles on the glass. The more dust particles you remove, the easier the job of editing your image in Elements.

✔ **Clean the source material.** Be certain that the print or film you want to scan is free of dust and spots.

If you have old negatives that are dirty or that have water spots or debris that you can't remove with a cloth and film cleaner, soak the film in photo *flo* (a liquid you can purchase at a photo reseller). Be certain that your hands are clean and then run the filmstrip between two fingers to remove the excess liquid. Turn on your shower full force with hot water only and hang film nearby to dry it. Remove the film when it's dry, and you should see a surprisingly clean filmstrip compared with your soiled original.

✔ **Get to know your scanner software.** When you scan in Elements, the software supplied with your scanner takes charge, and you use the options in this software before it finally drops into an Elements image window.

✔ **Prepare the artwork.** If you plan on scanning pages in a book or pamphlet, remove the pages or try to make photocopies so that the piece you scan lies flat on the scanner platen. Make sure that you observe copyright laws if you're scanning printed works. For faxes and photocopies, try to improve originals by recopying them on a photo-copier by using darker settings.

✔ **Find the scanner's sweet spot.** Every scanner has an area where you can acquire the best scans. This area is often called the *sweet spot.* To find the scanner's sweet spot, scan a blank piece of paper. The sweet spot is the brightest area on the resultant scan. Other areas should be darker. The sweet spot is most often in the upper-left quadrant, the lower-right quadrant, or the middle of the page. Note the area and plan to place your source material within this area when scanning pictures.

Understanding image requirements

All scanning software provides you with options for determining resolution and color mode before you start a new scan. You should decide what output you intend to use and scan originals at target resolutions designed to accommodate a given output. Some considerations include the following:

✔ **Scan the artwork or photo at the size and resolution for the final output.** If you have a 3-x-5 photo that needs to be 1.5 x 2.5 inches on a

Web page, scan the original with a 50-percent reduction in size at 72 ppi. (See Chapter 3 for information about resizing images.)

✓ **Size images with the scanner software.** If you have a 4-x-6 photo that needs to be output for prepress and commercial printing at 8 x 12 inches, scan the photo at 4 x 6 inches at 600 ppi (enough to size to 200 percent for a 300 dpi image).

✓ **Scan properly for line art.** *Line art* is 1-bit black and white only. When you print line art on laser printers or prepare files for commercial printing, the line art resolution should match the device resolution. For example, printing to a 600 dpi (dots per inch) laser printer requires 600 ppi for a 1-bit line-art image. When you're printing to an image setter at a print shop, or when an image is going directly to plate or press, the resolution should be 1200 dpi.

✓ **Scan grayscale images in color.** In some cases, it doesn't matter, but with some images and scanners, you can get better results by scanning in RGB (red, green, and blue) color and converting to grayscale by using the Hue/Saturation dialog box or the Convert to Black and White dialog box, as we explain in Chapter 3.

✓ **Scan in high bit depths.** If your scanner is capable of scanning in 16- or 32-bit, by all means, scan at the higher bit depths to capture the most data. See Chapter 3 for more information about working with higher-bit images.

Using scanner plug-ins (Windows)

Generally, when you install your scanner software, a standalone application and a plug-in are installed to control the scanning process. *Plug-ins* are designed to work inside other software programs, such as Photoshop Elements. When you're using the plug-in, you can stay right in Elements to do all your scanning. Here's how it works:

1. **After installing a new scanner and the accompanying software, launch Elements and then open the Organizer by clicking Organize on the Welcome screen.**

2. **From the Organizer, open the Preferences dialog box by pressing Ctrl+K.**

3. **Click Scanner in the left column and adjust the Scanner preferences, as we describe in Chapter 2.**

When the Preferences dialog box sees your scanner, you know that the connection is properly set up and you're ready to scan. Here's how to complete your scan:

1. **To open the scanner software from within Elements, choose File⇨Get Photos⇨From Scanner.**

   You must be in the Organizer window on Windows to access the File⇨Get Photos⇨From Scanner menu command.

2. **In the Get Photos from Scanner dialog box that appears, as shown in Figure 4-3, make your choices and click OK.**

Here you make a choice for your scanner in the Scanner drop-down menu, a location on your hard drive for saving the scanned images, a quality setting, and an option to automatically correct red-eye.

Elements may churn a bit, but eventually your scanner software appears atop the Organizer window, as you can see in Figure 4-4. The window is the scanner software provided by your scanner manufacturer. (Your window looks different than Figure 4-4 unless you use the same scanner we use.)

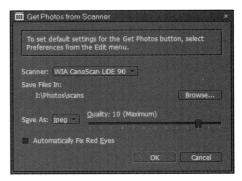

Figure 4-3: Make choices in the Get Photos from Scanner dialog box and click OK.

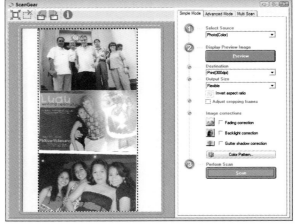

3. **Preview the scan.**

Regardless of which software you use, you should have similar options for creating a preview; selecting resolution, color mode, and image size; scaling; and other options. If you

Figure 4-4: When you scan from within Elements, your scanner software loads on top of the Elements workspace.

click the Preview button, you see a preview before scanning the photo(s).

4. **Adjust the options according to your output requirements and the recommendations made by your scanner manufacturer.**

5. **When everything is ready to go, click the Scan button.**

The final image drops into an Elements image window.

Scanning on the Macintosh

Photoshop Elements doesn't support scanning on the Macintosh as it does for Windows. On the Mac, you have a few different options. You can use your scanner software and open the resultant scan in the Elements Editor, or you can use Image Capture. With Image Capture, you can complete a scan and open the file directly in Elements without having to first save the scan to disk.

Scanning many photos at a time

If you have several photos to scan, you can lay them out on the scanner platen and perform a single scan to acquire all images in one pass. Arrange the photos to scan on the glass and set up all the options in the scanner window for your intended output. When you scan multiple images, they form a single scan, as you can see in Figure 4-5.

Figure 4-5: You can scan multiple images with one pass.

After you scan multiple images, Elements makes it easy for you to separate each image into its own image window, where you can save the images as separate files. In Edit Full mode, choose Image➪Divide Scanned Photos to make Elements magically open each image in a separate window while your original scan remains intact. The images are neatly tucked away in the Project Bin, where you can select them for editing, as shown in Figure 4-6.

Getting Files from Storage Media

When you acquire images in Elements from media sources, such as CD-ROMs, DVDs, external hard drives, and your internal hard drive, the process is very similar to opening files from digital cameras, which we explain in the section, "Grabbing Images from Your Camera," earlier in this chapter. Insert a CD or DVD into the CD/DVD drive, and the Windows AutoPlay Wizard opens just like when you insert a media cartridge or connect a cable from your camera to your computer.

Just cancel out of the wizard if a wizard launches and follow these steps:

1. **Open the Organizer from the Welcome screen or click Photo Browser.**

2. **When the Organizer window opens, choose File➪Get Photos➪From Files and Folders.**

3. **Open the source drive from the listed drives.**

   You see the photos stored on the media.

Figure 4-6: After you choose Image➪Divide Scanned Photos, the scan is split into separate image windows.

 4. **Select images and click Get Photos (from the Organizer) or Open (from one of the editing modes) to open the files in the Organizer or an editor.**

    Now, you can edit the photos in Elements or save them to your hard drive.

Grabbing Photos from iPhoto (Macintosh Only)

If you insert a media device and your photos are automatically loaded up in iPhoto on the Mac, you can easily import the iPhoto images into the Organizer. Unique to the Macintosh is the File➪Get Photos and Videos➪From iPhoto command. A dialog box opens where you can choose to import photos as iPhoto Events or convert imported photos to Albums. You can convert Events or just simply import photos from your iPhoto library. All photos contained within iPhoto are imported into the Organizer.

Using Online Services

Online printing and sharing services require you to set up an account with a service. You can access services provided by Adobe Partner Services by clicking the Share tab above the Panels Bin in the Organizer and clicking either Order Prints or Online Album. To use a service, you begin by setting up an account, as we explain in Chapter 2.

You can create digital photo albums with your images and share them with friends, family, and coworkers. To initiate a sharing service, you send an e-mail invitation to others. Each member of your sharing group needs to set up an account individually. After everyone has an account, you and your friends can then order prints that are mailed from the online service center. All the kinds of prints you might order from a local superstore or photo lab are available from online services, including specialty items, such as calendars.

After setting up an account and choosing a service, you handle sharing services by using the Share panels, as we explain in Chapter 16.

Phoning In Your Images

You can acquire images from cell phones, iPhones, iPods, iPads and a variety of different handheld devices. As a matter of fact there's quite a bit you can do with uploading, downloading, and preparing photos for handheld devices.

If you want to add images from a cellphone to the Organizer or open images in one of the editing modes, you need to copy files via a USB or Bluetooth connection or e-mail photos if your phone is cabable of using e-mail.

After copying files to your hard drive on Windows, choose File⇨Get Photos and Video⇨From Files and Folders or press Ctrl+G (⌘+G on the Mac). Locate the folder into which you copied the files and add them to your Organizer or open them in one of the editing modes.

With an iPhone, iPod, or iPad you can use the Photo Downloader to get media. Hook up the device with a USB cable and the Photo Downloader automatically opens. Follow the same procedures for downloading photos as explained in the section "Using Adobe Photoshop Elements 9.0 – Photo Downloader" earlier in this chapter.

For iPhone and iPad, you can also hook up your device via a USB cable and choose Get Photos and Videos From Camera or Card Reader. Elements recognizes the device and the Photo Downloader opens (shown in Figure 4-7) where you have options for importing all photos or selected images.

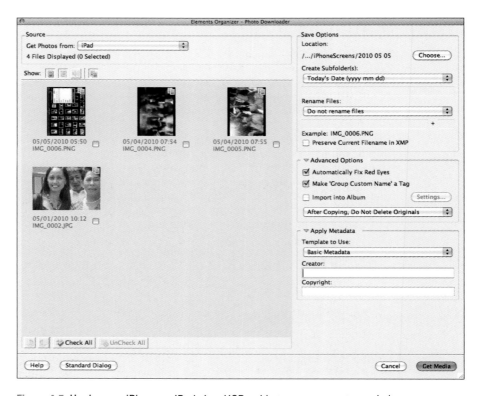

Figure 4-7: Hook up an iPhone or iPad via a USB cable to your computer and choose Get Photos and Videos from Camera or Card Reader.

To upload Elements creations and edited photos to iPhone or iPad, use Apple's iTunes. In iTunes choose File➪Add Files to Library and select the images and videos from a folder on your hard drive that you want to upload to the device. Next hook up the iPhone or iPad and click the Photos and/or Videos tab at the top of the iTunes window. Select the check boxes adjacent to each item you want to upload and click the Sync button. Your files are uploaded to your device while the Sync is in progress.

When uploading photos to an iPhone or iPad, use only the supported formats such as JPEG, TIFF, GIF, and PNG.

You can bypass iTunes with the iPad using the Camera Connection Kit provided by Apple for $29.95. The kit only supports SD cards, but you can attach many different types of card readers to the USB port on the Camera Connection Kit and use other media cards. Copy files from the Organizer to the media card and use it like you would use an external media source to share photos back and forth between your computer and the iPad.

Creating Images from Scratch

You may want to start from scratch by creating a new document in Elements. New, blank pages have a number of uses. You can mix and merge images in a new document, as we explain in Chapter 8; create a canvas where you can draw and paint, as we explain in Chapter 12; or use the New dialog box to find out a file's size, dimensions, and resolution.

Creating a new document

You can create new, blank documents by using one of several options. On the Welcome screen, which appears when you first launch Elements, click Edit to launch the Edit Full mode. Choose File⇨New Blank File to open the New dialog box, in which you choose the document size, resolution, and other attributes. You can also click the New button on the Macintosh at the top of the Edit Full window. Likewise, you can create new files while working in either Edit Quick mode or in the Organizer.

Follow these steps to create a new document while working in any editing mode:

1. **Open Elements and select an editing mode.**

   Click Edit (Start from Scratch on the Macintosh) on the Welcome screen.

2. **Choose File⇨New⇨Blank File in any workspace or press Ctrl+N (⌘+N).**

   Either way, the New dialog box opens, as shown in Figure 4-8.

3. **Select the attributes for the new file.**

   You have several options from which to choose:

   Figure 4-8: Regardless of the method used to create a new, blank document, the New dialog box opens.

   - *Name:* Type a name for your file.

   - *Preset:* From the drop-down list, you can select from a number of different sizes.

   - *Size:* You can select a preset size from a long drop-down list. This is optional because you can change the file attributes in the other text boxes and drop-down menus.

   - *Dimensions (Width/Height):* Values in the Width and Height text boxes are independent. Either box can be edited without affecting the other. Adjacent to the values in the Width and Height text boxes, you find drop-down menus that offer many different options for units of measure, such as the default units of pixels followed by inches, centimeters (cm), millimeters (mm), points, picas, and columns.

- *Resolution:* Resolution here is similar to editing the resolution value in the Image Size dialog box when the Resample check box is selected. The resolution is an independent value and isn't linked to the dimensions. If you want to know how resolution changes dimensions without resampling, create a new, blank file at the known values and click OK. Then, choose Image⇨Resize⇨Image Size and change the values in the Image Size dialog box, which we discuss in Chapter 3.

- *Color Mode:* Your choices are Bitmap, Grayscale, and RGB Color. (See Chapter 3 for more information about color modes.)

- *Background Contents:* You have three choices: White, Background Color, and Transparent. The selection you make results in the color of the blank image. If you choose Background Color, the current background color assigned on the Tools panel is applied to the background. See Chapter 12 for information on changing background color. If you choose Transparent, the image is created as a layer, and the layer name changes to Layer 0, as we explain in Chapter 8.

- *Image Size:* This value (displayed in the lower-right corner of the dialog box) dynamically changes when you change the Width, Height, and Resolution values. The reported value is how much file space is required to save the uncompressed file.

 4. Click OK after setting the file attributes to create the new document.

Finding file specs in the New dialog box

In addition to creating new, blank files, the New dialog box can be a helpful source of information for all your work in Elements. Suppose that you want to know how many images you can copy to a USB storage device with 2,656MB free space, or how large your digital camera files will print with a 150 ppi resolution. All you have to do is press Ctrl+N (⌘+N on the Mac) to open the New dialog box, plug in the values, and read the Image Size number or examine the file dimensions. If your files will be converted to grayscale, choose Grayscale from the Color Mode drop-down menu and check the Image Size number to see how much your file size is reduced. Because this number is *dynamic,* it updates with each change you make to the file attributes.

Adding pages to an existing project

Rather than create a new, blank file, you can add pages to an existing file in the form of a project. Just follow these steps:

1. **Open an image in Edit Full mode.**

2. **Right-click the photo thumbnail in the Project Bin. By default, the Project Bin opens.**

   The context menu, as shown in Figure 4-9, appears.

3. **Choose either Add Blank Page (for adding a new, blank page) or Add Page Using Current Layout (to duplicate the current photo as a new page).**

4. **Save the file by choosing File⇨Save As and selecting Photoshop Multiple Project as your file format.**

   Note that the default format in the Save As dialog box is Photo Project Format (*.PSE).

   All the pages you add to a project are saved as separate files in a folder created automatically by Elements. When you open any one of the images, it appears separately in the Project Bin. To open an image in the stack, click the image you want to open in the Project Bin. Clicking an image in the Project Bin opens that image in the image window.

Figure 4-9: Right-click and then choose an option for adding a page to the photo selected in the Project Bin.

In Figure 4-10, you can see thumbnails of a project where the original RGB image appears on the left, followed by a grayscale image, a sepia-tone image, and a bitmap image — all contained in the same photo project.

Figure 4-10: Click one of the thumbnails in the Project Bin to open the respective photo in the image window.

A Basic Primer on Camera Raw

We include the elaborate description of Camera Raw in the following sections, after sharing with you all the other options you have for getting images in Elements. We recognize that you may not have a digital camera capable of capturing Camera Raw images, so this information may not be of much interest to you now.

If you don't have a camera capable of capturing Camera Raw images, you might want to look over the following sections to understand how this file format can benefit you. If you purchase a camera equipped with Camera Raw support, you'll have some understanding of the advantages of using this format.

Understanding Camera Raw

Camera Raw images enable you to post-process your pictures. When you take a picture with a digital camera in Camera Raw format, the camera's sensor records as much information as it can. When you open a Camera Raw file in Elements, you decide what part of that data is opened as a new image.

Suppose that your camera is set for exposure in tungsten lighting, which is used with tungsten flash photography in a studio. If you take this camera outside in daylight and shoot an image, all your images appear with a blue cast because tungsten lighting produces a cooler temperature than daylight.

If you acquire images that are saved in JPEG format, you need to do a lot of color correction after the image opens in Elements. If you shoot the image in Camera Raw format, you just process the image with a warmer temperature (consistent with conditions when the shot was taken), and your color correction in Elements is a fraction of what it is to fix a JPEG image.

Post-processing Camera Raw images requires a plug-in that's installed with Photoshop Elements. When you open a Camera Raw image, the Camera Raw plug-in takes over and provides you with a huge set of options for post-processing the image before you open it in one of the Elements editors.

Each camera developer uses a different flavor of Camera Raw, and some developers use different Raw formats between different models in their product line. Although Adobe tries to keep up with all the various Raw formats, you may find a camera using a format not supported by the Raw plug-in. Be sure to check updates online for Photoshop Elements. As new developments occur, Adobe makes an effort to update plug-ins to support newer formats.

Acquiring Camera Raw images

If you read through the first part of this chapter, you know how to acquire images from your camera and copy them to your hard drive. We don't bother going through those steps again; we just assume that you have some Camera Raw images on your hard drive. That's where you want them, anyway. Opening files from your hard drive is much faster than working off media cards.

To open a Camera Raw image, follow these steps:

1. **Open the image by pressing Ctrl+O (⌘+O on the Mac) and select the image in the Open dialog box.**

   If you want to select several images in a row, click the first image, hold down the Shift key, and then click the last image. If you want to select several nonadjacent images, Ctrl-click each image (⌘-click on the Mac).

2. **Click Open in the Open dialog box.**

   If you're selecting multiple images, only one image appears in the Camera Raw dialog box. When you click Open Image, the next image opens in the Camera Raw dialog box, as shown in Figure 4-11.

   As you can see in Figure 4-11, you can use a vast number of options to post-process your image before you drop it into Elements. This window is like a digital darkroom, where you can process the film and see what you're doing to the image before you accept the changes.

3. **Choose from the options to post-process your images.**

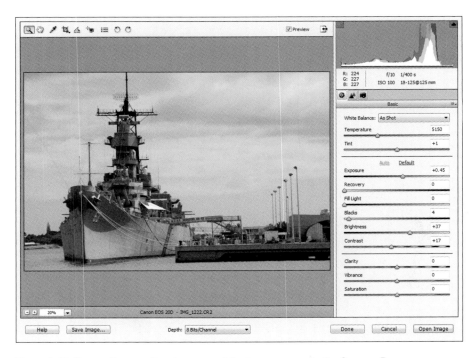

Figure 4-11: Open a Camera Raw image, and the image opens in the Camera Raw plug-in window.

If you have your monitor properly calibrated, as we explain in Chapter 2, all the adjustments you make for Camera Raw format are dynamically updated in the image preview. Don't be shy. Poke around and adjust settings to see the results in the preview area. The more you play with the settings, the more you find out how to get the best out of Camera Raw.

A large number of settings are in the Camera Raw window, as the following list describes; mark this section to refer to when you work with Camera Raw images:

✓ **Tools:** Nine tools appear in the window:

• *Zoom:* Zooms in and out of the image preview.

• *Hand:* Moves the image around, like it does in the Elements image window.

• *Eyedropper:* Samples color in the image. We cover using the Elements Eyedropper tools in Chapter 12, and that information also applies to using the Eyedropper in the Camera Raw window.

• *Crop tool:* Draw a marquee with the Crop tool and make your color and brightness adjustments. The adjustments are applied only to the area defined by the Crop tool. When you click Open Image, the photo opens cropped to the area you marked with the Crop tool.

• *Straighten tool:* The Straighten tool enables you to draw a horizontal axis to straighten a crooked photo.

• *Red Eye Removal:* Click the Red Eye Removal tool to remove red-eye caused by flash lighting.

• *Open Preferences dialog box:* Click this tool to open the Camera Raw Preferences dialog box, where you can make some choices for saving image settings, change default image settings, and use the Adobe Digital Negative (DNG) format. You can press Ctrl+K (⌘+K on the Macintosh) to open this dialog box.

• *Rotate Left:* This tool appears first to rotate counterclockwise.

• *Rotate Right:* The last tool you see below the title bar is used to rotate clockwise. These last two rotation tools are self-explanatory.

✓ **Preview:** Select the check box to show dynamic previews of your edits.

✓ **Shadow/Highlight Clipping:** The Shadow and Highlight buttons above the histogram denoted by up-pointing arrows show clipping in the *shadows* (dark areas of the image) and *highlights* (light areas of the image). *Clipping* means that, in a certain area, some data and, ultimately, some detail have been lost in an image. Think of clipping as something that you don't want to appear in your pictures. When you make adjustments, shadow clipping is shown in blue and highlight clipping is shown in red in the image preview. Take a look at Figure 4-12, in which we exaggerate clipping to show how the clipping preview appears.

✔ **RGB values:** These values appear below the histogram. When you first open an image, you don't see any values in the RGB area. Click the Zoom tool, the Hand tool, or the Eyedropper tool and move the cursor over the image preview. When you move any of these tools around the image, the RGB values corresponding to the point below the cursor are reported in this area.

Figure 4-12: Shadow clipping appears in blue, and highlight clipping appears in red.

✔ **Histogram:** This graph displays all three channels (red, green, and blue) in an image simultaneously. The histogram changes when you change other options in the Camera Raw window.

The histogram graphs how pixels in an image are distributed. The distribution includes the number of pixels at each color-intensity level (one of the 256 levels you can find out about in Chapter 3).

If images have pixels concentrated in the shadows, you see the histogram skewed to the left. Conversely, images with pixels concentrated in the highlights reveal a histogram skewed to the right.

When you begin to understand histograms better, you can develop your skill to the point where a quick glance at the histogram provides you with a clue to what adjustments you need to make to improve images.

✔ **Detail icons:** The three icons change the pane below the histogram. The Basic choices are shown earlier in Figure 4-11. Click the Detail icon to apply sharpening and noise reduction, as shown in Figure 4-13, or click the Camera Calibration icon to select a camera profile.

✔ **Settings (pop-up menu):** This pop-up menu opens when you click the small icon on the far right of the Basic tab. From this menu, you have choices for applying settings to the open image. If you change any setting, the menu option changes to *Custom*. If you previously made setting choices on a Camera Raw image and want to return to the shot as it was taken by the camera, open the image and select Camera Raw Defaults.

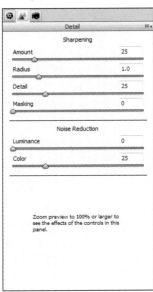

Figure 4-13: Click the triangle icon below the histogram to open the Detail tab, which includes options for sharpness and noise reduction.

Another option is Previous Conversion. This selection is handy if you have a collection of images that all require the same settings. After adjusting the first image, open additional images and select Previous Conversion. The Camera Raw plug-in applies the last settings you made to a Camera Raw image to the currently open file.

Sharpening sharpens images. You can choose to sharpen images in the Camera Raw window or in Elements. Try to avoid sharpening here and use the sharpening tools in Elements, as we explain in Chapter 9.

Noise Reduction includes options for adjusting the luminance and color. You've probably seen images with a lot of noise. In extreme cases, they look like the pictures were printed on sandpaper. Noise in an image is okay if that's an effect you intentionally apply to a picture. However, if you want a smooth-looking image, you have to eliminate any noise introduced by the camera. Luminance Smoothing reduces grayscale noise. The next setting is Color Noise Reduction, which is used to reduce color noise.

✔ **White Balance:** White Balance settings (available on the Basic tab — the far-left icon below the histogram, as shown in Figure 4-11) are used to adjust the color balance of an image to reflect the lighting conditions under which the shot was originally taken. Think of the sensor in a digital camera capable of capturing the entire range of white balance the sensor can see. You make a choice not necessarily for what you see, but rather for the white balance for the shot you took. Therefore, if your camera is set for taking pictures under one set of lighting conditions, and then you move to another set of lighting conditions and forget to change the settings, you can let the Camera Raw plug-in make a correction for the white balance because the sensor picked up the entire range, and the necessary data is contained in the file.

In Figure 4-14, you can see a picture taken with the camera set for tungsten lighting, but the shot was taken outdoors in daylight. By changing the White Balance in the Camera Raw dialog box, you can see how the settings affect the image color.

✔ **Temperature:** If one of the preset White Balance options doesn't quite do the job, you can move the Temperature slider or edit the text box to settle on values between one White Balance choice and another. Use this item to fine-tune the White Balance.

✔ **Tint:** Tint is another fine-tuning adjustment affected by White Balance. This slider and text box are used to correct any green or magenta tints that might appear in a photo.

Figure 4-14: Changing White Balance can dramatically change the image color.

✔ **Brightness adjustments:** Several adjustment sliders and text boxes help you control the image brightness and tonal range. Notice the Exposure setting. This item lets you correct photos taken at the wrong exposure. In analog darkrooms, you might ask technicians to push or pull film during processing, which results in longer and shorter processing times. Changing exposure times compensates for under- and overexposing film. A nice advantage of using Camera Raw is that you can change the exposure for one image and then later open the original raw image and change to a different exposure value. Analog film can't be reprocessed, but with Camera Raw, you can reprocess over and over again.

Other options for the brightness and tonal controls are similar to the choices you have in the Elements Edit Full mode. For more information on these adjustments, see Chapter 10.

✔ **Cancel/Reset:** When you open the Camera Raw window, the button you see by default is Cancel. Press the Alt (Option) key, and the button changes to Reset. If you want to scrub all the settings you made and start over, press Alt (Option) and click Reset.

✓ **Open Image/Open Copy:** This single button has two different purposes:

- *Open Image:* This button is the default. Click Open after you choose all your settings to process the photo and open it in Elements.

- *Open Copy:* Press the Alt (Option) key, and the button changes to Open Copy. Click Open Copy to open a copy of the raw image.

✓ **Done:** Clicking Done doesn't open the image in Edit Full mode. Click Done after making changes to the settings, and the new settings become the new defaults for your Raw image. You can clear the defaults by opening the pop-up menu and selecting Camera Raw Defaults.

✓ **Zoom:** In this drop-down menu, you can choose from several zoom presets. You can also edit the text box, click the minus (–) button to zoom out, or click the plus (+) button to zoom in. Using any option zooms the image preview.

✓ **Help:** Clicking this button opens a Help document to assist you in understanding more about Camera Raw.

✓ **Save Image:** Click the Save Image button to open the Save Options dialog box, where you can rename the image to save a copy and make choices for saving in Adobe's DNG format.

✓ **Depth:** If your camera is capable of shooting higher bit depths, they're listed here. If you want to convert to 8-bit images for printing, you can select the option from the drop-down menu.

On the Macintosh, you have two additional tools:

✓ **Spot Removal tool:** Use this tool to remove dust and scratches before opening the file in Elements.

✓ **Adjustment Brush tool:** Use this tool to adjust brightness, contrast and color to sections of the image before opening in Elements.

All we can hope to provide in this book is a simple cursory view for using Camera Raw. Several entire books have been written exclusively covering the Camera Raw format and how to open files in the Camera Raw plug-in window. For a more detailed look at using Camera Raw, see *Color Management for Digital Photographers For Dummies,* by Ted Padova and Don Mason.

5

Viewing and Finding Your Images

*T*he Organizer is a powerful tool that helps you locate files and keeps your photos arranged and organized. You can easily access the Organizer in Windows by clicking the Organizer button on the menu bar while you're in one of the editing modes. Or when you open the Welcome screen, click the Organize button.

Great news for Macintosh users! In Elements 9, Mac users see a return appearance of the Organizer. Many of the options that Windows users have had in previous versions of Elements are now within the reach of the Macintosh user.

In this chapter, you can discover how to view and organize your pictures in the Organizer and the image window, and how the many options help speed up your work in Photoshop Elements.

The Many Faces of the Organizer

The default Organizer view is like a slide sorter, and this view is one you're likely to use in all your Elements work sessions. The Organizer provides an efficient means to access the photos you want to open in one of the editors. Just double-click a photo in the Organizer, and you see the image zoom in size to fill an Organizer window. You can carefully examine the photo to be certain that it's the one you want and then just select which editor you want to use from the Editor drop-down menu on the menu bar, from the contextual menu you open on the image in the Organizer window, or by clicking the Fix button in the Panels Bin.

In addition to the default view in the Organizer, you have other ways to view your pictures: in a slide show or side-by-side to compare them.

Adding files to the default Organizer view

Before you explore alternative viewing options in the Organizer, take a look at how you add photos to the thumbnail images you see in the Organizer window.

After copying the photos to your hard drive, as we explain in Chapter 4, here's how you add those files to an existing group of images in the Organizer:

1. **Open the Organizer.**

2. **In the Organizer, choose File⇨Get Photos and Videos⇨From Files and Folders.**

   The Get Photos and Videos from Files and Folders dialog box opens, as shown in Figure 5-1.

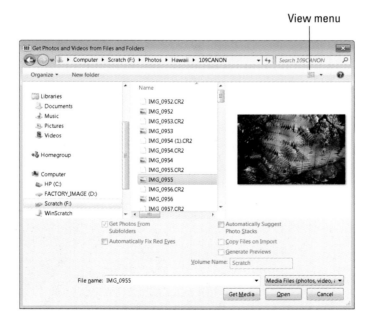

Figure 5-1: The Get Photos and Videos from Files and Folders dialog box.

3. **From the View menu (shown in Figure 5-1), choose Large icons (or Medium icons).**

   In Large icon (or Medium icon) view, thumbnail images of most files appear in a scrollable list large enough to see some detail. (***Note:*** You might not see Camera Raw files and some files saved in different formats.) This view makes it easy to locate the files you want to add to the Organizer. For example, if you want to load only Camera Raw images, you can easily see them represented as icons, rather than the image previews.

4. **Select files to add to the Organizer window.**

   Click a thumbnail and use either the Shift key or the Ctrl key (⌘ on the Macintosh) to select additional photos. When you hold down Shift and click, all photos between the first thumbnail and the thumbnail you Shift-click are selected. When you Ctrl-click (⌘-click on the Macintosh), you can select/deselect noncontiguous photos.

5. **Click Get Media to add the selected photos to the Organizer window.**

6. **To view all photos (new and old), click the Back button in the upper-left corner.**

   The photos you add to the Organizer may appear out of order when you're viewing them in the Organizer. Depending on the sort order, which we explain in the section "Sorting Your Photos," later in this chapter, the additional photos you add to the Organizer can appear before or after, or integrated within, the original photos. Use the scroll bar in the Organizer to view the added photos.

Changing the Organizer display

When you open the Organizer, the default view is a Thumbnail display. Your photos, videos, projects, audio files, and so on are shown with a mini image or icon that can be adjusted to different sizes. On the Shortcuts bar, a slider can be moved left to create smaller thumbnail views or right to create larger thumbnail views in the Organizer window.

The Thumbnail display is one of many options for browsing photos and other files in the Organizer. A quick glance at the Display drop-down menu shows alternative views available to you, as shown in Figure 5-2.

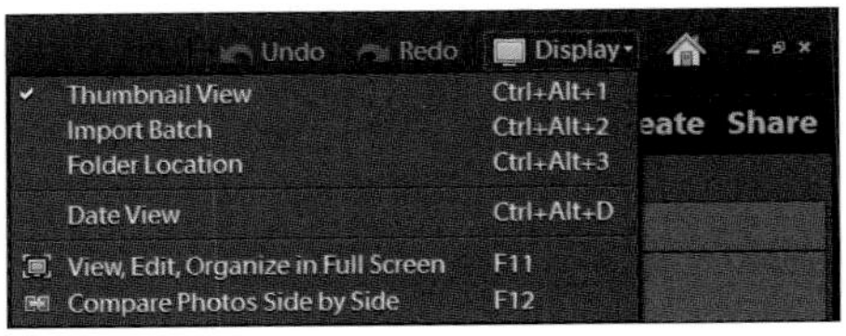

Figure 5-2: Click Display on the menu bar to see the options for alternative views in the Organizer.

Import Batch view

Below the default option for Thumbnail views, you find Import Batch. Open the Display menu and then select Import Batch, or press Ctrl+Alt+2 (⌘+Option+2 on the Macintosh) on your keyboard. The display in the Organizer keeps the view set to thumbnails, but the order of your files changes to reflect the date you imported files with the Get Photos and Videos command, which we discuss in Chapter 4. This view can be helpful if you want to organize images according to the dates you imported them.

Folder Location view

What's nifty about the Folder Location display is that you can peruse your hard drive for all files and folders while you remain in the Organizer window. Just select Folder Location from the Display menu or press Ctrl+Alt+3 (⌘+Option+3 on the Macintosh) to make an Explorer sidebar show you your hard drive(s), network locations, and offline media.

For Macintosh users, when you see a reference to *Windows Explorer* type of view, you see a hierarchy of folders along the left side of the Elements window. Where you see a right pointing arrow, you find a collapsed folder. Click the arrow, and a nest of subfolders is revealed below the parent folder.

Choose Folder Location to change the view to the one shown in Figure 5-3. When you want to poke around a folder, right-click and select Reveal in Explorer (Reveal in Finder on the Mac) from the contextual menu. Windows Explorer opens on top of the Organizer window and shows you all the files contained in that folder. On the Macintosh, a Finder view opens and displays the selected folder contents.

When you find an image you want to edit, right-click and choose Open With⇨Adobe Photoshop Elements 9.0 (Editor). On the Macintosh, choose Open With⇨Adobe Photoshop Elements. The image then opens in Edit Full mode in Elements.

When you want more of the screen window dedicated to seeing the files in the Organizer, hide the Panels Bin by clicking the separator bar. One click on the tiny right-pointing arrow on the separator bar hides the panel. Click the arrow on a collapsed panel to reopen that panel. In Figure 5-3, you see the Organizer window with the Panels Bin hidden, thereby displaying more thumbnail images in the Organizer window.

Date view

Choose Date View (Ctrl+Alt+D, ⌘+Option+D on the Macintosh) from the Display menu to change your Organizer window to a calendar showing you the dates your images were shot. The date information is derived from meta-data imported with your images that were recorded by your camera. (For more information on metadata, see "Searching metadata," later in this chapter.)

Figure 5-3: Choose Folder Location from the Display menu and then right-click to open a contextual menu.

If you shoot many pictures on a given date, the images are stacked on the calendar for that date. In the right panel, you find arrows that are used to scroll the stacked images left or right, and a number appears in the lower-left corner of the image thumbnail in view. In Figure 5-4, the numbers appear as 5 of 6; on April 13, 2008 (the date at the top of the thumbnail), six photos were taken, and the current view is the fifth photo in the stacked order.

To return to the Organizer thumbnail display, click the binoculars icon or press Ctrl+Alt+O (the letter O, not zero) or ⌘+Option+O on the Macintosh.

Figure 5-4: The right panel shows a thumbnail view of a photo with scroll arrows and numbers.

Show Map (Windows only)

How would you like to see a visual display of where your photos were taken geographically? Photoshop Elements provides you the answer with Yahoo! Maps and an option for placing your photos on a world map.

To see the Yahoo! Map, you first need to place photos on a map. Unlike earlier versions on Elements, Elements 9 doesn't have a Show Map command in the Display menu. All photo placement on a map and viewing the map is handled in the Edit menu or from a contextual menu opened from a photo in the Organizer.

You must have an Internet connection active on your computer to work with Yahoo! Maps.

To begin, select a photo or several photos in the Organizer and choose Edit⇨Place on Map. You're prompted in a dialog box to identify the location. Type a city name and click OK, and the city is verified in the dialog box. If multiple cities are shown, click the one you want and click OK. After you place a photo on a map, you can open the Maps panel by selecting a photo and choose Edit⇨Show on Map. The map and a thumbnail of the photo appears in the Map panel as shown in Figure 5-5.

Figure 5-5: Select a file in the Organizer and choose Edit⇨Place on Map.

To map the location of additional photos in the Organizer to Yahoo! Maps, you can choose from a couple different options:

- ✓ **Select photos in the Organizer and drag them to a map location on the map in the Map panel.** You must first have at least one file placed on the Map and choose Edit⇨Show on Map to open the Map panel.

- ✓ **Select photos in the Organizer and right-click one of the selected photos.** From the menu options, choose Place on Map. In the dialog box that opens, type a city name and click the Find button. If more than one city is reported in the dialog box, click the city name you want to use for the mapped photos.

To move around the map, place the cursor inside the Yahoo! Map panel and drag the map with the Hand tool within the panel window. If you go too far left, don't worry; the Asian, Indian, and Eastern European countries are found by dragging right across the Atlantic and eastward. Dragging left stops somewhere around the International Date Line; so, if you live in Singapore, you need to keep dragging right to find your country.

Zooming in the Map panel is handled by the tools you see at the bottom of the map. Use the Zoom In tool to find cities and road maps in a detailed view. Use the Zoom Out tool after you find the location you want to use.

After you add photos to the map, you can view the images by clicking the red pin placed on the map each time that you add photos to a location. Click the red pin to open a pop-up window that shows a thumbnail view of the current photo with smaller photos in a slide organizer below the primary image thumbnail, as shown earlier in Figure 5-5. Click the left and right arrows in the pop-up window to scroll the slides. Clicking the current image thumbnail in the pop-up window opens the image in a slide show view. To find out more about slide show views, see the following section.

In the Map panel, you can choose from several display options in the drop-down menu on the bottom-right side of the panel. Choose from the default Map, a Hybrid map, or Satellite map. Choose Satellite to locate Uncle Jeremy's house, where the last family reunion took place and you shot all those wonderful pictures.

To close the Map panel, click the x (close box) in the top right corner of the Map panel. The panel collapses, and you're back to the standard Organizer view.

When you view panels in Elements, drag the vertical separator bar on a panel to widen the panel or reduce the panel size. Look for the arrowhead on the vertical bar separating the Organizer window from a panel; click and drag left or right to change panel widths.

Viewing photos in a slide show (Full Screen view)

Are you ready for some exciting viewing in Photoshop Elements? To take an alternative view of your Organizer files, you can see your pictures in a self-running slide show (in Full Screen view), complete with transition effects and background music. Full Screen view takes you to a slide show view. For the purposes of clarity, think of Full Screen view and viewing a slide show as the same thing. Full-screen viewing temporarily hides the Elements tools and menus, and gives you the most viewing area on your monitor to see your pictures.

Viewing files in slide show mode can be helpful for quickly previewing the files you want to edit for all kinds of output, as well as for previewing photos that you might use for an exported slide show, which we explain in Chapter 15.

Creating slide shows and outputting to a file is supported only on Windows. However, viewing slide shows in Elements is supported for both Windows and Macintosh users.

Taking a quick view of the slide show

To set up your slide show and/or enter Full Screen view, follow these steps:

1. **Open the Organizer.**

2. **Select images that you want to see in a slide show or use all the images in the Organizer for your slide show.**

   If no images are selected when you enter Full Screen view, all photos in the Organizer window are shown in Full Screen view.

3. **Choose Display⇨View, Edit, Organize in Full Screen.**

   After choosing the menu command you jump right into the Full Screen view with some panels and tools displayed, as shown in Figure 5-6.

4. **View the slides.**

   Click the arrow keys at the bottom of the screen to move forward and back through the slides. You can also click the Toggle Film Strip icon (first icon on the left at the bottom of the screen) to show a filmstrip on the right side of the screen. It displays your slides as shown in Figure 5-6. Click a slide, and the main window displays the slide.

5. **Exit the Full Screen view. Press the Esc key on your keyboard to return to the Organizer window.**

You can also open Full Screen view by clicking the Full Screen View of Photos icon in the Shortcuts Bar. Look for the monitor icon with a right arrow.

Figure 5-6: Elements takes you right to Full Screen view after you press the F11 key (⌘+F11) on the Macintosh).

Getting fancy with self-running slide shows

Manually clicking arrows to view slides is more work than you need to do. With just a few adjustments, Elements can autoplay a slide show complete with a music background. To sit back and enjoy your slides without clicking a mouse button to advance slides, do the following:

1. **Select images that you want to see in a slide show in the Organizer window.**

2. **Press the F11 key (⌘+F11 on the Macintosh) to change the view to Full Screen mode.**

3. **Click the Change Settings tool on the toolbar at the bottom of the window, as shown in Figure 5-7.**

   Change Settings

   Figure 5-7: Click the Change Settings tool.

   The Full Screen View Options dialog box opens.

4. **Make adjustments in the Full Screen View Options dialog box.**

Select the Start Playing Automatically check box shown in Figure 5-8. When the box is selected, the slide show plays automatically. By default, you also have an audio file play for the duration of the slide show.

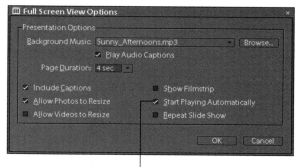

Select the Start Playing Automatically check box.

Figure 5-8: Play the slide automatically.

5. **Click OK and watch the show.**

6. **Press Esc when you're finished viewing the slide show.**

You can make choices for the music you want played when viewing a slide show by clicking the Browse button and selecting an audio file from your hard drive. You can determine the slide interval by editing the value in the Page Duration text box and make choices for viewing captions and resizing photos before dismissing the Full Screen View Options dialog box.

Working with the panels and toolbar

Full Screen view provides you with several editing tools. When you open selected photos from the Organizer in Full Screen view, you'll find two panels on the left side of the screen. The Quick Edit panel provides Quick Edit tools for editing photos, such as sharpening images and removing red-eye. The Quick Organize panel permits you to add keywords for easily organizing photos with keyword identifiers. (See Chapter 6 for more on adding keywords to photos.)

The toolbar shown in Figure 5-7 offers options for slide viewing. These tools include (from left to right):

✔ **Toggle Filmstrip:** Click this tool to show/hide the filmstrip on the right side of the window.

✔ **Toggle Quick Edit panel:** Shows/hides the Quick Edit panel.

✔ **Toggle Quick Organize panel:** Shows/hides the Quick Organize panel.

✔ **Previous Photo:** Click the left arrow to open the previous photo.

- **Play/Pause:** Click to play or pause a slide show.

- **Next Photo:** Click the right arrow to advance to the next photo.

- **Change Settings:** Click to open the Settings dialog box. (Refer to Figure 5-9.)

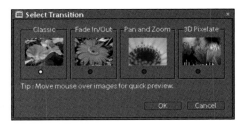

- **Transitions:** Click the Transitions tool, and the Select Transition dialog box opens, as shown in Figure 5-9. When you enter Full Screen view, this tool is selected. Four different transition effects are displayed in the dialog box. You can preview a

Figure 5-9: If you click the Transitions tool, the Select Transition dialog box opens.

transition effect by placing the cursor over one of the images. When you find an effect you like, click the image and click OK to change the transition.

- **Toggle Properties panel:** Click this tool to open the Properties dialog box. For more information about changing properties, see Chapter 6.

- **Show all controls (right arrow):** Click the tiny right-pointing arrow on the far right side of the toolbar, and the toolbar expands to reveal additional tools. Here you find a large display icon used for showing the Full Screen default view. The double monitors icon to the right is used to show two slides adjacent to each other in the slide show. Click the down-pointing arrow to open a pop-up menu that offers choices for two slide views (side-by-side or above and below). The chain link icon is used to lock panning and zooming together.

The main thing to keep in mind is that the Full Screen view is a temporary viewing option you have in Elements. It's not permanent. You use the view for a quick display method on your computer when you want to show off some photos to family and friends. Windows users have more permanent options for saving files as slide shows that can be shared with other users, as we explain in Chapter 15.

Comparing the Organizer on Windows and the Macintosh

As we said, the Macintosh version of Elements 9 introduces the Organizer. You have many great opportunities on the Macintosh for an assortment of tasks that were not available in earlier versions of Elements.

Unfortunately, not all the options available to Windows users are available to Macintosh users in the Organizer. Therefore, we thought it would be helpful to list features that are Windows only things you can do with Elements. Look over Table 5-1 for a quick glance of the differences between the Windows version and the Macintosh version according to supported features in the Organizer.

Table 5-1	Comparing the Organizer on Windows and Macintosh		
Feature	*Covered In*	*Windows*	*Macintosh*
Burn data to CD/DVD	Chapter 6	Yes	No
Create flipbooks	Chapter 15	Yes	No
Create slide shows	Chapter 15	Yes	No
HTML-based photo mail	Chapter16	Yes	No
Visual similarity searches of images	"Searching faces" section, this chapter	Yes	No
GEO maps	"Changing the Organizer display" section, this chapter	Yes	No
Watched folders functionality	Photoshop Elements Help document	Yes	No

The reason you find an assortment of differences between the features available on Windows and not available on the Macintosh is because of significant technical issues related to the platform differences. There are some native supported OS issues on Windows that aren't supported on the Mac.

Moving around the Image Window

When you edit images in either Edit Quick or Edit Full mode, you continually interact with the image window. Whether you're zooming in and out of a single window or viewing multiple windows, you need to work comfortably in this area for all your editing tasks. To help you move around the image window, Elements provides a rich set of tools.

If you become familiar with the many viewing options and keyboard shortcuts available in Elements, all your editing jobs will be much easier. The tools, menu commands, and panels we describe in the following sections are essential for just about everything you do in Elements.

Zooming in and out of images

Zooming in and out of images is a task you perform routinely while editing images in the image window, and also when working in other windows, such as the Camera Raw window and the Full Screen view. Zooming in is necessary when you want to precisely edit a section of an image or examine detail in a small area. You then need to zoom out to see the edits as they compare to the entire image.

Zoom by clicking

The Zoom tool appears on the Tools panel. To use the tool for zooming in and out, follow these steps to take a look at how it all works:

1. **Click the Zoom tool on the Tools panel to select it (or simply press Z).**

2. **Move the cursor, now loaded with the Zoom tool, to the image window and click the place where you want to zoom.**

   To zoom in more, click again; keep clicking until you zoom in far enough.

3. **To zoom out of an image, keep the Zoom tool selected, hold down the Alt key (Option key on the Macintosh), and click.**

   The cursor changes to a magnifying glass tool with a minus (–) symbol when you hold down the Alt key (Option key on the Macintosh).

Zoom to a selection

Another way to change a view is to zoom to a target area in an image. Here's how:

1. **Click the Zoom tool on the Tools panel.**

2. **Drag a box around the area you want to zoom.**

   Keep the mouse button pressed, and as you drag the mouse, a dashed rectangle marquee appears, as shown in Figure 5-10.

3. **Move the rectangle marquee if you need to adjust the selection.**

   Now, it's time to get fancy. If you have a marquee drawn with the Zoom tool and the size appears just right, but you want to move the rectangle, press the space-bar while you keep the mouse button pressed. You can drag the marquee rectangle anywhere

Figure 5-10: Click the Zoom tool on the Tools panel and drag around an area you want to zoom in on.

in the image to zoom to the area defined by the rectangle boundary.

4. **Release the mouse button.**

The view zooms to fit the space defined by the marquee rectangle.

Using the Options bar

Above the image window and below the Shortcuts bar, you find the Options bar. The Options bar is ever-changing, offering different options when you select different tools on the Tools panel. When you click the Zoom tool, the Options bar changes, as shown in Figure 5-11. You have many similar choices for zooming in and out of images and a few options unique to the Options bar:

Figure 5-11: Click the Zoom tool on the Tools panel to make the Options bar change to reflect choices for zooming in and out of images.

✐ **Zoom In/Zoom Out tools:** You can choose Zoom In or Zoom Out as separate tools to avoid using the Alt key (Option key on the Macintosh) to toggle between the two.

✐ **Zoom percentage:** This figure shows you the current zoom level as a percentage. You can edit the text by typing values between 5 and 3200.

✐ **Zoom slider:** Click the down-pointing arrow to open a slider bar. Drag the slider left to zoom out or right to zoom in.

✐ **Resize Windows to Fit:** Select this check box to resize the window along with the image zoom. Deselect the box to zoom in and out of an image while the image window remains at a fixed size.

✐ **Zoom All Windows:** If you have multiple images open and select this check box, zooming with the Zoom tool zooms all open documents simultaneously.

✐ **1:1:** Zooms the current window to a 1-to-1 ratio, showing the zoom level at which the file will be printed.

✐ **Fit Screen:** Click this button to fit the image within the image window.

✐ **Fill Screen:** Zooms the current window to fill the screen.

✐ **Print Size:** Often, this option shows you the same size as 1:1, where the image is zoomed to the size of the print file.

Viewing multiple documents

To work on any image in one of the editors, you need to become familiar with moving around the Elements interface and bring photos in view in the main image window.

While in Edit Full mode, you'll notice that when several images are open their filenames are listed at the top of the image window, as shown in Figure 5-12.

Figure 5-12: Multiple files opened in Edit Full mode are listed at the top of the image Window according to filename.

The list appears similar to tabs you find in Web browsers. Notice that adjacent to each filename you see an X. Click the X, and the file closes. Click any filename, and the file opens in the image window.

Additional viewing options are available from menu commands found on the Window menu. Choose Window⇨Images to open a submenu of viewing options used for viewing multiple files. The Window menu also provides a list of all your open documents. Here's a list of options you find on the submenu:

- ✔ **Tile:** Tiling images reduces image window sizes to a size that accommodates viewing all images in scrollable windows within the Elements workspace. Choose Window⇨Images⇨ Tile when multiple images are open to get a view similar to the one shown in Figure 5-13.

- ✔ **Cascade:** Choose Window⇨Images⇨ Cascade to make the image windows overlap each other in a cascading view.

Figure 5-13: Open several images in one of the editing modes and choose Window⇨Images⇨Tile to show all image windows.

- **Float in Window:** When photos are opened in the image window, they appear attached to the center area of your monitor. Choose this option to detach the photo from the image window, where you can click and drag the title bar around the image window area.

- **Float All in Windows:** When you have multiple photos open, use this option to detach all photos from the image window. After selecting this option, all the photos lose the tab view shown in Figure 5-13.

- **Consolidate All to Tabs:** If you choose Float All Windows and want to return to the tab view, choose this option.

- **New Window:** When you choose this option, you open a duplicate window for the photo in the foreground in the image window. You might use this option to create two views of the same image, where one view is zoomed in to edit some detail work and the other view shows the image in a reduced size for an overall look at the editing results.

- **Match Zoom:** Set the zoom level for one of several images open in Elements and choose Window➪Images➪Match Zoom. All open documents are zoomed to the same level as the foreground image.

- **Match Location:** If you zoom in to, for example, the upper-right corner and then select Match Location, all open images zoom to the same location in the respective photos.

You can also select and bring forward photos in the image window by double-clicking image thumbnails in the Project Bin.

Using pan and zoom

When you zoom in on a document larger than the image window can accommodate, scroll bars provide a means for moving the image inside the window. Moving the image around a window is *panning* the image.

You can also use the Hand tool to pan the image. Zoom in to an image and click the Hand tool. Click and drag the image around the window. If you want to zoom in or out while the Hand tool is selected, hold down the Ctrl key (⌘ key on the Mac), and the Hand tool temporarily changes to the Zoom In tool. Hold down Ctrl+Alt (⌘+Option on the Mac) to temporarily change the Hand tool to the Zoom Out tool.

Using the Navigator panel

The Navigator panel affords you several different options for both zooming and panning an image.

To open the Navigator panel, choose Window➪Navigator. The Navigator panel, as shown in Figure 5-14, opens as a floating panel in the Elements workspace. (For more information on floating panels, see Chapter 1.)

While you select options for zooming in the Navigator panel, the image preview in the panel stays fixed to show you the entire image. When you zoom in and out inside the panel, the corresponding zoom is applied to the active document.

Figure 5-14: The Navigator panel.

 Either use the zoom tools on the panel or drag the slider left and right to zoom in and out. If you place the cursor inside the image preview thumbnail, you can drag a rectangle and zoom into the image.

 Using the Navigator panel can be particularly helpful if you use two monitors. Just drag the Navigator panel to your second monitor, where you can change zoom levels without having the panel obscure the background image.

Sorting Your Photos

With all the Photoshop Elements modes and workspaces, you need a consistent starting place to handle all your editing tasks. Think of the Organizer as Grand Central Station, and from this central location, you can take the Long Island Railroad to any destination you desire. In Elements terms, rather than head out to Port Washington, you travel to an editing mode. Rather than go to the Hamptons, you journey through all the creation areas. In short, the Organizer is the central depot on the Photoshop Elements map.

In addition to being a tool to navigate to other workspaces, the Organizer is a management tool you can use to organize, sort, search, and describe photos with identity information. In terms of sorting and organizing files, Elements provides many different options, and we cover them all in the following sections.

Using sort commands

One quick way to sort images in the Organizer is to use the menu in the Shortcuts bar in the Organizer window for date sorting. Two options are available to you, as shown in Figure 5-15.

The sorting options available to you from the menu are

Figure 5-15: You can quickly sort files in ascending or descending order by date.

- ✔ **Date (Newest First):** Select this option to view images according to the date you took the photos, beginning with the most recent date.
- ✔ **Date (Oldest First):** This option displays photos in chronological order, starting with the oldest file.

As we mention in the section "Changing the Organizer display," earlier in this chapter, you can also view files according to the Import Batch date and Folder Locations. Under the Display menu, you have options for

- ✔ **Import Batch:** You might import a batch of photos in one Photoshop Elements session and import another batch in the same session or in another session. When you select Import Batch, the images appear organized in groups, according to the date the batch was created.
- ✔ **Folder Location:** Click Folder Location to make an Explorer (Finder) pane appear on the left side of the Organizer window. You can browse your hard drive for folder locations and select a folder containing images you imported into the Organizer.

Sorting media types

Photos can also be sorted according to media type. Elements supports viewing photos, video files, audio files, projects, and Adobe PDF files. To select different media types, choose View➪Media Types, and a submenu offers options for viewing the different media types. Select a menu item from the submenu to make all media types matching the menu command appear in the Organizer window.

Using Search Options

The Organizer's Find menu is devoted entirely to searching photos. From the Find menu, you can locate photos in collections, catalogs, and the Organizer window according to a variety of different search criteria.

To use the commands on the Find menu, you need to have photos loaded in the Organizer window, or create collections or catalogs, which we explain in Chapter 6. The categories in the following sections can be searched in the Organizer.

Searching by date

When you have a number of different files in an Organizer window from photos shot on different dates, you can narrow your search to find photos, and all other types of files supported by Elements, through a date search.

In the Organizer, the date is taken from the camera metadata; but if a date isn't available from the camera data, the date is taken from the file creation date. The creation date isn't likely to be the date you shot the photo.

To search files by date in the Organizer, follow these steps:

1. **Open files in the Organizer by choosing File⇨Get Photos and then choosing a submenu command for acquiring files.**

   To open files stored on your hard drive, choose the From Files and Folders submenu command.

2. **Select a date range by choosing Find⇨Set Date Range.**

   The Set Date Range dialog box, shown in Figure 5-16, opens.

3. **Specify the dates.**

   Type a year in the Start Date Year text box. Select the month and day from the Month and Day drop-down menus. Repeat the same selections for the end date.

Figure 5-16: Open the Set Date Range dialog box and specify the start and end dates.

4. **Click OK.**

   The thumbnails shown in the Organizer window include only files created within the specified date range.

Searching for untagged items

You can tag files with a number of different criteria, as we explain in Chapter 6. When tags are added to images, you can sort files according to tag labels. We cover sorting by tag labels in Chapter 6, too. For now, take a look at the Find menu and notice the Untagged Items command. If you haven't added tags to some items and want to show only the untagged files so that you can begin to add tags, choose Find⇨Untagged Items or press Ctrl+Shift+Q on Windows. Elements displays all files without tags in the Organizer window.

Searching collections

Collections are among many items we address in Chapter 6. You can create collections and then select a collection on the Collections panel. Selecting a collection is like having a first level of sorting. You can then search by date or other sort options discussed in the preceding and following sections to narrow the choices.

Searching captions and notes

In Chapter 6, we talk about adding captions and notes to your files. When captions or notes are added to files, you can search for the caption name, contents of a note, or both. To search caption names and notes, follow these steps:

1. **Open files in the Organizer by choosing File⇨Get Photos and Videos, and then choosing a submenu command for acquiring files.**

   If you're opening files stored on your hard drive, choose the From Files and Folders submenu command.

2. **Choose Find⇨By Caption or Note.**

   The Find by Caption or Note dialog box opens, as shown in Figure 5-17.

   Options in the dialog box are

   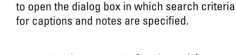

   Figure 5-17: Choose Find⇨By Caption or Note to open the dialog box in which search criteria for captions and notes are specified.

   - *Find Items with Caption or Note:* In the text box, type the words you want to locate.

   - *Match Only the Beginning of Words in Captions and Notes:* Click this radio button when you know that your caption or note begins with words you type in the text box.

   - *Match Any Part of Any Word in Captions or Notes:* Click this radio button if you're not sure whether the text typed in the box is used at the beginning of a caption or note, or whether it's contained within the caption name or note text.

3. **Click OK.**

   The Results appear in the Organizer window.

Searching by history

Elements keeps track of what you do with your photos, such as printing, e-mailing, sharing, and performing a number of other tasks. You can search for files based on the file history by choosing Find⇨By History. Selecting options on the By History submenu reports files found on date searches meeting the history criteria.

Searching metadata

Metadata includes information about your images that's supplied by digital cameras as well as custom data you add to a file. *Metadata* contains descriptions of the image, such as your camera name, the camera settings you used to take a picture, copyright information, and much more.

Searching metadata is easy. Just choose Find⇨By Details (Metadata) in the Organizer. The Find by Details (Metadata) dialog box opens. The first two groups in the dialog box offer a number of different choices for search criteria and options according to the criteria. In the third column, you specify exactly what you want to search by typing search criteria in the text box. Clicking the plus button adds new lines to add more criteria to the search, as shown in Figure 5-18, and clicking the minus button deletes a line.

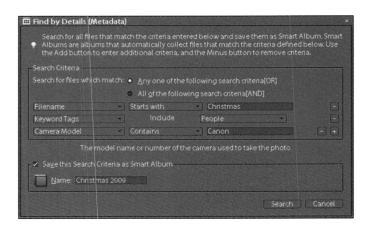

Figure 5-18: Choose Find⇨By Details (Metadata) in the Organizer to open the dialog box in which metadata are specified.

Searching faces

If a magical method is available to you for searching files in Elements, it has to be searching for faces. When you choose Find➪Find Faces for Tagging, Elements searches through files you select in the Organizer window and examines each image for a face — *Homo sapiens* faces, to be exact.

Note that you should first select image thumbnails in the Organizer window and then choose Find➪Find Faces for Tagging. If you don't select files, Elements searches the entire catalog. Be aware that if you search through a large catalog, Elements takes some time to complete the search.

The results of the search magically include all photos containing faces in a new Organizer window. Although the command is intended to identify images you can tag, you can use the command for invoking a search and choosing to view all files containing faces.

6
Organizing and Managing Your Photos (Windows)

*D*ownloading a bunch of media cards filled with photos and leaving them in folders distributed all over your hard drive is like having a messy office with papers stacked haphazardly all over your desk. Trying to find a file, even with all the great search capabilities we cover in Chapter 5, can take you as much time as sorting through piles of papers. What you need is a good file-management system.

In this chapter, we talk about organizing and annotating files and the important task of backing up files. Be certain to take a little time to understand the organizational methods that Elements offers, keep your files organized when you copy them to your hard drive, and back up files to CDs or DVDs. The time you invest in organizing your pictures helps you quickly locate files when you need them.

Macintosh users have full advantage of using all the Organizer tools and methods in Photoshop Elements 9.

Organizing Groups of Images with Keyword Tags

Elements provides you with a great opportunity for organizing files, in the form of keyword tags. After you acquire your images in the Organizer, as we discuss in Chapter 4, sort them out and add keyword tags according to the dates you took the pictures, the subject matter, or some other categorical arrangement.

In the Organizer window, the Keywords Tags panel helps you sort your pictures and keep them well organized. You use the Keyword Tags panel (which we talk about in the section "Working with keyword tags," later in this chapter) to identify individual images by using a limitless number of options for categorizing your pictures. On the Keyword Tags panel, you can create keyword tags and collection groups to neatly organize files.

In the following sections, you can find out how to create and manage keyword tags.

Creating and viewing a new keyword tag

To create a new keyword tag and add photos to the tag, follow these steps:

1. **Open photos in the Organizer.**

   Open the Organizer window by clicking the Organizer button in an editing mode or by selecting Organize on the Welcome screen. Choose File⇨Get Photos and Videos⇨From Files and Folders. Note that you should have first copied some photos to your hard drive, as we explain in Chapter 4.

2. **To create a new keyword tag, click the plus sign (+) icon in the Keyword Tags panel to open a drop-down menu and then choose New Keyword Tag. Alternatively, you can press Ctrl+N (⌘+N) to create a new Keyword Tag.**

   The Create Keyword Tag dialog box opens, as shown in Figure 6-1.

3. **Specify a category.**

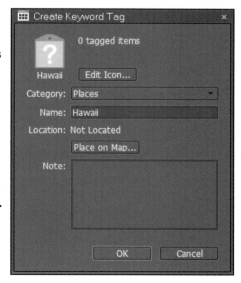

Figure 6-1: The Create Keyword Tag dialog box.

Click the Category drop-down menu and choose one of the preset categories listed in the menu. (See the next section for instructions on customizing these categories.)

4. **Type a name for the tag in the Name text box and add a note to describe the keyword tag.**

   You might use the location where you took the photos, the subject matter, or other descriptive information for the note.

5. **(Optional and Windows-only) If you want to assign the keyword tag to a map location on the Yahoo! Maps, as we discuss in Chapter 5, click the Place on Map button. If you want to add a Note, type in the Note text box.**

   When you click Place on Map, a dialog box opens in which you type a city name for placing the image on Yahoo! Maps. Type a city name and select the correct city from options provided in a second dialog box.

   Notes offer an opportunity to add descriptions for your tags.

6. **Click OK in the Create Keyword Tag dialog box.**

   You return to the Organizer window.

7. **In the Organizer window, select the photos you want to keyword tag.**

   Click a photo and Shift-click another photo to select photos in a group. Click a photo and Ctrl-click (⌘-click on the Mac) different photos scattered around the Organizer window to select nonsequential photos.

8. **To add a new keyword tag to a photo (or selection of photos), click one of the selected photos in the Organizer window and drag the photo thumbnail to the New Tag icon on the Keyword Tags panel.**

   Alternatively, you can drag a tag to the selected photos.

   When you release the mouse button, the photos are added to the new keyword tag.

9. **Repeat Steps 2 through 6 to create keyword tags for all the images you want to organize.**

To view one or more keyword tags, click the empty square adjacent to a keyword tag icon to show the photos within that group in the Organizer window. When you click the empty square, an icon in the shape of a pair of binoculars appears inside the square, as shown in Figure 6-2. All photos matching the keyword tags are shown in the Organizer window.

Figure 6-2: A binocular icon appears when you click an empty square.

To return to viewing all photos in the Organizer, click the binoculars in the Tags panel. The square returns to empty and turns off viewing the tagged files.

Working with keyword tags

You can manage keyword tags by using menu commands from the New drop-down menu and other commands from a contextual menu that you open by right-clicking a keyword tag on the Keyword Tags panel.

In the New drop-down menu, you can access these commands:

- **New Keyword Tag:** Create a new keyword tag, as we describe in the steps in the preceding section.

- **New Sub-Category:** A *subcategory* is like a nested bookmark. Create a subcategory by selecting New Sub-Category from the New menu; a dialog box opens, prompting you to type a name for the new subcategory. As an example of how you might use keyword tags and subcategories, you might have a keyword tag named Uncle Joe's Wedding. Then, you might create subcategories for Bride Dressing Room, Ceremony, Family Photos, Reception, and so on.

- **New Category:** Choose New Category from the New menu in the Keyword Tags panel to open a dialog box that prompts you to type a name for the new category. By default, you can find predefined category names for People, Places, Events, and Other. If you want to add your own custom categories, use this menu command.

- **From File:** If you export a keyword tag, the file is written as XML (eXtensible Markup Language). When you choose From File, you can import an XML file of a keyword tags file.

- **Save Keyword Tags to a File:** You can save keyword tags to a file that can be retrieved with the From File command. This option is handy when you open a different catalog file and want to import the same collection names created in one catalog file to another catalog file. (See the section "Cataloging Files," later in this chapter.)

- **Collapse All Keyword Tags:** Keyword tags appear like bookmark lists that can be collapsed and expanded. An expanded list shows you all the subcategory keyword tags. Choose Collapse All Keyword Tags to collapse the list.

- **Expand All Keyword Tags:** This command expands a collapsed list.

When you create a new keyword tag, you see a large icon in the Keyword Tags panel. The default tags appear with small icons. You can access the items that appear below default tags by clicking the right-pointing arrow to expand the list.

Right-click a collection name to make the following menu commands appear:

- **Change *<keyword tag name>* keyword tag to a sub-category:** Choose this menu command to change a keyword tag to a keyword tag subcategory.

- **Edit *<keyword tag name>* keyword tag:** This menu command opens the Edit Keyword Tag dialog box. You can rename a keyword tag, change the note, or change the map location in this dialog box. Alternatively, you can click the Pencil tool on the Keyword Tags panel to open the same dialog box.

- **Delete *<keyword tag name>* keyword tag:** Select a keyword tag and select this menu option to delete a keyword tag. Alternatively, click the Trash icon on the panel to delete a keyword tag. Note that deleting a keyword tag doesn't delete files.

- **Place on Map (Windows only):** Choose Place on Map to add images to a Yahoo! Map location, as we describe in Chapter 5.

- **Remove from Map (Windows only):** Choose this command to remove tags from Yahoo! Maps.

- **Show on Map (Windows only):** This command opens the Yahoo! Maps panel and shows the red pin at the map location with which the image(s) are associated.

- **New Search Using *<keyword tag name>* keyword tag:** This command searches through a catalog and displays all the photos assigned the keyword tag in the Organizer window.

- **Add Media with *<keyword tag name>* keyword tag to search results:** Select media in the Organizer window that you want to add to the search results.

- **Exclude Photos with *<keyword tag name>* keyword tag from search results:** Select photos in the Organizer window and choose this command to exclude the selected photos from the search.

- **Attach *<keyword tag name>* keyword tag to *<n>* selected items:** Select a file in the Organizer window and choose this command to attach the keyword tag to the file. If you select one photo in the Organizer, the number *<n>* is one. Selecting more than one photo changes the number to the total number of selected images. When you open a contextual menu, the selected images are added to the keyword tag where the contextual menu is opened.

Keyword tags are saved automatically with the catalog you work with. By default, Elements creates a catalog and auto-saves your work to it. If you happen to create another catalog, as we explain in the next section, your keyword tags disappear. Be aware of which catalog is open when you create keyword tags in order to return to them.

Getting your head in the clouds

Elements 8 introduced another way to view and search for photos in a catalog: *tag clouds,* that is, a hierarchical list of tags. You can access the Tags Cloud feature by clicking the View Tags Cloud icon in the Tags panel, as shown in Figure 6-3. When you click the icon, an alphabetical list of your tags appears in the panel.

Figure 6-3: Click the Tags Cloud icon to display a hierarchical list of the tags categories.

Click a tag name in the list to select a tag and view all photos tagged with the respective name. When you look over the tag cloud, you find names in large, medium, and small text. This order displays the hierarchy of the tags. The large text is the parent name, the medium text is a category within the parent, and the small text is the tag item below a category.

To return to the default tags view, click the View Tag Hierarchy icon to the left of the View Tags Cloud icon on the Keyword Tags panel.

Cataloging Files

When you open files in the Organizer, all your files are saved automatically to a catalog. The files themselves aren't really saved to the catalog; rather, links from the catalog to the individual files are saved. *Links* are like pointers that tell the catalog where to look for a file. When you add and delete files within the Organizer, the catalog is continually updated.

When you open more files in the Organizer, the default catalog file grows, and the maximum size of the catalog file is limited only by your available hard drive space. Working with a single catalog file has some disadvantages. For example, if your catalog file becomes corrupted and unrecoverable, you lose all the work you've done organizing files into keyword tags. If you work with many files, the Organizer performance slows down.

Rather than work with a single catalog file, you can fine-tune your file organization by creating several catalogs. You might want to organize files according to subject matter, dates, locations, or some other division of categories, and then create separate catalogs for each category. You can find all the details in the sections that follow.

Importing photos to a new catalog

To keep your photos organized and your catalog files small, you can start a completely new catalog before you import photos. Follow these steps:

1. **Choose File⇨Catalog and click the New button in the Catalog Manager dialog box that appears, as shown in Figure 6-4.**

2. **When the New Catalog dialog box opens, type a name for the new catalog in the File Name text box and then click Save.**

3. **(Optional) If you want to add free music files installed with Elements, select the Import Free Music into All New Catalogs check box.**

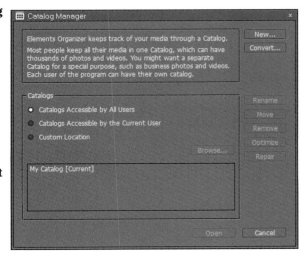

Figure 6-4: Choose File⇨Catalog to open the Catalog Manager dialog box.

4. **Choose File⇨Get Photos and Videos to add files to the new catalog.**

   When the Get Photos from Files and Folders dialog box opens, a list of media files appears in the dialog box when the Import Free Music into All New Catalogs check box is selected.

5. **(Optional) Select the free music files to add to your collection; then navigate your hard drive and select the photos you want to add. After you identify all the files, click Open.**

   The selected music files and photos are added to your new collection of media contained in the catalog.

Splitting a big catalog into smaller catalogs

Unfortunately, Elements doesn't provide you a command to split large catalogs into smaller ones. It's best to understand first how you want to organize your photos before creating your first catalog. However, if you've created a large catalog and want to split it into two or more separate catalogs, you need to manually add new photos to a new catalog and delete photos from the older catalog.

Switching to a different catalog

When you need to open a different catalog file, choose File➪Catalog and select the name of the catalog you want to open. Click Open at the bottom of the dialog box to open the selected catalog. The Organizer window changes to reflect files contained in that catalog.

Notice the Repair and Optimize buttons in Figure 6-4. If you can't see thumbnail previews of images or open them in one of the editing modes, your catalog file might be corrupted. Click the Repair button to try to fix the problem. When catalogs get sluggish, you might need to optimize a catalog to gain better performance. Click Optimize in the Catalog Manager routinely to keep your catalog operating at optimum performance.

Backing up your catalog (Windows only)

Computer users often learn the hard way about the importance of backing up a hard drive and the precious data they spent time creating and editing. We can save you some aggravation right now, before you spend any more time editing your photos in Elements.

We authors are so paranoid when we're writing a book that we back up our chapters on multiple drives, CDs, and DVDs when we finish them. The standard rule is that if you spend sufficient time working on a project and it gets to the point where redoing your work would be a major aggravation, it's time to back up files.

When organizing your files, adding keyword tags and creating albums, and creating stacks and version sets, you want to back up the catalog file in case your catalog becomes corrupted.

Here's how you can use Elements to create a backup of your data log:

1. **Choose File➪Backup Catalog to CD/DVD or Hard Drive to open the Backup Catalog to CD/DVD or Hard Drive Wizard.**

   This wizard has three panes that Elements walks you through to painlessly create a backup of your files.

2. **Select the source to back up.**

   The first pane in the Burn/Backup Wizard offers two options:

- *Full Backup:* Click this radio button to perform your first backup or write files to a new media source.

- *Incremental Backup:* Use this option if you've already performed at least one backup and you want to update the backed-up files.

3. **Click Next and select a target location for your backed-up files.**

Active drives, including CD/DVD drives attached to your computer, appear in the Select Destination Drive list, as shown in Figure 6-5. Select a drive, and Elements automatically assesses the write speed and identifies a previous backup file if one was created. The total size of the files to copy is reported in the wizard. This information is helpful so that you know whether more than one CD or DVD is needed to complete the backup.

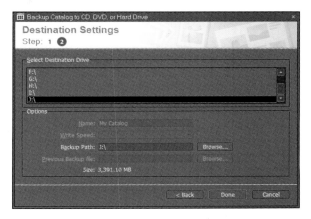

Figure 6-5: The wizard provides options for selecting the destination media for the backup.

4. **If you intend to copy files to your hard drive or to another hard drive attached to your computer, click the Browse button and identify the path.**

If you use a media source, such as a CD or DVD, Elements prompts you to insert a disc and readies the media for writing.

5. **Click Done, and the backup commences.**

Be certain to not interrupt the backup. It might take some time, so just let Elements work away until you're notified that the backup is complete.

Backing up photos and files (Windows)

With files stored all over your hard drive, manually copying files to a second hard drive, CD-ROM, or DVD would take quite a bit of time. Fortunately, Elements makes finding files to back up a breeze.

Choose File➪Make a CD/DVD and then in the dialog box that opens, click Yes to confirm the action. The Make a CD/DVD dialog box opens. Select a hard drive or a CD/DVD drive, type a name for the backup folder, and click OK. Elements goes about copying all files shown in the Organizer window to your backup source.

Macintosh users don't have an option for backing up photos from the Organizer. On the Mac you can create a burn folder in the Finder, select all photos in the Organizer window and drag the selected files to the burn folder. Click Burn and the files are copied to a CD/DVD-Rom.

Creating Albums

With keyword tags, you can organize files into categories and subcategories, which help keep your files neatly organized within a catalog. Elements offers additional organizing control in the Albums panel. You might want to organize an album for sharing photos with others on www.photoshop.com, assemble an album and rate each photo with a range from one to five stars, create a slide show, or just use the Albums panel to further segregate images within different categories.

Think of a catalog as a parent item, and think of keyword tags albums as its children. Within keyword tags, you can use the sort options (discussed in Chapter 5) to sort files according to date. If you still have a number of files in an Organizer window that are hard to manage, you can create tags that form subcategories within the keyword tags. Additionally, you can create an album out of a number of photos within a given keyword tag. For example, you might have a huge number of photos taken on a European vacation. Your catalog contains all the images taken on that trip. You can then create keyword tags for files according to the country visited. You then might rate the photos according to the best pictures you took on your trip. The highest-rated images could then be assembled in an album and viewed as a slide show.

Rating images

You can rate photos in the Organizer by tagging images with one to five stars. You might have some photos that are exceptional, which you want to give five-star ratings, whereas poor photos with lighting and focus problems might be rated with one star.

Rating photos is handled in the Properties panel. To assign a star rating to a file, open a contextual menu by right-clicking a photo and select Properties from that menu. The Properties – General panel, shown in Figure 6-6, opens. Click a star to rate the photo. Alternatively, you can click a photo, choose Edit⇨Ratings, and choose a star rating from the submenu that appears.

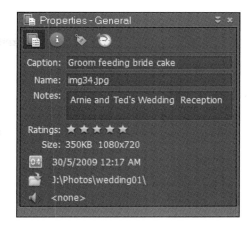

Figure 6-6: Rating photos with stars in the Properties panel.

When you select the Details check box on the Shortcuts bar, all your rated photos appear with the number of stars according to the rating you provided, as shown in Figure 6-7. You can easily sort files according to ratings by choosing the Edit⇨Ratings command and select a star rating from the submenu.

Adding rated files to an album

You might want to rate images with star ratings and then add all your images to an album. Within the album, you can still choose to view your pictures according to star ratings.

Figure 6-7: When the Details check box is selected, all rated photos appear with stars.

Creating an album

In the section "Organizing Groups of Images with Keyword Tags," earlier in this chapter, we discuss how creating keyword tags and assigning tags to photos help you organize a collection of photos and how sub-categories help you break down a collection into additional categories. With albums and star ratings, you can further break down a collection into groups that you might want to mark for printing, sharing, or onscreen slide shows.

To create an album, follow these steps:

1. **Click the plus sign (+) icon on the Albums panel and choose New Album from the drop-down menu shown in Figure 6-8.**

   The Albums panel expands to show the Album Details.

2. **Name the new album.**

   Type a name for the album in the Album Name text box, as shown in Figure 6-9.

3. **Drag photos from the Organizer to the items window in the Album Content panel, shown in Figure 6-9.**

   Alternatively, you can select photos in the Organizer and click the plus sign (+) icon to add them to the album.

4. **Click Done at the bottom of the panel.**

   Your new album now appears listed in the Albums panel.

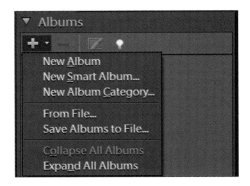

Figure 6-8: Click the plus sign (+) icon to open the drop-down menu and then choose New Album.

That's it! Your new album is created, and the photos you drag to the album are added to it. You can isolate all the photos within a given album by clicking the album name in the Albums panel.

Creating multiple albums uses only a fraction of the memory that would be required if you wanted to duplicate photos for multiple purposes, such as printing, Web hosting, sharing, and so on.

Creating a Smart Album

You can perform a search based on a number of different criteria, as we explain in Chapter 5. The Smart Album feature enables you to save the search results in an album. After you have all the files shown in the Organizer based on the searches you perform, you can create a Smart Album as follows:

Figure 6-9: Drag photos to the Items area in the Album Contents panel.

1. **Open the New menu on the Albums panel and choose New Smart Album.**

   The New Smart Album dialog box opens, as shown in Figure 6-10.

2. **Type a name for your new Smart Album.**

3. **Make selections for the search criteria below the Name text box.**

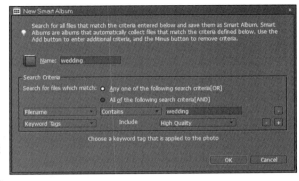

Figure 6-10: Type a name for your new Smart Album, add the search criteria, and click OK to add the album to the Albums panel.

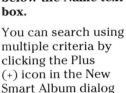

You can search using multiple criteria by clicking the Plus (+) icon in the New Smart Album dialog box. Click the icon, and a new line appears. Choose options from the Filename drop-down menu, the Contains drop-down menu, and the last drop-down menu to help narrow your search.

4. **Click OK.**

   The Smart Album is listed above the albums in the Albums panel.

Creating an Album Category

The Albums panel contains all the albums and Smart Albums you create in an organized list. By default, the albums are listed in alphabetical order. If you add many albums to the panel, the list can be long, making it difficult to find the album you want to use for a given editing session.

If you're a user of Photoshop Elements prior to version 8, New Album Category was previously referred to as a New Album Group.

An *Album Category* is no more than a divider shown in the Albums panel. You don't add photos to the group. You nest albums within a group in a hierarchical manner. To understand how to create an Album Category, follow these steps:

1. **Create several albums.**

   To begin, you should have two or more albums added to the Albums panel. For example, suppose that you have many photos of a vacation trip to Hawaii. You want to divide the photos by images taken at a luau, a diving trip, a day on Waikiki Beach, or other similar events that you want to group together. For each category, such as Luau, Diving, or Waikiki, you create a separate album.

2. **Create an Album Category by clicking the New menu on the Albums panel and choosing New Album Category.**

   The Create Album Category dialog box, as shown in Figure 6-11, opens.

3. **Type a name for the group in the Album Category Name text box.**

4. **Click OK.**

   You new Album Category is added to the Albums panel.

5. **Click and drag an album onto the Album Category name in the Albums panel.**

   The albums you drag to the Album Category are nested within the group, as shown in Figure 6-12.

Figure 6-11: Type a name for your new Album Category in the Create Album Category dialog box.

Figure 6-12 shows an expanded Album Category, as denoted by the list (below Trips) and the disclosure triangle. To collapse a group, click the down-pointing arrow. The group names remain visible and provide you with more viewing space on the Albums panel, making it easier to scroll long lists.

Like keyword tags, albums can be saved to an XML (eXtensible Markup Language) file, and the files can be loaded in the Albums panel. Open the New menu, where you find commands for Save Albums to File and

Figure 6-12: Albums are nested below an Album Category.

From File. You can export an album to a file and then copy the file to another computer, making it easy to organize photos on several computers.

Hiding Files That Get in the Way

Elements offers a few ways to hide files so that you can keep your images organized and easy to find.

With a simple menu command, you can mark selected files in the Organizer as *hidden*. You might have several files of the same subject and want to keep only one file visible in the Organizer window. However, you may not want to delete the other photos. As such, you can hide files in the Organizer window and show the hidden files by using menu commands.

Select files you want to hide, and from either the Edit menu or a contextual menu, choose Visibility➪Mark as Hidden. To see the files you mark for hiding, return to the same Visibility menu and choose Show Hidden. Essentially, you remove the check mark for Show Hidden, resulting in hiding the files. To easily toggle between showing and hiding files marked for hiding, choose View➪Hidden Files. Selecting this menu command toggles between showing and hiding the files you marked for hiding.

Stacking 'em up

Think of *stacks* like a stack of cards that is face up. You see only the front card, and all the other cards are hidden behind that card. Stacks work the same way. You hide different images behind a foreground image. At any time, you can sort the images or display all images in the stack in the Organizer window.

To create a stack, follow these steps:

1. **In the Organizer, select several photos.**

   You can select any number of photos. However, you can't stack audio or movie files.

2. **Choose Edit➪Stack➪Stack Selected Photos.**

   Elements stacks your photos. The first image you select remains in view in the Organizer window. In the upper-right area, an icon that looks like a stack of cards appears on the image thumbnail when you've stacked some images. Double-click the photo to open the stack in the Organizer, and you find the same icon in the top-right corner, as shown in Figure 6-13.

After you stack a group of images, you can use the Stack submenu commands to manage the photos. Click a stack to select it and then choose Edit➪Stack. The submenu commands that are available include

✔ **Automatically Suggest Photo Stacks (Windows-only):** Select this command to make Elements search the photos in the Organizer window for visually similar appearances. Photos that have visually similar appearances are opened in a separate window, where you can select photos you want to stack. Make a selection of two or more photos, and select Stack Selected Photos.

Photo courtesy Leah Valle (www.13thwitch.com)

Figure 6-13: Viewing a stack in the Organizer.

✔ **Stack Selected Photos:** This command remains grayed out unless you have several photos selected to create a stack.

✔ **Unstack Photos:** Click a stack in the Organizer and choose this command to return all images to the Organizer window and eliminate the stack.

✔ **Expand Photos in Stack:** This command expands the stack to show all thumbnail images in the Organizer window.

✔ **Collapse Photos in Stack:** This command collapses a stack to show only the top photo in the Organizer window.

✔ **Flatten Stack:** After you stack some photos, this command becomes available.

Be careful with this command. When you flatten a stack, all photos except for the top photo are deleted from the catalog (not from your hard drive).

✔ **Remove Photo from Stack:** Choosing this command removes the selected photos from the stack.

✔ **Set as Top Photo:** You also need to first choose Expand Photos in Stack before accessing this command. If you don't like the topmost photo, select another and choose this menu command to move the selected photo to the top of the stack.

If you want to view all stacks in an Organizer window in expanded form, choose View➪Expand All Stacks. Using this command doesn't require you to individually select stacks in the Organizer before expanding them.

Creating versions

Versions are similar to stacks, but you create versions from only one file. You can edit an image and save both the edited version and the original as a version set. Also, you can make additional edits in either editing mode and saved to a version set. To create a version set, follow these steps:

1. **Select an image by clicking it in the Organizer window.**

2. **Apply an edit.**

   For example, right in the Organizer, you can correct some brightness problems in your image. Choose Edit➪Auto Smart Fix to adjust contrast and brightness. See Chapter 10 for more details on adjusting contrast and brightness.

3. **View the items in the version set by clicking the image in the Organizer and choosing Edit➪Version Set➪Expand Items in Version Set.**

   Elements automatically creates a version set for you when you apply the Auto Smart Fix to the file. A new Organizer window opens and shows two thumbnail images — one representing the original image and the other representing the edited version.

4. **To open the original in Edit Full mode, select the original image and then select Edit Full from the Display drop-down menu on the Organizer menu bar.**

5. **Edit the image in Edit Full mode.**

   You can choose from many different menu commands to edit the image. For example, change the color mode to Indexed Color by choosing Image➪Mode➪Indexed Color, as we explain in Chapter 3.

6. **Save a version by choosing File➪Save As.**

7. **In the Save Options area of the Save As dialog box, select the Include in the Organizer and Save in Version Set with Original check boxes.**

8. **Click Save.**

   The edit made in Edit Full mode is saved as another version in your version set.

TIP

When you have a version set, you can open the Edit⇨Version Set submenu and choose menu commands that are similar to commands available with stacks. (See the preceding section for details.)

After you create a version set, you find additional submenu commands you can use to manage the version set. Choose Edit⇨Version Set, or open a contextual menu on a version set and then choose Version Set. The submenu, as shown in Figure 6-14, opens.

Figure 6-14: Use the Edit menu or a contextual menu opened on a version set, and then choose Version Set to open the submenu.

Items listed in the Version Set submenu include:

- ✔ **Expand Items in Version Set:** Click a version set and choose this menu command to expand the items in the version set.

- ✔ **Collapse Items in Version Set:** When items are expanded, you can return them to a collapsed view by selecting this command.

- ✔ **Flatten Version Set:** Be careful here. If you choose this command, you lose all items in the version set except the top image.

- ✔ **Convert Version Set to Individual Items:** This command removes items from the version set and adds each version as a separate image to the Organizer window.

- ✔ **Revert to Original:** This command deletes the version set and returns you to the original, unedited version of the file.

- ✔ **Remove Item(s) from Version Set:** As stated, this option removes an item from a version set.

- ✔ **Set as Top Item:** When viewing an expanded version set, click one of the images and choose this item to move it to the top.

Sticking Digital Notes on Your Photos

A way to identify your files beyond the tagging capabilities, which we discuss in the section "Organizing Groups of Images with Keyword Tags," earlier in this chapter, is to add captions and notes. When you add a caption or note, you can search captions or notes by choosing the Find⇨By Caption or Note menu command. Captions and notes are also helpful when you create different keyword tags — such as slide presentations and photo albums — by using the Create panel, as we explain in Chapter 16.

Text captions are easy to create. Although you can select a thumbnail image in the Organizer window and choose Edit➪Add Caption, a better way is to use the Properties panel. Just follow these steps:

1. **To open the Properties panel, select a thumbnail image in the Organizer, right-click it, and choose Show Properties from the contextual menu that appears.**

   Alternatively, you can choose Window➪Properties or press Alt+Enter. In either case, the Properties – General panel opens, as shown in Figure 6-15.

2. **Type a caption by adding text to the Caption text box.**

3. **Type text in the Notes area on the panel to add a note.**

   That's all there is to it. You can also record audio notes about an image.

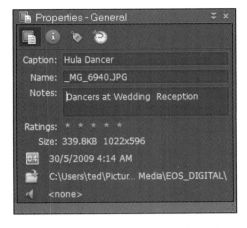

Figure 6-15: The Properties – General panel.

Automating Your Organization

If you have a number of common edits you want to make on a collection of photos, Elements lets you perform common changes to multiple files. With a single menu command, you can change file formats, change file attributes, and add common file base names. File renaming can be part of the Export command, or you can use a menu option for renaming files in the Organizer.

Automating common tasks when you export

You might use the Export Selected Items dialog box frequently when you're acquiring images from digital cameras. What you may not know is that this dialog box can automate other common tasks, too.

- **Add common base names for the filenames.** (For example, change names, such as DSC000001, DSC000002, and so on, to more descriptive filenames, such as Dallas 001 and Dallas 002.)
- **Change the file format.**
- **Change the file size and quality.**

Follow these steps to use options in the Export dialog box:

1. **Select files and open the Export New Items dialog box by choosing File➪Export➪As New File(s) or pressing Ctrl+E (⌘+E on the Mac).**

   The Export New Files dialog box opens, as shown in Figure 6-16.

   You don't have to select files beforehand. You can identify files in another dialog box that's accessible from within the Export New Files dialog box. If you know ahead of time which files you want to export, go ahead and select them in the Organizer window.

2. **Select a file type.**

   From the File Type options, select the format you want to use for the exported images. For more information on file formats, see Chapter 3.

Figure 6-16: The Export New Files dialog box permits you to rename and change formats for batches of files.

3. **Select a size and quality.**

   If you select Use Original Format in Step 2, resizing options are grayed out. You use this setting when you want to retain the original sizes while you rename files. If you select JPEG, you can move the quality slider, as we explain in Chapter 3, to set the image quality of JPEG images. None of the other format options provides a quality option.

   For sizing images, select commands from the Photo Size drop-down menu, where you find several fixed dimensions and an option for using a custom size.

4. **Select a target location for the new files by clicking the Browse button and selecting a folder.**

If you want to create a new folder, you can click the Make New Folder button (New Folder button on Mac) in the Browse for Folder dialog box, which opens after you click the Browse button.

5. **If you want to keep the original filenames, click the Original Names radio button. If you want to rename files with a common base name, select Common Base Name and type a name in the text box.**

The resultant files are *<base name>*001.extension, *<base name>*002. extension, *<base name>*003.extension, and so on.

6. **If you want to add files to the list for exporting, click the plus sign (+) symbol in the lower-left corner.**

This step opens the Add Media dialog box, as shown in Figure 6-17, which offers a number of different options for selecting files to export.

Among your choices in this dialog box are

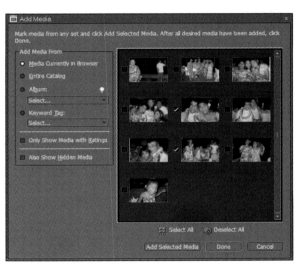

- *Media Currently in Browser:* Click this radio button when you want to export all files shown in the Organizer window.

Figure 6-17: The Add Media dialog box offers a number of options for exporting photos.

- *Entire Catalog:* Click this radio button if you're viewing a catalog, tagged files, or a sorted group in which some files are temporarily hidden. When you select this option, all hidden files are included in the export.

- *Album:* Click the Album radio button and select an album from the drop-down menu.

You can search albums and save the results as a Smart Album. To create a Smart Album, just perform any kind of search and then click New Smart Album below the plus sign (+) icon in the Albums panel.

- *Keyword Tag:* Click this radio button to select files marked with keyword tags. All files with the same tag are exported.

- *Only Show Media with Ratings:* All photos and other supported media with star ratings are shown on the window.

- *Also Show Hidden Media:* Any file that might be hidden in the Organizer can be made visible in the file list and included in the export.

- *Select All:* When you add files to the list window, you can choose to export all files from the selected category. Click the Select All button to mark all the files for export.

- *Deselect All:* If you want some files from the list window exported while others remain behind, click the Deselect All button and then individually click the check boxes for all files you want to export.

- *Add Selected Media:* When you add photos and other media by using the options found in the Add Photos From area in the dialog box, the thumbnails for the images appear in a scrollable window inside the dialog box. You can select individual photos to be included in the export by selecting the check boxes adjacent to each photo. After selecting the photos you want to include, click this button. The button action doesn't dismiss the dialog box; it merely marks the files for inclusion.

- *Done:* Click this button to return to the Export Selected Items dialog box.

- *Cancel:* Click to cancel out of the dialog box.

 7. **Select any images you don't want included in the export by clicking the check box to remove a check mark.**

 8. **Click Done Add Selected Media in the Add Media dialog box and you are returned to the Export New Files dialog box,**

 9. **Click Export in the Export New Files dialog.**

Elements automatically exports the images to the selected folder.

Renaming files

If you load an Organizer window and want to rename files, you don't need to use the Export command and wade through the options in the Export Selected Files dialog box. Just select the files you want to rename and then choose File⇨Rename. In the Rename dialog box that opens, type a base name for the files and click OK. The selected files are renamed using a common base name. This is a quick and easy way to rename those digital camera images.

Part III
Selecting and Correcting Photos

In this part . . .

The wide array of editing features in Elements permit you to change, optimize, perfect, and combine images into composite designs. In this part, you discover how to select image content and then alter that content for a variety of purposes, such as correcting the color, changing the appearance, and extracting the content so that you can introduce it in other photos. Because photos are composed of many thousands of tiny pixels, you need to develop some skill in selecting just the pixels you want to use for any given editing task.

In addition to describing how to create image selections, this part covers photo correction for image contrast and brightness, color correction, and color conversions from one color mode to another. Rarely do you encounter digital images that don't require some kind of correction. In the chapters ahead, you can find out how to quickly master some powerful correction techniques.

7

Making and Modifying Selections

*I*f all you want to do is use your photos in all their unedited glory, feel free to skip this chapter and move on to other topics. But if you want to occasionally pluck an element out of its environment and stick it in another, or apply an adjustment to just a portion of your image, this chapter's for you.

Finding out how to make accurate selections is one of those skills that's well worth the time you invest. In this chapter, we cover all the various selection tools and techniques. We give you tips on which tools are better for which kinds of selections. But remember that you usually have several ways to achieve the same result. Which road you choose is ultimately up to you.

Defining Selections

Before you dig in and get serious about selecting, let us clarify for the record what we mean by defining a selection. When you *define* a selection, you specify which part of an image you want to work with. Everything within a selection is considered selected. Everything outside the selection is unselected. After you have a selection, you can then adjust only that portion, and the unselected portion remains unchanged. Or you can copy the selected area into another image altogether. Want to transport yourself out of your background and onto a white sandy beach? Select yourself out of that backyard BBQ photo, get a stock photo of the tropical paradise of your choice, and drag and drop yourself onto your tropics photo with the Move tool. It's that easy.

When you make a selection, a dotted outline — variously called a *selection border,* an *outline,* or a *marquee* — appears around the selected area. Elements, the sophisticated imaging program that it is, also allows you to partially select pixels, which allows for soft-edged selections. You create soft-edged selections by feathering or anti-aliasing the selection or by using a mask. Don't worry: We cover these techniques in the section "Applying marquee options," later in this chapter.

For all the selection techniques described in this chapter, be sure that your image is in Edit Full mode in the Editor and not in Edit Quick or Edit Guided modes or in the Organizer.

Creating Rectangular and Elliptical Selections

If you can drag a mouse, you can master the Rectangular and Elliptical Marquee tools. These two tools are the easiest selection tools to use, so if your desired element is rectangular or elliptical, by all means, grab one of these tools.

The Rectangular Marquee tool, as its moniker states, is designed to define rectangular or square selections. This tool is great to use if you want to home in on the pertinent portion of your photo and eliminate unnecessary background.

Here's how to make a selection with this tool:

1. **Select the Rectangular Marquee tool from the Tools panel.**

   It looks like a dotted square. You can also press M to access the tool. If it isn't visible, press Shift+M.

2. **Drag from one corner of the area you want to select to the opposite corner.**

   While you drag, the selection border appears. The marquee follows the movement of your mouse cursor.

3. Release your mouse button.

You now have a completed rectangular selection, as shown in Figure 7-1.

The Elliptical Marquee tool, which shares the same flyout menu as the Rectangular Marquee tool, is designed for elliptical or circular selections. This tool is perfect for selecting balloons, clocks, and other rotund elements.

Here's how to use the Elliptical Marquee:

1. Select the Elliptical Marquee tool from the Marquee flyout menu on the Tools panel.

It looks like a dotted ellipse. You can also press M to access this tool, if it's visible. If it isn't, press Shift+M.

2. Position the crosshair near the area you want to select and then drag around your desired element.

With this tool, you drag from a given point on the ellipse. While you drag, the selection border appears.

3. When you're satisfied with your selection, release the mouse button.

Your elliptical selection is done, as shown in Figure 7-2. If your selection isn't quite centered around your element, simply move the selection border by dragging inside the border.

You can move a selection while you're making it with either of the Marquee tools by holding down the spacebar while you're dragging.

Figure 7-1: Use the Rectangular Marquee tool to create rectangular selections.

Flat Earth

Figure 7-2: The Elliptical Marquee is perfect for selecting round objects.

Perfecting squares and circles with Shift and Alt or Option

Sometimes, you need to create a perfectly square or circular selection. To do so, simply press the Shift key after you begin dragging. After you make your selection, release the mouse button first and then release the Shift key.

When you're making an elliptical selection, making the selection from the center outward is often easier. To draw from the center, first click the mouse button where you want to position the center, press Alt (Option on the Mac), and then drag. When you make your selection, release the mouse button first and then release the Alt (Option on the Mac) key.

If you want to draw from the center outward *and* create a perfect circle or square, press the Shift key, as well. After you make your selection, release the mouse button and then release the Shift+Alt (Shift+Option on the Mac) keys.

Applying marquee options

The Marquee tools offer additional options when you need to make precise selections at specific measurements. You also find options for making your selections soft around the edges.

The only thing to remember is that you must select the options on the Options bar, as shown in Figure 7-3, before you make your selection with the Marquee tools. Options can't be applied after the selection has already been made. The exception is that you can feather a selection after the fact by choosing Select⇨Feather.

Figure 7-3: Apply marquee settings on the Options bar.

Here are the various marquee options available to you:

- ✓ **Feather:** Feathering creates soft edges around your selection. The amount of softness depends on the value, from 0 to 250 pixels, you enter. The higher the value, the softer the edges, as shown in Figure 7-4.
  Very small amounts of feathering can be used to create subtle transitions between selected elements in a collage or for blending an element into an existing background. Larger amounts are often used when you're combining multiple layers so that one image gradually fades into another. If you want a selected element to have just a soft edge without the background, simply choose Select⇨Inverse and delete the background. See more on inversing selections in the "Modifying Your Selections" section, later in this chapter. For more on layers, see Chapter 8.

Feather 6 pixels   Feather 50 pixels

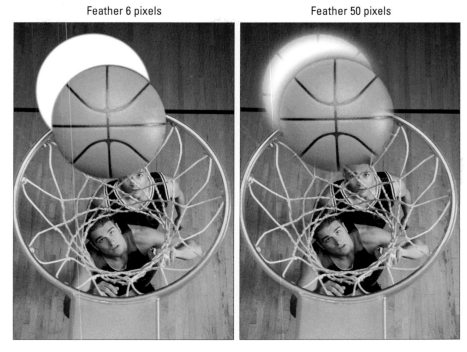

Corbis Digital Stock

Figure 7-4: Feathering creates soft-edged selections.

Don't forget that those soft edges represent partially selected pixels.

✔ **Anti-Alias:** Anti-aliasing barely softens the edge of an elliptical or irregularly shaped selection so that the jagged edges aren't quite so obvious. An anti-aliased edge is always only 1 pixel wide. We recommend leaving this option selected for your selections. It can help to create natural transitions between multiple selections when you're creating collages.

✔ **Mode:** The Mode drop-down menu contains three settings:

• *Normal:* The default setting, which allows you to freely drag a selection of any size.

• *Fixed Ratio:* Lets you specify a fixed ratio of width to height. For example, if you enter **3** for width and **1** for height, you get a selection that's three times as wide as it is high, no matter what the size.

• *Fixed Size:* Lets you specify desired values for the width and height. This setting can be useful when you need to make several selections that must be the same size.

> ✐ **Width and Height:** When you select Fixed Ratio or Fixed Size from the Mode drop-down menu, you must also enter your desired values in the Width and Height text boxes. To swap the Width and Height values, click the double-headed arrow button between the two measurements.

The default unit of measurement in the Width and Height text boxes is pixels (px), but that doesn't mean that you're stuck with it. You can enter any unit of measurement that Elements recognizes — pixels, inches (in), centimeters (cm), millimeters (mm), points (pt), picas (pica), or percentages (%). Type your value and then type the word or abbreviation of your unit of measurement.

Making Freeform Selections with the Lasso Tools

You can't select everything with a rectangle or an ellipse. Life is just way too freeform for that. Most animate, and many inanimate, objects have undulations of varying sorts. Luckily, Elements anticipated the need to capture these and provided the Lasso tools.

The Lasso tools enable you to make any freehand selection you can think of. Elements generously provides three types of lasso tools:

✐ Lasso

✐ Polygonal

✐ Magnetic

Although all three tools are designed to make freeform selections, they differ slightly in their methodology, as we explain in the sections that follow.

To use these tools, all that's really required is a steady hand. You'll find that the more you use the Lasso tools, the better you become at your tracing technique. Don't worry if your initial lasso selection isn't super accurate. You can always go back and make corrections by adding and deleting from your selection. To find out how, see the section "Modifying Your Selections," later in this chapter.

If you find that you really love the Lasso tools, you may want to invest in a digital drawing tablet and stylus. This device makes tracing, and also drawing and painting, on the computer more comfortable. It better mimics pen and paper, and many users swear that they'll never go back to a mouse after trying it out.

Selecting with the Lasso tool

Using the Lasso tool is the digital version of tracing an outline around an object on a piece of paper. It's that easy. And you have only three choices on the Options bar — Feather, Anti-Alias, and Refine Edge. To find out more about Feather and Anti-Alias, see the section "Applying marquee options," earlier in this chapter. For the scoop on Refine Edge, see the section "Wielding the wand to select," later in this chapter.

Here's how to make a selection with the Lasso tool:

1. **Select the Lasso tool from the Tools panel.**

   It's the tool that looks like a rope. You can also just press the L key. If the Lasso tool isn't visible, press Shift+L to cycle through the various Lasso flavors.

2. **Position the cursor anywhere along the edge of the object you want to select.**

   The leading point of the cursor is the protruding end of the rope, as shown in Figure 7-5. Don't be afraid to zoom in to your object if you need to see the edge more distinctly. In this figure, we started at the upper-left corner of the butterfly's wing.

Lasso cursor

Corbis Digital Stock

Figure 7-5: The Lasso tool makes freeform selections.

3. **Hold down the mouse button and trace around your desired object.**

Try to include only what you want to select. While you trace around your object, an outline follows the mouse cursor.

Try not to release the mouse button until you return to your starting point. When you release the mouse button, Elements assumes that you're done and closes the selection from wherever you released the mouse button to your starting point, creating a straight line across your image.

4. **Continue tracing around the object and return to your starting point; release the mouse button to close the selection.**

You see a selection border that matches your lasso line. Look for a small circle that appears next to your lasso cursor when you return to your starting point. This icon indicates that you're closing the selection at the proper spot.

Getting straight with the Polygonal Lasso tool

The Polygonal Lasso tool has a specific mission in life: to select any element whose sides are straight. Think pyramids, stairways, skyscrapers, barns — you get the idea. It also works a tad differently from the Lasso tool. You don't drag around the element with the Polygonal Lasso. Instead, you click and release the mouse button at the corners of the element you're selecting. The Polygonal Lasso tool acts like a stretchy rubber band.

Follow these steps to select with the Polygonal Lasso tool:

1. **Select the Polygonal Lasso tool from the Tools panel.**

You can also press the L key and then press Shift+L until you get the Polygonal Lasso tool.

2. **Click and release at any point to start the Polygonal Lasso selection line.**

We usually start at a corner.

3. **Move (don't drag) the mouse and click at the next corner of the object. Continue clicking and moving to each corner of your element.**

Notice how the line stretches out from each point you click.

4. **Return to your starting point and click to close the selection.**

Be on the lookout for a small circle that appears next to your lasso cursor when you return to your starting point. This circle is an indication that you're indeed closing the selection at the right spot.

Note that you can also double-click at any point, and Elements closes the selection from that point to the starting point.

After you close the polygonal lasso line, a selection border should appear, as shown in Figure 7-6.

Snapping with the Magnetic Lasso tool

The third member of the Lasso team is the Magnetic Lasso. We aren't huge fans of this Lasso tool, which sometimes can be hard to work with. But we show you how it works so that you can decide whether to use it. The Magnetic Lasso tool works by defining the areas of the most contrast in an image and then snapping to the edge between those areas, as though the edge has a magnetic pull.

Corbis Digital Stock

Figure 7-6: After closing the polygonal lasso line, Elements creates a selection border.

You have the most success using the Magnetic Lasso tool on an image that has a well-defined foreground object and high contrast between that element and the background — for example, a dark mountain range against a light sky.

The Magnetic Lasso tool also has some unique settings, which you can adjust on the Options bar before you start selecting:

- **Width:** Determines how close to the edge (between 1 and 256 pixels) you have to move your mouse before the Magnetic Lasso tool snaps to that edge. Use a lower value if the edge has a lot of detail or if the contrast in the image is low. Use a higher value for high-contrast images or smoother edges.

- **Contrast:** Specifies the percentage of contrast (from 1 percent to 100 percent) that's required before the Magnetic Lasso snaps to an edge. Use a higher percentage if your image has good contrast between your desired element and the background.

- **Frequency:** Specifies how many fastening points (from 1 to 100) to place on the selection line. The higher the value, the greater number of points. As a general rule, if the element you want to select has a smooth edge, keep the value low. If the edge has a lot of detail, try a higher value.

- **Tablet Pressure (pen icon):** If you're the proud owner of a pressure-sensitive drawing tablet, select this option to make an increase in stylus pressure cause the edge width to decrease.

Follow these steps to use the Magnetic Lasso tool:

1. **Select the Magnetic Lasso tool from the Tools panel.**

   You can also press the L key and then press Shift+L until you select the Magnetic Lasso tool. The tool looks like a straight-sided lasso with a little magnet on it.

2. **Click the edge of the object you want to select to place the first fastening point.**

   Fastening points anchor the selection line, as shown in Figure 7-7. You can start anywhere; just be sure to click the edge between the element you want and the background you don't want.

Corbis Digital Stock

Figure 7-7: The Magnetic Lasso tool snaps to the edge of your element and places fastening points to anchor the selection.

3. **Continue to move your cursor around the object, without clicking.**

   While the selection line gets pinned down with fastening points, only the newest portion of the selection line remains active.

If the Magnetic Lasso tool starts veering off the desired edge of your object, back up your mouse and click to force down a fastening point. Conversely, if the Magnetic Lasso tool adds a fastening point where you don't want one, press your Backspace (Delete on the Mac) key to delete it. Note that successive presses of the Backspace or Delete key continues to remove the fastening points.

If the Magnetic Lasso isn't cooperating, you can temporarily switch to the other Lasso tools. To select the Lasso tool, hold down Alt (Option on the Mac) and then click the mouse button and drag. To select the Polygonal Lasso tool, hold down Alt (Option on the Mac) and click.

 4. **Return to your starting point and click the mouse button to close the selection.**

You see a small circle next to your cursor, indicating that you're at the right spot to close the selection. You can also double-click, whereby Elements closes the selection from where you double-clicked to your starting point. The selection border appears when the selection is closed.

Working Wizardry with the Magic Wand

The Magic Wand tool is one of the oldest tools in the world of digital imaging. This beloved tool has been around since Photoshop was in its infancy and Elements was not yet a twinkle in Adobe's eye. It's extremely easy to use, but a little harder to predict what selection results it will present.

Here's how it works: You click inside the image, and the Magic Wand tool makes a selection. This selection is based on the color of the pixel you clicked. If other pixels are similar in color to your target pixel, Elements includes them in the selection. What's sometimes hard to predict, however, is how to determine *how* similar the color has to be to get the Magic Wand tool to select it. Fortunately, that's where the Tolerance setting comes in. In the sections that follow, we first introduce you to this setting and then explain how to put the Magic Wand to work.

Talking about tolerance

The Tolerance setting determines the range of color that the Magic Wand tool selects. It's based on brightness levels that range from 0 to 255:

 ✓ Setting the Tolerance to 0 selects one color only.

 ✓ Setting the Tolerance to 255 selects all colors, or the whole image.

The default setting is 32, so whenever you click a pixel, Elements analyzes the value of that base color and then selects all pixels whose brightness levels are between 16 levels lighter and 16 levels darker.

What if an image contains a few shades of the same color? It's not a huge problem. You can make multiple clicks of the Magic Wand to pick up additional pixels that you want to include in the selection. You can find out how in the section "Modifying Your Selections," later in this chapter. Or, you can try a higher Tolerance setting. Conversely, if your wand selects too much, you can also lower your Tolerance setting.

TIP

So, you can see by our talk on tolerance that the Magic Wand tool works best when you have high-contrast images or images with a limited number of colors. For example, the optimum image for the Wand would be a solid black object on a white background. Skip the wand if the image has a ton of colors and no real definitive contrast between your desired element and the background.

Wielding the wand to select

To use the Magic Wand tool to adjust Tolerance settings, follow these steps:

1. **Select the Magic Wand tool from the Tools panel.**

   You can't miss it. It looks like a wand with a starburst on the end. You can also just press W.

2. **Click anywhere on your desired element, using the default Tolerance setting of 32.**

   Remember that the pixel you click determines the base color.

   If the pixel gods are with you and you selected everything you want on the first click, you're done. If your selection needs further tweaking, like the top image shown in Figure 7-8, continue to Step 3.

Tolerance 32

Tolerance 80

Corbis Digital Stock

Figure 7-8: The Magic Wand selects pixels based on a specified Tolerance setting.

3. **Specify a new Tolerance setting on the Options bar.**

   If the Magic Wand selects more than you want, lower the Tolerance setting. If the wand didn't select enough, increase the value. While you're poking around the Options bar, here are a couple more options to get familiar with:

   - *Anti-Alias:* Softens the edge of the selection by one row of pixels. See the section "Applying marquee options," earlier in this chapter, for details.

   - *Contiguous:* Forces the Magic Wand to select only pixels that are adjacent to each other. Without this option, the tool selects all pixels within the range of tolerance, whether or not they're adjacent to each other.

   - *Sample All Layers:* If you have multiple layers and enable this option, the Magic Wand selects pixels from all visible layers. Without this option, the tool selects pixels from the active layer only. For more on layers, see Chapter 8.

   - *Refine Edge:* Clean up your selection by moving the Smooth slider to reduce the amount of jagginess in your edges. Feather works like the feather option discussed in the "Applying marquee options" section, earlier in the chapter. Move the Contract/Expand slider to the left or right to decrease or increase the selected area, respectively. Click the custom overlay color button to preview your selection with your edges hidden and an overlay of screen-only color in your unselected area. For even more details, see the section "Refining the edges of a selection," later in this chapter.

4. **Click your desired element again.**

   Unfortunately, the Magic Wand tool isn't magical enough to modify your first selection automatically. Instead, it deselects the current selection and makes a new selection based on your new Tolerance setting. If it still isn't right, you can adjust the Tolerance setting again. Try, try again.

Modifying Your Selections

It's time for a seventh-inning stretch in this chapter on selection tools. In this section, you can find out how to refine that Marquee, Lasso, or Magic Wand selection to perfection. Although these tools do an okay job of capturing the bulk of your selection, if you take the time to add or subtract a bit from your selection border, you can ensure that you get only what you really want.

You're not limited to the manual methods described in the following sections, or even to keyboard shortcuts. You can also use the four selection option buttons on the left side of the Options bar to create a new selection (the default), add to a selection, subtract from a selection, or intersect one selection with another. Just choose your desired selection tool, click the selection option button you want, and drag (or click if you're using the Magic Wand or Polygonal Lasso tool). The Add to Selection and Subtract from Selection buttons are also available when you're using the Selection Brush, explained later in this chapter. When you're adding to a selection, a small plus sign (+) appears next to your cursor. When you're subtracting from a selection, a small minus sign (–) appears. When you're intersecting two selections, a small multiplication sign (×) appears.

Adding to a selection

If your selection doesn't quite contain all the elements you want to capture, you need to add those portions to your current selection border. To add to a current marquee selection, simply press the Shift key and drag around the area you want to include. If you're using the Polygonal Lasso, click around the area. And, if you're wielding the Magic Wand, just press the Shift key and click the area you want.

You don't have to use the same tool to add to your selection that you used to create the original selection. Feel free to use whatever selection tool you think can get the job done. For example, it's very common to start off with the Magic Wand and fine-tune with the Lasso tool.

Subtracting from a selection

Got too much? To subtract from a current selection, press the Alt (Option on the Mac) key and drag the marquee around the pixels you want to subtract. With the Alt (Option on the Mac) key, use the same method for the Magic Wand and Polygonal Lasso as you do for adding to a selection.

Intersecting two selections

Get your fingers in shape. To intersect your existing selection with a second selection, press Shift+Alt (Shift+Option on the Mac) and drag with the Lasso tool. Or, if you're using the Magic Wand or Polygonal Lasso, press those keys and click rather than drag.

Avoiding key collisions

If you read the beginning of this chapter, you found out that by pressing the Shift key, you get a perfectly square or circular selection. We tell you in the section "Adding to a selection," earlier in this chapter, that if you want to add to a selection, you press the Shift key. What if you want to create a perfect square while adding to the selection? Or, what if you want to delete part of a selection while also drawing from the center outward? Both require the use of the Alt (Option on the Mac) key. How in the heck does Elements know what you want? Here are a few tips to avoid keyboard collisions — grab your desired Marquee tool:

- **To add a square or circular selection, press Shift and drag.** While you drag, keep the mouse button pressed, release the Shift key for just a second, and then press it again. Your added selection area suddenly snaps into a square or circle. You must then release the mouse button first and then release the Shift key.

- **To delete from an existing selection while drawing from the center outward, press Alt (Option on the Mac) and drag.** While you drag, keep the mouse button pressed, release the Alt (Option on the Mac) key for just a second, and then press it down again. You're now drawing from the center outward. Again, release the mouse button first and then release the Alt (Option on the Mac) key.

Painting with the Selection Brush

If you like the organic feel of painting on a canvas, you'll appreciate the Selection Brush. Using two different modes, you can either paint over areas of an image that you want to select or paint over areas you don't want to select. This great tool also lets you make a basic, rudimentary selection with another tool, such as the Lasso, and then fine-tune the selection by brushing additional pixels into or out of the selection.

Here's the step-by-step process of selecting with the Selection Brush:

1. **Select the Selection Brush from the Tools panel.**

   Or simply press the A key. Press Shift+A if the Quick Selection tool is visible.

   This tool works in either Edit Full or Edit Quick mode.

2. **Specify your Selection Brush options on the Options bar.**

   Here's the rundown on each option:

- *Brush Presets:* Choose a brush from the presets drop-down panel. To load additional brushes, click the downward-pointing arrow to the left of Default Brushes and choose the preset library of your choice. You can select the Load Brushes command from the panel pop-up menu.

- *Brush Size:* Specify a brush size, from 1 to 2500 pixels. Enter the value or drag the slider.

- *Mode:* Choose between Selection and Mask. Choose Selection if you want to paint over what you *want* to select. Choose Mask if you want to paint over what you *don't* want. If you choose Mask mode, you must choose some additional overlay options. An *overlay* is a layer of color (that shows onscreen only) that hovers over your image, indicating protected or unselected areas. You must also choose an overlay opacity between 1 and 100 percent (which we describe in a Tip paragraph at the end of this section). You can change the overlay color from the default red to another color. This option can be helpful if your image contains a lot of red.

- *Hardness:* Set the hardness of the brush tip, from 1 to 100 percent.

3. **If your mode is set to Selection, paint over the areas you *want* to select.**

   You see a selection border. Each stroke adds to the selection. (The Add to Selection button in the Options bar is automatically selected.) If you inadvertently add something you don't want, simply press the Alt (Option on the Mac) key and paint over the undesired area. You can also select the Subtract from Selection button on the Options bar. After you finish painting what you want, your selection is ready to go.

4. **If your mode is set to Mask, paint over the areas that you *don't* want to select.**

   When you're done painting your mask, choose Selection from the Mode drop-down menu, or simply choose another tool from the Tools panel, in order to convert your mask into a selection border. Remember that your selection is what you *don't* want.

   While you paint, you see the color of your overlay. Each stroke adds more to the overlay area, as shown in Figure 7-9. In my example, I masked the sky because I wanted to replace it with a different sky. When working in Mask mode, you're essentially covering up, or *masking,* the areas you want to protect from manipulation. That manipulation can be selecting, adjusting color, or performing any other Elements command. Again, if you want to remove parts of the masked area, press Alt (Option on the Mac) and paint.

Figure 7-9: The Selection Brush allows you to make a selection (right) by creating a mask (left).

If you painted your selection in Mask mode, your selection border is around what you *don't* want. To switch to what you do want, choose Select➪Inverse.

Which mode should you choose? Well, it's up to you. But one advantage to working in Mask mode is that you can partially select areas. By painting with soft brushes, you create soft-edged selections. These soft edges result in partially selected pixels. If you set the overlay opacity to a lower percentage, your pixels are even less opaque, or "less selected." If this partially selected business sounds vaguely familiar, it's because this is also what happens when you feather selections, as we discuss in the section "Applying marquee options," earlier in this chapter.

Painting with the Quick Selection Tool

Think of the Quick Selection tool as a combination Brush, Magic Wand, and Lasso tool. Good news — it lives up to its "quick" moniker. Better news — it's also easy to use. The best news? It gives pretty decent results, so give it a whirl.

Here's how to make short work of selecting with this tool:

1. **Select the Quick Selection tool from the Tools panel.**

   The tool looks like a wand with a marquee around the end. It shares the same flyout menu with the Selection Brush tool. You can also press the A key. Press Shift+A if the Selection Brush is visible.

   This tool works in either Edit Full or Edit Quick mode.

2. **Specify the options on the Options bar.**

   Here's a description of the options:

   - *New Selection:* The default option enables you to create a new selection. There are also options to add to and subtract from your selection.

   - *Brush Picker:* Choose your desired brush settings. Specify the diameter, from 1 to 2500 pixels. You can also specify hardness, spacing, angle, and roundness settings. For details on these settings, see Chapter 12.

   - *Sample All Layers:* If your image has layers and you want to make a selection from all the layers, select this option. If you leave it deselected, you will select only from the current layer.

   - *Auto-Enhance:* Select this option to have Elements automatically refine your selection by implementing an algorithm.

3. **Drag, or paint, the desired areas of your image.**

   Your selection grows as you drag, as shown in Figure 7-10. If you stop dragging and click in another portion of your image, your selection includes that clicked area.

www.istockphoto.com

Figure 7-10: Paint a selection with the Quick Selection tool.

4. **Add to or delete from your selection, as desired:**

    - *To add to your selection:* Press the Shift key while dragging across your desired image areas.

    - *To delete from your selection:* Press the Alt (Option on the Mac) key while dragging across your unwanted image areas.

    You can also select the Add to Selection and Subtract from Selection options on the Options bar.

5. **If you need to fine-tune your selection, click the Refine Edge option on the Options bar and then change the settings, as desired.**

    The settings are explained in detail in the "Refining the edges of a selection" section, later in this chapter.

    Note that if your object is fairly detailed, you may even need to break out the Lasso or another selection tool to make some final cleanups. Eventually, you should arrive at a selection you're happy with.

Resizing Smartly with the Recompose Tool

The Recompose tool is like an über-intelligent crop-and-transform tool. You can move elements closer together or even change the orientation of a landscape shot from horizontal to vertical without sacrificing your most vital content.

Here's how this great tool works:

1. **In the Editor, in Edit Full mode, select the Recompose tool from the Tools panel.**

    This tool shares the same flyout menu with the Crop tool. You can also press the C key. Press Shift+C if the Crop tool is visible.

    When you select the tool, you're presented with a dialog box describing what the tool does and also giving you the option of viewing an online tutoring video. Click Ok.

2. **(Optional) Using the Brushes and Erasers in the Options bar, mark the areas you want to protect and eliminate.**

    Although this step isn't mandatory, it will help to give you better results.

Here's a description of these tools:

- *Mark for Protection Brush:* Brush over the areas of the image you want to protect or retain. (Strokes will be green.) You don't have to be super precise; just give Elements an inkling of what you want to keep (or remove, in the case of the next brush), as shown in Figure 7-11.

Purestock

Figure 7-11: Mark areas that you want to retain or remove.

- *Mark for Removal Brush:* Brush over those areas you want to remove first. (Strokes will be red.) Make sure to choose the area you don't mind eliminating at all.

- *Erase Highlight Marked for Protection:* Use this tool to erase any area you erroneously marked to retain.

- *Erase Highlights Marked for Removal:* Use this tool to erase any area you erroneously marked to remove.

3. **Specify the other options on the Options bar.**

   Here's a description of those options:

   - *Brush Size:* Click the down-pointing arrow and drag the slider to make the brush diameter smaller or larger.

   - *Suggest Skin Tone Region:* Select this option to prevent skin tones from being distorted when scaled.

   - *Presets:* Use a preset ratio or size to which to recompose your image. Or leave on the default of No Restriction.

   - *Width and Height:* Enter width and height scale percentages if desired.

   - *Amount:* Set a recomposition threshold to help minimize distortion. Start with a higher percentage, and then adjust as needed.

4. **Grab an image handle and resize your image.**

   As you drag, the red areas are removed first, and the green areas remain intact. After all the red areas have been removed, Elements begins to "carve" out areas you didn't mark to protect.

5. **After you've recomposed your image as desired, click the Commit (green) check mark icon to accept the composition.**

Retouch any areas as needed with the Clone Stamp or Healing tools. For our example, shown in Figure 7-12, we cloned noticeable seams near the man's feet and some of the sandy areas.

Purestock

Figure 7-12: A recomposed image.

Working with the Cookie Cutter Tool

The Cookie Cutter tool is a cute name for a pretty powerful tool. You can think of it as a Custom Shape tool for images. But, whereas the Custom Shape tool creates a mask and just hides everything outside the shape, the Cookie Cutter cuts away everything outside the shape. The preset libraries offer you a large variety of interesting shapes, from talk bubbles to Swiss cheese. (We're not being funny here — check out the food library.)

Here's the lowdown on using the Cookie Cutter:

1. **Choose the Cookie Cutter tool from the Tools panel.**

    There's no missing it; it looks like a star. You can also press the Q key.

2. **Specify your options on the Options bar.**

    Here's the list:

    - *Shape:* Choose a shape from the preset library. To load other libraries, click the panel pop-up menu and choose one from the submenu.

    - *Shape Options:* These options let you draw your shape with certain parameters:

        Unconstrained: Enables you to draw freely.

        Defined Proportions: Enables you to keep the height and width proportional.

        Defined Size: Crops the image to the original, fixed size of the shape you choose. You can't make it bigger or smaller.

        Fixed Size: Allows you to enter your desired width and height.

        From Center: Allows you to draw the shape from the center outward.

- *Feather:* This option creates a soft-edged selection. See the section "Applying marquee options," earlier in this chapter, for more details.

- *Crop:* Click this option to crop the image into the shape. The shape will fill the image window.

3. **Drag your mouse on the image to create your desired shape, size the shape by dragging one of the handles of the bounding box, and position the shape by placing the mouse cursor inside the box and dragging.**

   You can also perform other types of transformations, such as rotating and skewing. For more on transformations, see Chapter 9.

4. **Click the Commit button on the Options bar or press Enter to finish the cutout.**

   See Figure 7-13 to see my image cut into an elephant shape. If you want to bail out of the bounding box and not cut out, you can always click the Cancel button on the Options bar or press Esc.

Corbis Digital Stock

Figure 7-13: Crop your photo into interesting shapes with the Cookie Cutter.

Eliminating with the Eraser Tools

The Eraser tools let you erase areas of your image. Elements has three eraser tools: the regular Eraser, the Magic Eraser, and the Background Eraser. The Eraser tools look like those pink erasers you used in grade school, so you can't miss them. If you can't locate them, you can always press E and then Shift+E to toggle through the three tools.

When you erase pixels, those pixels are history — they're gone. So, before using the Eraser tools, you should probably have a backup of your image stored somewhere. Think of it as a cheap insurance policy in case things go awry.

The Eraser tool

The Eraser tool enables you to erase areas on your image to either your background color or, if you're working on a layer, a transparent background, as shown in Figure 7-14. For more on layers, check out Chapter 8.

Corbis Digital Stock

Figure 7-14: Erase either to your background color (left) or to transparency (right).

To use this tool, simply select it and drag through the desired area on your image, and you're done. Because it isn't the most accurate tool on the planet, remember to zoom way in and use smaller brush tips to do some accurate erasing.

You have several Eraser options to specify on the Options bar:

- **Brush Presets:** Click the drop-down panel to access the Brush presets. Choose the brush of your choice. Again, additional brush libraries are available on the Brushes pop-up menu.

- **Size:** Click the down-pointing arrow to access the Size slider. Choose a brush size between 1 and 2500 pixels.

- **Mode:** Select from Brush, Pencil, and Block. When you select Block, you're stuck with one size (a 16-x-16-pixel tip) and can't select other preset brushes.

- **Opacity:** Specify a percentage of transparency for your erased areas. The lower the Opacity setting, the less it erases. Opacity isn't available in Block mode.

The Background Eraser tool

The Background Eraser tool, which is more savvy than the Eraser tool, erases the background from an image while being mindful of leaving the foreground untouched. The Background Eraser tool erases to transparency on a layer. If you use this tool on an image with only a background, Elements converts the background into a layer.

The key to using the Background Eraser is to carefully keep the *hot spot,* the crosshair at the center of the brush, on the background pixels while you drag. The hot spot samples the color of the pixels and deletes that color whenever it falls inside the brush circumference. But, if you accidentally touch a foreground pixel with the hot spot, it's erased as well. And the tool isn't even sorry about it! This tool works better with images that have good contrast in color between the background and foreground objects, as shown in Figure 7-15. If your image has very detailed or wispy edges (such as hair or fur), you're better off using the Magic Extractor command, which we describe in the section "Using the Magic Extractor Command," later in this chapter.

Corbis Digital Stock

Figure 7-15: The Background Eraser erases similarly colored pixels sampled by the hot spot of your brush cursor.

Here's the rundown on the Background Eraser options:

- **Brush Preset Picker:** This option provides settings to customize the size and appearance of your brush tip. The Size and Tolerance settings at the bottom are for pressure-sensitive drawing tablets.

- **Limits:** *Discontiguous* erases all similarly colored pixels wherever they appear in the image. *Contiguous* erases all similarly colored pixels that are adjacent to those under the hot spot.

- **Tolerance:** The percentage determines how similar the colors have to be to that of the color under the hot spot before Elements erases them. A higher value picks up more colors, whereas a lower value picks up fewer colors. See the section "Talking about tolerance," earlier in this chapter, for more details.

The Magic Eraser tool

You can think of the Magic Eraser tool as a combination Eraser and Magic Wand tool. It selects *and* erases similarly colored pixels simultaneously. Unless you're working on a layer with the transparency locked (see Chapter 8 for more on locking), the pixels are erased to transparency. If you're working on an image with just a background, Elements converts the background into a layer.

The Magic Eraser shares most of the same options with the other erasers. Here are the unique options:

- **Anti-Alias:** Creates a slightly soft edge around the transparent area.

- **Sample All Layers:** Samples colors using data from all visible layers but erases pixels on the active layer only.

Using the Magic Extractor Command

The last selection tool in the Elements repertoire is the Magic Extractor command. This command enables you to make selections based on your identification of the foreground and background portions of your image. The way this tool works is you specify your foreground and background by simply clicking these areas with the brush tool and "marking" them. Click the magic OK button, and your object or objects are neatly and painlessly extracted.

Although it isn't mandatory, you can make a rough selection first before selecting the Magic Extractor command. This technique obviously restricts what's extracted and can result in a more accurate selection.

Follow these steps to magically extract your element:

1. **Choose Image⇨Magic Extractor.**

   The huge Magic Extractor dialog box appears.

2. **Grab the Foreground Brush tool and click or drag to mark your** *foreground* **areas — or the areas you want to select.**

   The default color of the Foreground Brush is red.

   Like with the Selection Brush, the more accurate the data you provide to the command's algorithm, the more accurate your extraction. Be sure to use the Zoom and Hand tools to help magnify and move around your image, as needed. For more on these tools, see Chapter 5.

You can also change the size of your brush tip (from 1 to 100 pixels) in the Tool Options area on the right side of the dialog box. If necessary, change the color of your foreground and background colors by clicking the swatch and choosing a new color from the Color Picker.

3. **Select the Background Brush tool and then click or drag to mark the background area or the portions you don't want to select, as shown in Figure 7-16.**

   The default color of the Background Brush is blue.

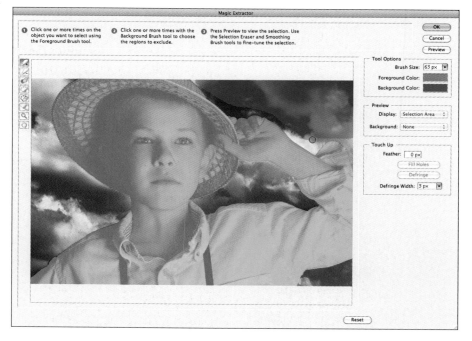

Figure 7-16: The Magic Extractor allows you to identify foreground and background areas.

4. **Click Preview to view your extraction.**

   Elements churns for a few seconds before presenting you with a look at your extraction. You can change the preview by choosing either Selection Area or Original Photo from the Display pop-up list.

   If you want to see your selection against a different background, choose one, such as black matte for a black background, from the Background pop-up list.

5. **If you aren't happy with the preview of your selection, you can refine the selection:**

   - *To erase any markings:* Select the Point Eraser tool and click or drag over the offending areas.

   - *To add areas to the selection:* Click or drag over your desired areas with the Add to Selection tool.

   - *To delete areas from the selection:* Drag with the Remove from Selection tool.

   - *To smooth the edges of your foreground selection:* Drag over the edges with the Smoothing Brush tool.

   - *To soften the edges of your selection:* Enter a value in the Feather box. ***Remember:*** The higher the value, the softer the edge.

   - *To fill a hole:* Click the aptly named Fill Holes button.

   - *To remove the halo of pixels between the foreground and background areas:* Click Defringe. Enter a value in the Defringe Width box.

   If things start to get messy, you can always start over by clicking Reset at the bottom of the dialog box.

6. **When you're pleased with the results, click OK to finish the selection process and close the Magic Extractor dialog box.**

   The newly extracted image appears, as shown in Figure 7-17.

www.istockphoto.com

Figure 7-17: A boy selected with the Magic Extractor.

Using the Select Menu

In the following sections, we breeze through the Select menu. Along with the methods we describe in the "Modifying Your Selections" section, earlier in this chapter, you can use this menu to further modify selections by expanding, contracting, smoothing, softening, inversing, growing, and grabbing similarly colored pixels. If that doesn't satisfy your selection needs, nothing will.

Selecting all or nothing

The Select All and Deselect commands are no-brainers. To select everything in your image, choose Select⇨All or press Ctrl+A (⌘+A on the Mac). To deselect everything, choose Select⇨Deselect or press Ctrl+D (⌘+D on the Mac). Remember that you usually don't have to Select All. If you don't have a selection border in your image, Elements assumes that the whole image is fair game for any manipulation.

Reselecting a selection

If you sacrifice that second cup of coffee to steady your hand and take the time to carefully lasso around your desired object, you don't want to lose your selection before you have a chance to perform your next move. But all it takes is a mere inadvertent click of your mouse while you have an active selection border to obliterate your selection. Fortunately, Elements anticipated such a circumstance and offers a solution. If you choose Select⇨Reselect, Elements retrieves your last selection.

One caveat: The Reselect command works only for the last selection you made, so don't plan to reselect a selection you made last Tuesday or even just five minutes ago, if you selected something else after that selection. If you want to reuse a selection for the long term, save it as we explain in "Saving and loading selections," later in this chapter.

Inversing a selection

You know the old song lyric: "If you can't be with the one you love, love the one you're with." Well, Elements is kind of like that. Sometimes, it's just easier to select what you don't want rather than what you do want. For example, if you're trying to select your beloved in his or her senior photo, it's probably easier to just click the studio backdrop with the Magic Wand and then inverse the selection by choosing Select⇨Inverse.

Feathering a selection

In the "Applying marquee options" section earlier in this chapter, we describe how to feather a selection when using the Lasso and Marquee tools by entering a value in the Feather box on the Options bar. Remember that this method of feathering requires that you set the Feather value *before* you create your selection. What we didn't tell you is that there's a way to apply a feather *after* you make a selection.

Choose Select⇨Feather and enter your desired amount from 0.2 to 250 pixels. Your selection is subsequently softened around the edges.

This method is actually a better way to go. Make your selection and fine-tune it by using the methods we describe earlier in this chapter. Then, apply your feather. The problem with applying the feather before you make a selection happens when you want to modify your initial selection. When you make a selection with a feather, the marquee outline of the selection adjusts to take into account the amount of the feather. So, the resulting marquee outline doesn't resemble your precise mouse movement, making it harder to modify that selection.

Refining the edges of a selection

The Refine Edge option enables you to fine-tune the edges of your selection. It doesn't matter how you got the selection, just that you have one. You can find the command in the Options bar of the Magic Wand, Lasso, and Quick Selection tools. And, of course, you can find it in the Select menu. Here's the scoop on each of the settings in this option, as shown in Figure 7-18:

- **Smooth:** Reduces jaggedness along your selection edges.
- **Feather:** Moves the slider to create an increasingly softer, more blurred edge.
- **Contract/Expand:** Decreases or increases the selected area. The contract and expand features are discussed in more detail in the next section, "Using the Modify commands."
- **Background icons:** Enables you to preview your selection in Standard or Overlay mode. Click the custom overlay color button to preview your selection with your edges hidden and a semi-opaque layer of color (that shows onscreen only) in your unselected area. Double-click this icon to change the color and opacity of the overlay. Press F to cycle between standard and overlay views. And press X to hide your selection edges.
- **Zoom tool:** Allows you to zoom in to your image to see the effects of your settings.
- **Hand tool:** Enables you to pan around your image window to see the effects of your settings.

www.istockphoto.com

Figure 7-18: Fine-tune your selection with Refine Edge.

Using the Modify commands

Although the commands on the Modify submenu definitely won't win any popularity contests, they may occasionally come in handy. Here's the scoop on each command:

- ✔ **Border:** Selects the area, from 1 to 200 pixels, around the edge of the selection border. By choosing Edit➪Fill Selection, you can fill the border with color.

- ✔ **Smooth:** Rounds off any jagged, raggedy edges. Enter a value from 1 to 100 pixels, and Elements looks at each selected pixel and then includes or deselects the pixels in your selection based on your chosen value. Start with a low number, like 1, 2, or 3 pixels. Otherwise, it may make your selection worse.

- ✔ **Expand:** Enables you to increase the size of your selection by a given number of pixels, from 1 to 100. This command is especially useful if you just barely missed getting the edge of an elliptical selection and need it to be a little larger.

- ✔ **Contract:** Decreases your selection border by 1 to 100 pixels. When you're compositing multiple images, you often benefit by slightly contracting your selection if you plan on applying a feather. That way, you avoid picking up a fringe of background pixels around your selection.

Applying the Grow and Similar commands

The Grow and Similar commands are often used in tandem with the Magic Wand tool. If you made an initial selection with the Magic Wand but didn't quite get everything you want, try choosing Select➪Grow. The Grow command increases the size of the selection by including adjacent pixels that fall within the range of tolerance. The Similar command is like Grow except that the pixels don't have to be adjacent to be selected. The command searches throughout the image and picks up pixels within the tolerance range.

These commands don't have their own tolerance options. They use whatever Tolerance value is displayed on the Options bar when the Magic Wand tool is selected. You can adjust that Tolerance setting to include more or fewer colors.

Saving and loading selections

At times, you toil so long over a complex selection that you really want to save it for future use. Saving it isn't only possible, but also highly recommended. It's also a piece a cake. Here's how:

1. **After you perfect your selection, choose Select⇨Save Selection.**

2. **In the Save Selection dialog box, leave the Selection option set to New and enter a name for your selection, as shown in Figure 7-19.**

   The operation is automatically set to New Selection.

3. **Click OK.**

Figure 7-19: Save your selection for later use to save time and effort.

4. **When you want to access the selection again, choose Select⇨Load Selection and choose a selection from the Selection drop-down menu.**

Working with Layers

*U*sing Elements without ever using layers would be like typing a book on an old IBM Selectric typewriter: Sure, you could do it, but it wouldn't be fun. An even bigger issue would occur when it came time to edit that book and make changes. Correction tape, Wite-Out, and erasers would make that task downright tedious, not to mention messy. The benefit of using layers is that you have tremendous flexibility. You can quickly make as many edits as you want for as long as you want, as long as you keep your composite image in layers. Layers make working in Elements a lot more productive. Don't give a darn about productivity? Well, let's just say that layers also make it a breeze for you to bring out your more artsy side.

This chapter explains the tools and techniques you need to start working with layers. After you try them, you'll wonder how you ever lived without them.

Getting to Know Layers

Think of layers as sheets of acetate or clear transparency film. You have drawings or photographs on individual sheets. What you place on each sheet doesn't affect any of the other sheets. Any area on the sheet that doesn't have an image on it is transparent. You can stack these sheets on top of the others to create a combined image, or *composite* (or *collage,* if you prefer). You can reshuffle the order of the sheets, add new sheets, and delete old sheets.

In Elements, *layers* are essentially digital versions of these clear acetate sheets. You can place elements, such as images, text, or shapes on separate layers and create a composite, as shown in Figure 8-1. You can hide, add, delete, or rearrange layers. Because layers are digital, of course, they have added functionality. You can adjust how opaque or transparent the element on the layer is. You can also add special effects and change how the colors interact between layers.

To work with layers, you must be in the Editor in Edit Full mode.

Corbis, PhotoDisc/Getty Images

Figure 8-1: Layers enable you to easily create composite images.

When you create a new file with background contents of white or a background color, scan an image into Elements, or open a file from a CD or your digital camera, you basically have a file with just a *background.* There are no layers yet.

An image contains at most one background, and you can't do much to it besides paint on it and make basic adjustments. You can't move the background or change its transparency or blend mode. How do you get around all these limitations? Convert your background into a layer by following these easy steps:

1. **Choose Window⇨Layers to display the Layers panel.**

   The Layers panel is explained in detail in the next section.

2. **Double-click Background on the Layers panel.**

   Or, choose Layer⇨New⇨Layer From Background.

3. **Name the layer or leave it at the default name of Layer 0.**

   You can also adjust the blend mode and opacity of the layer in the New Layer dialog box. You can even do it via the Layers panel commands later.

4. **Click OK.**

   Elements converts your background into a layer, known also as an *image layer*.

   When you create a new image with transparent background contents, the image doesn't contain a background but instead is created with a single layer.

Anatomy of the Layers panel

Elements keeps layers controlled with a panel named, not surprisingly, the *Layers panel*. To display the Layers panel, as shown in Figure 8-2, choose Window⇨Layers in the Editor in Edit Full mode.

The order of the layers on the Layers panel represents the order in the image. We refer to this concept in the computer graphics world as the *stacking order*. The top layer on the panel is the top layer in your image, and so on. Depending on what you're doing, you can work either on a single layer or on multiple layers at one time. Here are some tips for working with the Layers panel:

Figure 8-2: The Layers panel controls layers in your image.

✓ **Select a layer.** Click a layer name or its thumbnail. Elements highlights the *active layer* on the panel.

✓ **Select multiple contiguous layers.** Click your first layer and then Shift-click your last layer.

✓ **Select multiple noncontiguous layers.** Ctrl-click (⌘-click on the Mac) your desired layers.

✓ **View and hide layers.** To hide a layer, click the eye icon for that layer so that the eye disappears. To redisplay the layer, click the blank space in the eye column. You can also hide all the layers except one by selecting your desired layer and Alt-clicking (Option-clicking on the Mac) the eye icon for that layer. Redisplay all layers by Alt-clicking (Option-clicking on the Mac) the eye icon again. Hiding all the layers except the one you want to edit can be helpful in allowing you to focus without the distraction of all the other imagery.

Only layers that are visible are printed. This can be useful if you want to have several versions of an image (each on a separate layer) for a project within the same file.

✓ **Select the actual element (the nontransparent pixels) on the layer.** Ctrl-click (⌘-click on the Mac) the layer's thumbnail (not the name) on the panel.

✓ **Create a new blank layer.** Click the Create New Layer icon at the bottom of the panel.

✓ **Add a layer mask.** Click the Add Layer Mask icon at the bottom of the panel. A layer mask enables you to selectively show and hide elements or adjustments on your layer, as well as creatively blend layer together. For more details, see "Adding Layer Masks" later in this chapter.

✓ **Create an adjustment layer.** Click the Create Adjustment Layer icon at the bottom of the panel. *Adjustment layers* are special layers that modify contrast and color in your image. You can also add *fill layers* — layers containing color, gradients, or patterns — by using this command. We give you more details on adjustment and fill layers in the section "Working with Different Layer Types," later in this chapter.

✓ **Duplicate an existing layer.** Drag the layer to the Create New Layer icon at the bottom of the panel.

✓ **Rearrange layers.** To move a layer to another position in the stacking order, drag the layer up or down on the Layers panel. While you drag, you see a fist icon. Release the mouse button when a highlighted line appears where you want to insert the layer.

If your image has a background, it always remains the bottommost layer. If you need to move the background, convert it to a layer by double-clicking the name on the Layers panel. Enter a name for the layer and click OK.

✐ **Rename a layer.** When you create a new layer, Elements provides default layer names (Layer 1, Layer 2, and so on). If you want to rename a layer, double-click the layer name on the Layers panel and enter the name directly on the Layers panel.

✐ **Adjust the interaction between colors on layers and adjust the transparency of layers.** You can use the blend modes and the opacity options at the bottom of the panel to mix the colors between layers and adjust the transparency of the layers, as shown in Figure 8-3.

Corbis Digital Stock

Figure 8-3: We created this effect by using blend modes and opacity options.

✐ **Link layers.** Sometimes, you want your layers to stay grouped as a unit to make your editing tasks easier. If so, link your layers by selecting the layers on the panel and then clicking the Link layers icon at the bottom of the panel. A link icon appears to the right of the layer name. To remove the link, click the Link Layers icon again.

✐ **Lock layers.** Select your desired layer and then click one of the two lock icons at the bottom of the panel. The checkerboard square icon locks all transparent areas of your layers. This lock prevents you from painting or editing any transparent areas on the layers. The lock icon locks your entire layer and prevents it from being changed in any way, including moving or transforming the elements on the layer. You can, however, still make selections on the layer. To unlock the layer, simply click the icon again to toggle off the lock.

By default, the background is locked and can't be unlocked until you convert the background into a layer by choosing Layer⇨New⇨Layer from Background.

✔ **Delete a layer.** Drag it to the trash can icon.

Using the Layer and Select menus

As with many features in Elements, you usually have more than one way to do something. This is especially true when it comes to working with layers. Besides the commands on the Layers panel, you have two layer menus — the Layer menu and the Select menu, both of which you can find on the main menu bar at the top of the application window (top of screen on the Mac).

The Layers menu

Much of what you can do with the Layers panel icons you can also do by using the Layer menu on the menu bar and the Layers panel menu connected to the Layers panel. (Click the horizontally lined button in the upper-right corner.) Commands, such as New, Duplicate, Delete, and Rename, are omnipresent throughout. But you find commands that are exclusive to the Layers panel, the main Layer menu, and the Layers menu, respectively. So, if you can't find what you're looking for in one area, just go to another. Some commands require an expanded explanation and are described in sections that follow. Here's a quick description of most of the commands:

✔ **Delete Linked Layers and Delete Hidden Layers:** These commands delete only those layers that have been linked or hidden from display on the Layers panel.

✔ **Layer Style:** These commands manage the styles, or special effects, you apply to your layers.

✔ **Arrange:** Enables you to shuffle your layer stacking order with commands, such as Bring to Front and Send to Back. Reverse switches the order of your layers if you have two or more layers selected.

✔ **Create Clipping Mask:** The Create Clipping Mask command (previously known as the Group with Previous command) creates a *clipping group,* which a group of layers is constrained to the boundaries of a base layer. Find more details in the section "Adjustment layers," later in this chapter.

✔ **Type:** The commands in the Type submenu control the display of type layers. For more on type, see Chapter 13.

✔ **Rename Layer:** Enables you to give a layer a new name. You can also simply double-click the name on the Layers panel.

- **Simplify Layer:** This command converts a type layer, shape layer, or fill layer into a regular image layer. Briefly, a *shape layer* contains a vector object, and a *fill layer* contains a solid color, a gradient, or a pattern.

- **Merge and Flatten:** The various merge and flatten commands combine multiple layers into a single layer or, in the case of flattening, combine all your layers into a single background.

- **Panel Options:** You can select display options and choose to use a layer mask on your adjustment layers. Leave this option selected.

The Select menu

Although the Select menu's main duties are to assist you in making and refining your selections, it offers a few handy layer commands. Here's a quick introduction to each command:

- **Select All Layers:** Want to quickly get everything in your file? Choose Select⇨All Layers.

- **Select Layers of Similar Type:** This command is helpful if you have different types of layers in your document, such as regular layers, type layers, shape layers, and adjustment layers, and you want to select just one type. Select one of your layers and then choose Select⇨Similar Layers. For details on different types of layers, see the following section.

- **Deselect All Layers:** Choose Select⇨Deselect Layers.

Working with Different Layer Types

Layer life exists beyond just converting an existing background into a layer, which we describe in the section "Getting to Know Layers," earlier in this chapter. In fact, Elements offers five kinds of layers. You'll probably spend most of your time creating image layers, but just so that you're familiar with all types, the following sections describe each one.

Image layers

The *image layer,* usually just referred to as a *layer,* is the type of layer we're referring to when we give the analogy of acetate sheets in the section "Getting to Know Layers," earlier in this chapter. You can create blank layers and add images to them, or you can create layers from images themselves. You can have as many image layers as your computer's memory allows. Just keep in mind that the more layers you have, the larger your file size and the slower your computer responds.

Each layer in an image can be edited without affecting the other layers. You can move, paint, size, or apply a filter, for example, without disturbing a single pixel on any other layer or on the background, for that matter. And, when an element is on a layer, you no longer have to make a selection to select it. (See Chapter 7 for selection info.) Just drag the element with the Move tool.

We tell you more about how to work with image layers in the section "Tackling Layer Basics," later in this chapter.

Adjustment layers

An *adjustment layer* is a special kind of layer used for modifying color and contrast. The advantage of using adjustment layers for your corrections, rather than applying them directly on the image layer, is that you can apply the corrections without permanently affecting the pixels. Adjustment layers are totally nondestructive. And, because the correction is on a layer, you can edit, or even delete, the adjustment at any time. Adjustment layers, as shown in Figure 8-4, apply the correction only to all the layers below them, without affecting any of the layers above them.

Another unique feature of adjustment layers is that when you create one, you also create a layer mask on that layer at the same time. If you are unfamiliar with layer masks, take a peek at the upcoming section, "Adding Layer Masks." The layer mask allows you to selectively and even partially apply the adjustment to the layers below it by applying shades of gray — from white to black — on the mask. For example, by default, the mask is completely white. This allows the adjustment to be fully applied to the layers. If you paint on a layer mask with black, the areas under those black areas don't show the adjustment. If you paint with a shade of gray, those areas partially show the adjustment, as shown in Figure 8-5. Note that if you have an active selection border in your

Corbis, PhotoDisc/Getty Images

Figure 8-4: Adjustment layers correct color and contrast in your image.

image before you add an adjustment layer, the adjustment is applied only to that area within the selection border.

Elements has eight kinds of adjustment layers, and you can use as many as you want. These adjustments are the same adjustments you find on the Enhance⇨Adjust Lighting and Enhance⇨Adjust Color and the Filter⇨Adjustments submenus. For specifics on each adjustment, see Chapters 9 and 10. Here's how to create an adjustment layer:

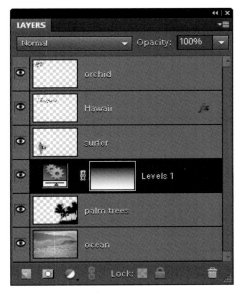

Corbis, PhotoDisc/Getty Images

Figure 8-5: Layer masks control the amount of adjustment applied to your layers.

1. **Open an image that needs a little contrast or color adjustment.**

   Note that you don't need to convert your background into a layer to apply an adjustment layer.

2. **Click the Create New Fill or Adjustment Layer icon at the bottom of the Layers panel, and from the drop-down menu, choose your desired adjustment.**

The Adjustment Layer icon and a thumbnail appear on the adjustment layer. The thumbnail represents the layer mask. And the dialog box specific to your adjustment appears in the Adjustments panel.

3. **Make the necessary adjustments in the Adjustments panel.**

You can paint on the layer mask to selectively allow only portions of your image to receive the adjustment. Use the Brush or Pencil tool to paint. Or, you can also make a selection and fill that selection with any shade of gray, from white to black. Finally, you can use the Gradient tool on the mask to create a gradual application of the adjustment.

As with image layers, you can adjust the opacity and blend modes of an adjustment layer. Reducing the opacity of an adjustment layer reduces the effect of the adjustment on the underlying layers.

Here are a few more tips on using adjustment layers:

- ✔ **To view your image without the adjustment:** Click the eye icon in the left column of the Layers panel to hide the adjustment layer.

- ✔ **To delete the adjustment layer:** Drag it to the trash can icon on the Layers panel.

- ✔ **To edit an adjustment layer:** Simply double-click the adjustment layer on the Layers panel. You can also choose Layer➪Layer Content Options. In the dialog box that appears in the Adjustment panel, make any desired edits. The only adjustment layer that you can't edit is the Invert adjustment. It's either on or off.

- ✔ **To use the adjustment panel controls:** Click an icon. From left to right, here's what the icons do:

  - • Have the adjustment layer clip to the layer below (will affect only the layer directly beneath it, not all the underlying layers in the stack).

  - • Toggle the adjustment layer on and off.

  - • View the previous state (how the image appeared before your most recent step).

  - • Reset the adjustment layer settings back to the default.

Fill layers

A *fill layer* lets you add a layer of solid color, a gradient, or a pattern. Like adjustment layers, fill layers also include layer masks. You can edit, re-arrange, duplicate, delete, and merge fill layers similarly to adjustment layers. You can blend fill layers with other layers by using the opacity and blend mode options on the Layers panel. Finally, you can restrict the fill layer to just a portion of your image by either making a selection first or painting on the mask later.

Follow these steps to create a fill layer:

1. **Open an image.**

   Use an image that will look good with a frame or border of some kind. Remember that if you don't have a selection, the fill layer covers your whole image.

2. **Click the Create New Fill or Adjustment Layer icon on the Layers panel. From the drop-down menu, choose a fill of a solid color, gradient, or pattern.**

   The dialog box specific to your type of fill appears.

3. **Specify your options, depending on the fill type you choose in Step 2:**

   - *Solid Color:* Choose your desired color from the Color Picker. See Chapter 12 for details on choosing colors and also gradients and patterns.

   - *Gradient:* Click the down-pointing arrow to choose a preset gradient from the drop-down panel or click the gradient preview to display the Gradient Editor and create your own gradient.

   - *Pattern*: Select a pattern from the drop-down panel. Enter a value to scale your pattern, if you want. Click Snap to Origin to make the origin of the pattern the same as the origin of the document. Select the Link with Layer option to specify that the pattern moves with the fill layer if you move that layer.

4. **Click OK.**

   The fill layer appears on the Layers panel, as shown in Figure 8-6. Notice the layer mask that was created on the fill layer.

 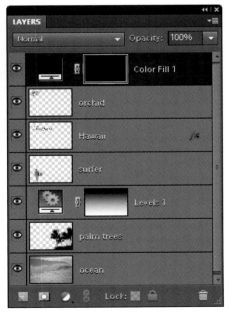

Corbis, PhotoDisc/Getty Images

Figure 8-6: Add a frame or border with a fill layer.

Shape layers

If you haven't made your way to Chapter 12 yet, you may be surprised to discover that Elements also lets you draw shapes with six different drawing tools. These shapes also have the bonus of being *vector*-based. This term means that the shapes are defined by mathematical equations, which create points and paths, rather than by pixels. The advantage of vector-based objects is that you can freely resize these objects without causing degradation. In addition, they're always printed with smooth edges, not with the jaggies you're familiar with seeing in pixel-based elements.

To create a shape layer, grab a shape tool from the Tools panel and drag it on your canvas. When you create a shape, it resides on its own, unique shape layer, as shown in Figure 8-7. As with other types of layers, you can adjust the blend modes and opacity of a shape layer. You can edit, move, and transform the actual shapes. However, to apply filters, you must first *simplify* the shape layer. This process converts the vector paths to pixels.

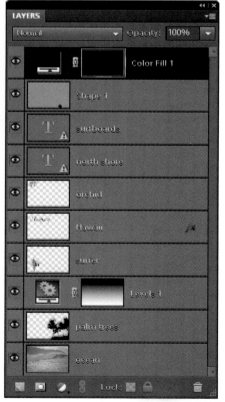

Figure 8-7: Shape layers are vector-based, allowing for smooth edges and optimum print quality.

Type layers

To add words to your images, as shown in Figure 8-7, click your canvas with the Type tool and just type. It's really as easy as that. Well, you can specify options, such as a font family and size, on the Options bar, but when you click the Commit button on the Options bar, you create a type layer. On the Layers panel, you see a layer with a T icon. For details on working with type, check out Chapter 13.

Tackling Layer Basics

Image layers are the heart and soul of the layering world. You can create multiple image layers within a single image. Even more fun is creating a composite from several different images. Add people you like; take out people you don't. Pluck people out of boring photo studios and put them in exotic locales. The creative possibilities are endless. In the following sections, we cover all the various ways to create image layers. We cover how to convert a background into a layer in the section "Getting to Know Layers," earlier in this chapter. The following sections describe how to create an image layer by using various other methods.

Creating a new layer from scratch

If you're creating a new, blank file, you can select the Transparent option for your background contents. Your new file is created with a transparent layer and is ready to go. If you have an existing file and want to create a new, blank layer, here are the ways to do so:

- ✔ Click the Create a New Layer icon at the bottom of the Layers panel.
- ✔ Choose New Layer from the Layers panel menu.
- ✔ Choose Layer➪New➪Layer.

Note that if you create a layer by using either of the menu commands, you're presented with a dialog box with options. In that dialog box, you can name your layer and specify options for grouping, blending, and adjusting opacity. Provide a name for your layer and click OK. You can always adjust the other options directly on the Layers panel later.

You can also use the Copy and Paste commands without even creating a blank layer first. When you copy and paste a selection without a blank layer, Elements automatically creates a new layer from the pasted selection. A better method of copying and pasting between multiple images, however, is to use the drag-and-drop method, which we describe in the section "Dragging and dropping layers," later in this chapter.

The Copy Merged command on the Edit menu creates a merged copy of all visible layers within the selection.

After you create your layer, you can put selections or other elements on that layer by doing one or more of the following:

- Grab a painting tool, such as the Brush or Pencil, and paint on the layer.

- Make a selection on another layer or on the background within the same document, or from another image entirely, and then choose Edit⇨Copy. Select your new, blank layer on the Layers panel and then choose Edit⇨Paste. You can also choose Select⇨All and then copy and paste to transfer an entire image to the new layer.

- Make a selection on another layer or on the background within the same document, or from another image, and then choose Edit⇨Cut. Select your new, blank layer and then choose Edit⇨Paste. Be aware that this action removes that selection from its original location and leaves a transparent hole, as shown in Figure 8-8.

Corbis Digital Stock

Figure 8-8: When you cut a selection from a layer, take note of the resulting hole in the original location.

Using Layer via Copy and Layer via Cut

Another way to create a layer is to use the Layer via Copy and Layer via Cut commands on the Layer menu. Make a selection on a layer or background and choose Layer⇨New⇨Layer via Copy or Layer via Cut. Elements automatically creates a new layer and puts the copied or cut selection on the layer. Remember that if you use the Layer via the Cut command, your selection is deleted from its original location layer, and you're left with a transparent hole. If you use the background for the source, your background color fills the space. A reminder: You can use these two commands only within the same image. You can't use them among multiple images.

Duplicating layers

Duplicating layers can be helpful if you want to protect your original image while experimenting with a technique. If you don't like the results, you can always delete the duplicate layer. No harm, no foul.

To duplicate an existing layer, select it on the Layers panel and do one of three things:

✔ Drag the layer to the Create a New Layer icon at the top of the panel. Elements creates a duplicate layer with *Copy* appended to the name of the layer.

✔ Choose Duplicate Layer from the Layers panel menu.

✔ Choose Layer⇨Duplicate Layer.

If you use the menu methods, a dialog box appears, asking you to name your layer and specify other options. Provide a name for your layer and click OK. You can specify the other options later, if you want.

Dragging and dropping layers

The most efficient way to copy and paste layers between multiple images is to use the drag-and-drop method. Why? Because it bypasses your Clipboard, which is the temporary storage area on your computer for copied data. Storing data, especially large files, can bog down your system. By keeping your Clipboard clear of data, your system operates more efficiently. If you already copied data and it's lounging on your Clipboard, choose Edit⇨Clear⇨Clipboard Contents to empty your Clipboard.

Here's how to drag and drop layers from one file to another:

1. **Select your desired layer in the Layers panel.**

2. **Grab the Move tool (the four-headed arrow) from the Tools panel.**

3. **Drag and drop the layer onto your destination file.**

   The dropped layer pops in as a new layer above the active layer in the image. You don't need to have a selection border to copy the entire layer. But, if you want to copy just a portion of the layer, make your selection before you drag and drop with the Move tool. If you want the selected element to be centered on the destination file, press the Shift key while you drag and drop.

 Here's a handy tip. If you have several elements (that aren't touching each other) on one layer and you want to select only one of the elements to drag and drop, use the Lasso tool to make a crude selection around the object without touching any of the other elements. Then press the Ctrl (⌘ on the Mac) key and press the up-arrow key once. The element then becomes perfectly selected. Drag and drop with the Move tool.

Using the Paste into Selection command

The Paste into Selection command lets you put an image on a separate layer while also inserting that image into a selection border. For example, in Figure 8-9, we used this command to make it appear as though our surfer is in the water.

Figure 8-9: Use the Paste into Selection command to make one element appear as though it's coming out of another element.

You can do the same by following these steps:

1. **Make your desired selection on the layer in your destination image.**

   In our figure, we selected the area in the water where the surfer would be positioned.

2. **Select the image that will fill that selection.**

   The image can be within the same file or from another file. Our surfer was in another file.

3. **Choose Edit⇨Copy.**

4. **Return to the destination image layer and choose Edit⇨Paste into Selection.**

   Elements converts the selection border on the layer into a layer mask. The pasted selection is visible only inside the selection border. In our example, the surfer only shows inside the selected area. His ankles and feet are outside the border and therefore are hidden.

Moving a Layer's Content

Moving the content of a layer is a piece of cake: Grab the Move tool from the Tools panel, select your layer on the Layers panel, and drag the element on the canvas to your desired location. You can also move the layer in 1-pixel increments by using the keyboard arrow keys. Press Shift with the arrows to move in 10-pixel increments.

The Auto-Select Layer option on the Options bar enables you to switch to a layer when you click any part of that layer's content with the Move tool. But be careful if you have a lot of overlapping layers because this technique can sometimes be more trouble than it's worth.

The Move tool has a couple of additional options. Here's the lowdown:

- **Show Bounding Box:** This option surrounds the contents of your layer with a dotted box that has handles, enabling you to easily transform your layer. Find details in the following section.

- **Show Highlight on Rollover:** Hover your mouse anywhere over the canvas to make an outline appear around the element on your layer. Click the highlighted layer to select it and then move it.

- **Arrange menu:** This menu enables you to change your selected layer's position in the stacking order.

- **Link Layers:** This option, which resides not on the Options bar, but in the Layers panel, connects the layers to allow ease in moving (or transforming) multiple layers simultaneously. Select a layer and then Ctrl-click (⌘-click on the Mac) to select more layers. Click the Link Layers option.

- **Align submenu:** Align your selected layers on the left, center, right, top, middle, and bottom. As with linking, select your first layer and then Shift-click to select more layers. Ctrl-click (⌘-click on the Mac) to select non-consecutive layers. Choose an alignment option.

- **Distribute submenu:** Use this menu to evenly space your selected layers on the left, center, right, top, middle, and bottom. Like with aligning, select your first layer and then Shift-click to select more layers. Ctrl-click (⌘-click on the Mac) to select non-consecutive layers. Choose your desired distribution option.

Transforming Layers

When working with layers, you may find the need to scale or rotate some of your images. You can do so easily by applying the Transform and Free Transform commands. The methods to transform layers and transform selections are identical.

Here's how to transform a layer:

1. **Select your desired layer.**

   You can also apply a transformation to multiple layers simultaneously by linking the layers first.

2. **Choose Image⇨Transform⇨Free Transform.**

   A bounding box surrounds the contents of your layer. Drag a corner handle to size the contents. Press Shift while dragging to constrain the proportions. To rotate the contents, move the mouse cursor just outside a corner handle until it turns into a curved arrow and then drag. To distort, skew, or apply perspective to the contents, right-click and choose the desired command from the context menu. You can also click the rotate, scale, and skew icons in the Options bar, as well as enter your transform values numerically in the fields.

   If you want to apply just a single transformation, you can also choose the individual Distort, Skew, and Perspective commands from the Image⇨Transform menu. Or, to rotate or flip, you can choose Image⇨ Rotate.

3. **When your layer is transformed to your liking, double-click inside the bounding box.**

Try to perform all your transformations in one execution. Each time you transform pixels, you put your image through the *interpolation process* (analyzing the colors of the original pixels and "manufacturing" new ones). Done to the extreme, this process can degrade the quality of your image. This is why it's prudent to use the Free Transform command, rather than individual commands — so that all transformations can be executed in one fell swoop.

When the Move tool is active, you can transform a layer without choosing a command. Select the Show Bounding Box option on the Options bar. This option surrounds the layer, or selection, with a box that has handles. Drag the handles to transform the layer or selection.

Adding Layer Masks

Elements once again inherits a feature that previously was exclusive to its big brother Photoshop. Full fledged *layer masks* have made their arrival in Photoshop Elements 9. *Masking* is essentially just another way of making a selection. Instead of making a selection with a single selection outline — either it is selected or it isn't — masks enable you to define your selection with up to 256 levels of gray (from white to black). You can therefore, have varying levels of a selection.

Here's how it works. First, think of a layer mask as a sheet of acetate that hovers over your layer. With any of the painting tools (Brush tool, Gradient tool, and others), you apply black, white, or any shade of gray onto the layer mask. Where the mask is white, the image on the layer is selected and shows. Where the mask is black, the image is unselected and is hidden. And where the mask is gray, the image is partially selected and therefore, partially shows. The lighter the gray, the more the image shows. By default, the mask starts out completely white so everything is selected and shows.

Here are some things you can do with layer masks:

- **Creatively blend one layer into another.** If you want one image to gradually dissolve into another, using a layer mask is the way to go, as shown in Figure 8-10 where we combined a couple of conversing dolphins and stuck them in a pool. Try using the gradient tool with the black to white gradient selected to create a soft dissolve.

- **Adjust your layer mask to selectively show and hide the effects of adjustment layer.** See the earlier section, "Adjustment layers."

- **Apply a filter to your layer mask to create an interesting special effect.**

One of the best aspects of layer masks is that you can endlessly edit them. Unlike just making a feathered selection, you can keep adjusting how much of your current layer or underlying images show. Or you can adjust how gradually one image blends into another: Just change the areas of white, black, and gray on the layer mask by painting with any of the painting tools. Just make sure you select the layer mask and not the image. When you select the layer mask thumbnail in the Layers panel, you see the appearance of an outline around the thumbnail.

You can't add a layer mask to a background layer. You must convert the background into a layer first.

Some other things to keep in mind when you use layer masks are:

- To load the mask as a selection outline, simply Ctrl-click (⌘-click on the Mac) the layer mask thumbnail in the Layers panel.

- To temporarily hide a mask, Shift-click the layer mask thumbnail in the Layers panel. Repeat to show the mask

- To view the mask without viewing the image, Alt-click (Option-click on the Mac) on the Layer Mask thumbnail in the Layers panel. This can be helpful when editing a layer mask.

- To unlink a layer from its layer mask, click the link icon in the Layers panel. Click again to reestablish the link. By default, Elements links a layer mask to the contents of the layer. This link enables them to move together.

Corbis, PhotoDisc/Getty Images

Figure 8-10: Add a layer mask to gradually blend one layer into another.

> ✔ To delete a layer mask, drag its thumbnail to the trash icon in the Layers panel.
>
> ✔ To apply a layer mask, drag the mask thumbnail to the trash icon in the Layers panel and be sure to click Apply in the dialog box. When you apply a layer mask, you fuse the mask to the layer so editing is no longer possible.

Note that many of the preceding commands are also available in the Layer⇨ Layer Mask submenu.

Flattening and Merging Layers

Layers are fun and fantastic, but they can quickly chew up your computer's RAM and bloat your file size. And sometimes, to be honest, having too many layers can start to make your file tedious to manage, thereby making you less productive. Whenever possible, you should merge your layers to save memory and space. *Merging* combines visible, linked, or adjacent layers into a single layer (not a background). The intersection of all transparent areas is retained.

In addition, if you need to import your file into another program, certain programs don't support files with layers. Therefore, you may need to flatten your file before importing it. *Flattening* an image combines all visible layers into a background, including type, shape, fill, and adjustment layers. You're prompted as to whether you want to discard hidden layers, and any transparent areas are filled with white. We recommend, however, that before you flatten your image, you make a copy of the file with all its layers intact and save it as a native Photoshop file. That way, if you ever need to make any edits, you have the added flexibility of having your layers.

By the way, the only file formats that support layers are native Photoshop (.psd); Tagged Image File Format, or TIFF (.tif); and Portable Document Format, or PDF (.pdf). If you save your file in any other format, Elements automatically flattens your layers into a background. See Chapter 3 for details on these file types.

Flattening layers

To flatten an image, follow these steps:

1. **Make certain that all layers you want to retain are visible.**

   If you have any hidden layers, Elements asks you whether you want to discard those hidden layers.

2. **Choose Flatten Image from the Layers panel menu or the Layer menu.**

   All your layers are combined into a single background, as shown in Figure 8-11.

   If you mistakenly flatten your image, choose Edit⇨Undo or use your Undo History panel. (If you're not familiar with the History panel, see Chapter 1 for details.)

Merging layers

You can merge your layers in a couple of ways. Here's how:

- **Select only those layers you want to merge.** Choose Merge Layers from the panel menu or the Layer menu.

- **Display only those layers you want to merge.** Click the eye icon on the Layers panel to hide those layers you don't want to merge. Choose Merge Visible from the Layers panel menu or the Layer menu.

- **Arrange the layers you want to merge so that they're adjacent to each other on the Layers panel.** Select the topmost layer of that group and choose Merge Down from the Layers panel menu or the Layer menu. Note that Merge Down merges your active layer with the layer directly below it.

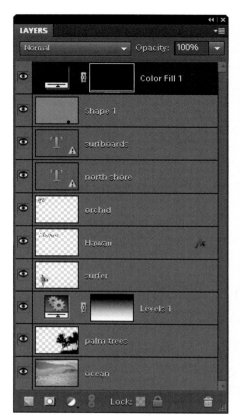

Figure 8-11: Flattening combines all your layers into a single background.

9

Simple Image Makeovers

▶ Cropping and straightening your images

▶ Using one-step auto fixes

▶ Editing in Edit Quick mode

▶ Fixing small imperfections

*F*ixing images quickly without pain or hassle is probably one of the most desirable features you'll find in Elements and one that we're sure you'll embrace frequently. Whether you're an experienced photographer or an amateur shutterbug, cropping away unwanted background, tweaking the lighting or color of an image, and erasing away the minor blemishes of a loved one's face are all editing tasks you'll most likely tackle. With these simple image-makeover tools in Elements, these tasks are as easy as clicking a single button or making a few swipes with a brush.

Cropping and Straightening Images

Cropping a photo is probably one of the easiest things you can do to improve the composition of your photo. Getting rid of the unnecessary background around your subject creates a better focal point. Another dead giveaway of amateurish photography is crooked horizon lines. Not a problem. Elements gives you several ways to straighten those images after the fact. So, after your next photo shoot, launch the Elements editor and then crop and straighten your images before you show them off.

Cutting away with the Crop tool

The most common way to crop a photo is by using the Crop tool. Simple, quick, and easy, this tool gets the job done. Here's how to use it:

1. **Select the Crop tool from the Tools panel in either Edit Full or Edit Quick mode.**

   You can also press the C key. For details on the different workspaces, see Chapter 1. For full details on Edit Quick mode, see the section "Editing with Edit Quick," later in this chapter.

2. **Specify your aspect ratio and resolution options on the Options bar.**

   Here are your choices:

   - *No Restriction:* Allows you to freely crop the image at any size.

   - *Use Photo Ratio:* Retains the original aspect ratio of the image when you crop.

   - *Preset Sizes:* Offers a variety of common photographic sizes. When you crop, your image then becomes that specific dimension.

   When you crop an image, Elements retains the original resolution of the file (unless you specify otherwise in the resolution option). Therefore, to keep your image at the same image size while simultaneously eliminating portions of your image, Elements must resample the file. Consequently, your image must have sufficient resolution so that the effects of the resampling aren't too noticeable. This is especially true if you're choosing a larger preset size. If all this talk about resolution and resampling is fuzzy, be sure to check out Chapter 3.

   - *Width and Height:* Enables you to specify a desired width and height to crop your image.

   - *Resolution:* Specify a desired resolution for your cropped image. Again, try to avoid resampling your image.

   - *Pixels/in or Pixels/cm:* Specify your desired unit of measurement.

3. **Drag around the portion of the image you want to retain and release the mouse button.**

   When you drag, a crop marquee bounding box appears. Don't worry if your cropping marquee isn't exactly correct. You can adjust it in Step 4.

   The area outside the cropping marquee (called a *shield*) appears darker than the inside in order to better frame your image, as shown in Figure 9-1. If you want to change the color and opacity of the shield, or if you don't want it at all, change your Crop preferences by choosing

Edit➪Preferences➪Display & Cursors. (On the Mac, choose Photoshop Elements➪Preferences➪Display & Cursors.)

Shield   Cropping marquee   Handle

Commit — └─ Cancel

Figure 9-1: The area outside the crop marquee appears darker to allow for easy framing of your image.

4. **Adjust the cropping marquee by dragging the handles of the crop marquee bounding box.**

   To move the entire marquee, position your mouse inside the marquee until you see a black arrowhead cursor and then drag.

   If you move your mouse outside the marquee, your cursor changes to a curved arrow. Drag with this cursor to rotate the marquee. This action allows you to both rotate and crop your image simultaneously — handy for straightening a crooked image. Just be aware that rotation, unless it's in 90-degree increments, also resamples your image.

5. **Double-click inside the cropping marquee.**

   You can also just press Enter or click the green Commit button next to the marquee. Elements then discards the area outside the marquee. To cancel your crop, click the red Cancel button.

You can also find the Crop command in the Organizer in the Fix pane.

Cropping with a selection border

You can crop an image by choosing Image➪Crop in either Edit Full or Edit Quick mode. First, make a selection with any of the selection tools and then choose the command. You can use this technique with any selection border shape. That is, your selection doesn't have to be rectangular. It can be round or even freeform. Your cropped image doesn't take on that shape, but Elements crops as close to the boundaries of the selection border as it can. For details about making selections, see Chapter 7.

Straightening images

There may be times when you just didn't quite get that horizon straight when you took a photo of the beach. Or maybe you scanned a photo and it wasn't quite centered in the middle of the scanning bed. It's not a big deal. Elements gives you several ways to straighten an image.

Using the Straighten tool

This tool enables you to specify a new straight edge, and it then rotates the image accordingly. Here's how to use the Straighten tool:

1. **Select the Straighten tool from the Tools panel (or press the P key) only in Edit Full mode.**

2. **Specify your desired setting from the Canvas Options on the Options bar.**

   Here are your choices:

   - *Grow or Shrink Canvas to Fit:* Rotates the image and increases or decreases the size of the canvas to fit the image area.

   - *Crop to Remove Background:* Trims off background canvas outside the image area. This choice is helpful if you scan an image and white areas appear around your photo that you want removed.

   - *Crop to Original Size:* Rotates your image without trimming off any background canvas.

3. **(Optional) Select Rotate All Layers.**

   If you have an image with layers and you want all of them rotated, select this option.

4. **Draw a line in your image to represent the new straight edge.**

   Your image is then straightened and, if you chose either of the crop options in Step 2, also cropped.

Using the Straighten menu commands

In addition to using the Straighten tool, you can straighten your images by using two commands on the Image menu, in either Edit Full or Edit Quick mode:

- ✔ **To automatically straighten an image without cropping:** Choose Image➪Rotate➪Straighten Image. This straightening technique leaves the canvas around the image.

- ✔ **To automatically straighten and crop the image simultaneously:** Choose Image➪Rotate➪Straighten and Crop Image.

Employing One-Step Auto Fixes

Elements has five automatic lighting-, contrast-, and color-correction tools that can improve the appearance of your images with just one menu command. These commands are available in either Edit Full or Edit Quick mode, and they're all on the Enhance menu. For more on Edit Quick mode, see the section "Editing with Edit Quick," later in this chapter.

The advantage of these one-step correctors is that they're extremely easy to use. You don't need to have one iota of knowledge about color or contrast to use them. The downside to using them is that sometimes the result isn't as good as you could get via a manual color-correction method. And sometimes these correctors may even make your image look worse than before by giving you weird color shifts. But because these correctors are quick and easy, give them a try on an image that needs help. Usually, you don't want to use more than one of the auto fixes. If one doesn't work on your image, undo the fix and try another. If you still don't like the result, move on to one of the manual methods we describe in Chapter 10.

Auto Smart Fix

This all-in-one command is touted to adjust it all. It's designed to improve lighting, improve the details in shadow and highlight areas, and correct the color balance, as shown in Figure 9-2. The overexposed image on the left was improved quite nicely with the Auto Smart Fix command.

Figure 9-2: In a hurry? Apply the Auto Smart Fix command to quickly improve an image.

The Auto Smart Fix command, as well as the Auto Color, Auto Levels, Auto Contrast, Auto Sharpen, and Auto Red Eye Fix, are also available in the Organizer (under the Fix pane), where you can apply the commands to several selected images simultaneously.

If the Auto Smart Fix was just too "auto" for you, you can crank it up a notch and try Adjust Smart Fix. This command is similar to Auto Smart Fix but gives you a slider that allows you, not Elements, to control the amount of correction applied to the image.

Auto Levels

The Auto Levels command adjusts the overall contrast of an image. This command works best on images that have pretty good contrast (even range of tones and detail in the shadow, highlight, and midtone areas) to begin with and need just a minor amount of adjustment. Auto Levels works by *mapping,* or converting, the lightest and darkest pixels in your image to black and white, thereby making highlights appear lighter and shadows appear darker, as shown in Figure 9-3.

Although Auto Levels can improve contrast, it may also produce an unwanted *colorcast* (a slight trace of color). If this happens, undo the command and try the Auto Contrast command instead. If that still doesn't improve the contrast, it's time to bring out the big guns. Try the Levels command we describe in Chapter 10.

Figure 9-3: Auto Levels adjusts the overall contrast of an image.

Auto Contrast

The Auto Contrast command is designed to adjust the overall contrast in an image without adjusting its color. This command may not do as good a job of improving contrast as the Auto Levels command, but it does a better job of retaining the color balance of an image. Auto Contrast usually doesn't cause the funky colorcasts that can occur when you're using Auto Levels. This command works great on images with a haze, as shown in Figure 9-4.

PhotoDisc/Getty Images

Figure 9-4: The Auto Contrast command works wonders on hazy images.

Auto Color Correction

The Auto Color Correction command adjusts both the color and contrast of an image, based on the shadows, midtones, and highlights it finds in the image and a default set of values. These values adjust the amount of black and white pixels that Elements removes from the darkest and lightest areas of the image. You usually use this command to remove a colorcast or to balance the color in your image, as shown in Figure 9-5. Occasionally, this command can also be useful in correcting oversaturated or undersaturated colors.

Figure 9-5: Use Auto Color Correction to remove a colorcast.

Auto Sharpen

Photos taken with a digital camera or scanned on a flatbed scanner often suffer from a case of overly soft focus. Sharpening gives the illusion of increased focus by increasing the contrast between pixels. Auto Sharpen attempts to improve the focus, as shown in Figure 9-6, without overdoing it. What happens when you oversharpen? Your images go from soft to grainy and noisy. For more precise sharpening, check out the Unsharp Mask and Adjust Sharpness features we cover in Chapter 10.

Always make sharpening your last fix after you make all your other fixes and enhancements.

Auto Red Eye Fix

This command is self-explanatory. The Auto Red Eye Fix command automatically detects and eliminates red-eye in an image. Red-eye happens when a person or an animal (where red-eye can also be yellow-, green-, or even blue-eye) looks directly into the flash.

If for some reason the Auto Red Eye Fix doesn't quite do the trick, you can always reach for the Red Eye Removal tool on the Tools panel. Here's how to remove red-eye manually:

Figure 9-6: Use Auto Sharpen to improve focus.

1. **Select the Red Eye Removal tool from the Tools panel.**
2. **Using the default settings, click the red portion of the eye in your image.**

   This one-click tool darkens the pupil while retaining the tonality and texture of the rest of the eye, as shown in Figure 9-7.

Figure 9-7: The Auto Red Eye Fix and the Red Eye Removal tool detect and destroy dreaded red-eye.

3. **If you're unhappy with the fix, adjust one or both of these options:**

- *Pupil Size:* Use the slider to increase or decrease the size of the pupil.

- *Darken Pupil:* Use the slider to darken or lighten the color of the pupil.

If you're trying to fix green-eye (or blue-eye) in animals, your best bet is to use the Color Replacement tool. See the section "Replacing one color with another," at the end of this chapter.

Editing with Edit Quick

Edit Quick mode is a pared-down version of Edit Full mode that conveniently provides basic fixing tools and tosses in a few unique features, such as a before-and-after preview of your image.

Here's a step-by-step workflow that you can follow in Edit Quick mode to repair your photos:

1. **Select one or more photos in the Organizer, click Fix in the upper-right side of the application window, and then choose the Quick Photo Edit from the drop-down menu.**

   Or, if you're in Edit Full mode, select your desired image(s) from the Project Bin and then select the Edit Quick button in the upper-right area of the application window.

   Note that you can also open images by simply choosing File➪Open.

2. **Specify your preview preference from the View pop-up menu at the bottom of the application window.**

   You can choose to view just your original image (Before Only), your fixed image (After Only), or both images side by side (Before & After) in either portrait (Vertical) or landscape (Horizontal) orientation, as shown in Figure 9-8.

3. **Use the Zoom and Hand tools to magnify and navigate around your image. (See Chapter 5 for more on these tools.)**

   You can also specify the Zoom percentage by using the Zoom slider at the bottom right of the application window.

4. **Choose your desired window view by selecting one of the following buttons located in the top-left corner of the application window: Actual Pixels, Fit Screen, Fill Screen (which zooms your image to fill your screen), or Print Size.**

Figure 9-8: Edit Quick mode enables you to view before-and-after previews of your image.

5. **Crop your image by using the Crop tool on the Tools panel.**

   You can also use any of the methods we describe in the "Cropping and Straightening Images" section, earlier in this chapter, except for the Straighten tool, which is exclusive to Edit Full mode.

6. **To rotate the image in 90-degree increments, click the Rotate Left or Rotate Right button at the bottom of the application window.**

7. **Apply any necessary auto fixes, such as Auto Smart Fix, Auto Levels, Auto Contrast, and Auto Color Correction.**

   All these commands are on the Enhance menu or in the Smart Fix, Lighting, Color, and Balance sections on the Quick Fix pane in the Panel bin.

   Each of these fixes is described in detail in the section "Employing One-Step Auto Fixes," earlier in this chapter. Remember that usually one of the fixes is enough. Don't stack them on top of each other. If one doesn't work, click the Reset button in the top-right corner of the image preview and try another. If you're not happy, go to Step 8. If you are happy, skip to Step 9.

8. **If the auto fixes don't quite cut it, get more control by using the sliders available for Smart Fix, Levels, Contrast, and Color, located in the Quick Fix pane.**

Here's a brief description of each available adjustment:

- *Shadows:* When you drag the slider to the right, lightens the darker areas of your image without adjusting the highlights.

- *Highlights:* When you drag the slider to the right, darkens the lighter areas of your image without adjusting the shadows.

- *Midtone:* Adjusts the contrast of the middle (gray) values and leaves the highlights and shadows as they are.

- *Saturation:* Adjusts the intensity of the colors.

- *Hue:* Changes all colors in an image. Make a selection first to change the color of just one or more elements. Otherwise, use restraint with this adjustment.

- *Temperature:* Adjusts the colors to make them warmer (red) or cooler (blue). You can use this adjustment to correct skin tones or to correct overly cool images (such as snowy winter photos) or overly warm images (such as photos shot at sunset or sunrise).

- *Tint:* Adjusts the tint after you adjust temperature to make the color more green or magenta.

If you still don't get the results you need, move on to one of the more manual adjustments that we describe in Chapter 10.

Note that you can also apply fixes to just selected portions of your image. Edit Quick mode offers the Quick Selection tool for your selection tasks. For details on using this tool, see Chapter 7.

9. **Add finishing fixes by using the remaining tools in the Tools panel.**

Here is a description of each tool:

- *Red Eye Removal tool:* Try the Auto Red Eye Fix to remove red eye from your peoples' eyes. But if it doesn't work, try using the Red Eye Removal tool. This method is described in the section "Auto Red Eye Fix," earlier in this chapter.

- *Whiten Teeth:* This fix does what it says — it whitens teeth. Be sure to choose an appropriate brush size from the Brushes drop-down panel before whitening. (For more on brush options, see Chapter 12.) Using a brush diameter that's larger than the area of the teeth also whitens/brightens whatever else it touches — lips, chin, and so on. Click the teeth. Note that this tool makes a selection and whitens simultaneously. After your initial click, your selection option converts from New Selection to Add to Selection in the Options bar. If you pick up too much in your dental selection, click the Subtract from Selection option and click the area you want to eliminate. When you're happy with the results of your whitening session, choose Select➪Deselect or press Ctrl+D (⌘+D on the Mac).

- *Make Dull Skies Blue:* Click or drag over areas of your sky that need brightening. Choosing a brush size and selection option is similar to using the Whiten Teeth fix, described in the preceding bullet. When you click your sky, it's selected and brightened at the same time. When you're done, choose Select➪Deselect or press Ctrl+D (⌘+D on the Mac).

- *Black and White–High Contrast:* This tool converts your image into a high-contrast grayscale image. The method and options are similar to those for the Whiten Teeth and Make Dull Skies Blue options, described in the preceding bullets. Figure 9-9 shows a color image converted into a grayscale image that looks like a vintage newspaper photo.

Note that you can find these same fixes (and many more) in Edit Full mode, under the Smart Brush and Detail Smart Brush tools. Check out Chapter 10 for the lowdown on these tools.

Figure 9-9: The Black and White–High Contrast fix converts a color image into a grayscale one.

10. **Sharpen your image either automatically (by clicking the Sharpen Auto button under Details in the Quick Fix pane) or manually (by dragging the slider on the Sharpen panel).**

This fix should always be the last adjustment you make on your image.

Fixing Small Imperfections with Tools

Photoshop Elements 9 provides you with several handy tools to correct minor imperfections in your photos. You can use the Clone Stamp tool to clone parts of your image, heal blemishes with the Healing Brush or Spot Healing Brush tools, lighten or darken small areas with the Dodge and Burn tools, soften or sharpen the focus with the Blur or Sharpen tools, and fix color with the Sponge or Color Replacement tools.

Cloning with the Clone Stamp tool

Elements enables you to clone elements without the hassle of genetically engineering DNA. In fact, the Clone Stamp tool works by just taking sampled pixels from one area and copying, or *cloning,* them onto another area. The advantage of cloning, rather than making a selection and then copying and pasting, is that it's easier to realistically retain soft-edged elements, such as shadows, as shown in Figure 9-10.

The Clone Stamp doesn't stop there. You can also use this tool for fixing flaws, such as scratches, bruises, date/time stamp imprints from cameras and other minor imperfections. Although the birth of the healing tools (discussed in the following sections) has somewhat pushed the Clone Stamp tool out of the retouching arena, it can still do a good repair job in many instances.

Here's how to use the Clone Stamp tool:

PhotoSpin

Figure 9-10: The Clone Stamp tool enables you to realistically duplicate soft-edged elements, such as shadows.

1. **Choose the Clone Stamp tool from the Tools panel in Edit Full mode.**

2. **On the Options bar, choose a brush from the Brush Preset drop-down menu and then use the brush as-is or adjust its size with the Size slider.**

   Keep in mind that the size of the brush you specify should be appropriate for what you're trying to clone or retouch. If you're cloning a large object, use a large brush. For repairing small flaws, use a small brush. Cloning with a soft-edged brush usually produces more natural results. For details on brushes, see Chapter 12.

3. **Choose your desired Blend Mode and Opacity percentage.**

   For more on blend modes, see Chapter 11. To make your cloned image appear ghosted, use an opacity percentage of less than 100 percent.

4. **Select or deselect the Aligned option.**

   With Aligned selected, the clone source moves when you move your cursor to a different location. If you want to clone multiple times from the same location, leave the Aligned option deselected.

5. **Select or deselect the Sample All Layers option.**

   This option enables you to sample pixels from all visible layers for the clone. If this option is deselected, the Clone Stamp tool clones from only the active layer. Check out Chapter 8 for details about working with layers.

6. **Click the double rectangle icon if you want to display an overlay.**

   Displaying an overlay can be helpful when what you're cloning needs to be in alignment with the underlying image. Adjust the opacity for your overlay. If you select Auto Hide, when you release your mouse, you will see a ghosted preview of how your cloned pixels will appear on the image. While you're cloning, however, the overlay is hidden. Select Clipped to have the overlay contained only within the boundaries of your brush. We think that this makes it easier to more precisely clone what you want. Finally, select Invert to reverse the colors and tones in your overlay.

7. **Alt-click (Option-click on the Macintosh) the area of your image that you want to clone to define the source of the clone.**

8. **Click or drag along the area where you want the clone to appear, as shown in Figure 9-11.**

   While you drag, Elements displays a crosshair cursor along with your Clone Stamp cursor. The crosshair is the source you're cloning from, and the Clone Stamp cursor is where the clone is being applied. While you move the mouse, the crosshair moves, as well, so you have a continuous reference to the area of your image that you're cloning. Watch the crosshair, or else you may clone something you don't want.

 If you're cloning an element, try to clone it without lifting your mouse. Also, when you're retouching a flaw, try not to overdo it. One or two clicks on each flaw is usually plenty. If you're heavy-handed with the Clone Stamp, you get a blotchy effect that's a telltale sign something has been retouched.

Figure 9-11: The crosshair and Clone Stamp cursor in action.

Retouching with the Healing Brush

The Healing Brush tool is similar to the Clone Stamp tool in that you clone pixels from one area onto another area. But the Healing Brush is superior in that it takes into account the tonality (highlights, midtones, and shadows) of the flawed area. The Healing Brush clones by using the *texture* from the sampled area (the *source*) and then using the *colors* around the brush stroke while you paint over the flawed area (the *destination*). The highlights, mid-tones, and shadow areas remain intact, giving you a realistic and natural repair that isn't as blotchy or miscolored as the repair you get with the Clone Stamp tool.

Here are the steps to heal a photo:

1. **Open an image in need of a makeover and select the Healing Brush tool from the Tools panel in Edit Full mode.**

   You can also heal between two images, but be sure that they have the same color mode: for example, both RGB (red, green, blue). We chose a guy who looks like he might like to lose a few years, as shown in Figure 9-12.

PhotoSpin

Figure 9-12: Wipe out ten years in two minutes with the Healing Brush tool.

2. **Specify a diameter and hardness for your brush tip from the Brush Picker drop-down panel on the Options bar.**

   You can also adjust the spacing, angle, and roundness. For details on these options, see Chapter 12. Don't be shy. Be sure to adjust the size of your brush, as needed. Using the appropriate brush size for the flaw you're retouching is critical to creating a realistic effect.

3. **Choose your desired blend mode.**

   For most retouching jobs, you probably should leave the mode as Normal. Replace mode preserves textures, such as noise or film grain, around the edges of your strokes.

4. **Choose one of these Source options:**

   - *Sampled:* Uses the pixels from the image. You use this option for the majority of your repairs.

   - *Pattern:* Uses pixels from a pattern chosen from the Pattern Picker drop-down panel.

5. **Select or deselect the Aligned option on the Options bar.**

   For most retouching tasks, you probably should leave Aligned selected. Here are the details on each option:

   - *With Aligned selected:* When you click or drag with the Healing Brush, Elements displays a crosshair along with the Healing Brush cursor. The crosshair represents the sampling point, also known as the *source.* When you move the Healing Brush tool, the crosshair also moves, providing a constant reference to the area you're sampling.

   - *With Aligned deselected:* Elements applies the source pixels from your initial sampling point, no matter how many times you stop and start dragging.

6. **Select the Sample All Layers option to heal an image by using all visible layers.**

   If this option is deselected, you heal from only the active layer.

    To ensure maximum editing flexibility later, select the Sample All Layers option and add a new, blank layer above the image you want to heal. When you heal the image, the pixels appear on the new layer and not on the image itself; so, you can adjust opacity and blend modes and make other adjustments to the healed layer.

7. **Establish the sampling point by Alt-clicking (Option-clicking on the Mac).**

   Make sure to click the area of your image that you want to clone from. In our example, we clicked a smooth area of the forehead.

8. **Release the Alt (Option on the Mac) key and click or drag over a flawed area of your image.**

   Keep an eye on the crosshair because that's the area you're healing from. We brushed over the wrinkles under and around the eyes and on the forehead. (Refer to Figure 9-12.) This guy never looked so good, and he endured absolutely no recovery time.

Zeroing in with the Spot Healing Brush

Whereas the Healing Brush is designed to fix larger flawed areas, the Spot Healing Brush is designed for smaller imperfections, with one exception — the new Content Aware option, which we explain in Step 4 in the following list. The Spot Healing Brush doesn't require you to specify a sampling source. It automatically takes a sample from around the area to be retouched. It's quick, easy, and often effective. But it doesn't give you control over the sampling source, so keep an eye out for less-than-desirable fixes.

Here's how to quickly fix flaws with the Spot Healing Brush tool:

1. **Open your image and grab the Spot Healing Brush tool in Edit Full mode.**

   The moles on this guy's face, as shown in Figure 9-13, are no match for the Spot Healing Brush.

PhotoSpin

Figure 9-13: Now you see it (left), and now you don't (right).

2. **On the Options bar, click the Brush Preset Picker and select a desired diameter and hardness for your brush tip from the drop-down panel.**

   Select a brush that's a little larger than the flawed area you're fixing.

3. **Choose a blend mode from the Options bar.**

   As with the Healing Brush, the most likely mode is Normal.

4. **Choose a Type from the Options bar:**

   - *Proximity Match:* Samples the pixels around the edge of the selection to fix the flawed area.

   - *Create Texture:* Uses all the pixels in the selection to create a texture to fix the flaw.

   - *Content-Aware:* If you want to eliminate something larger than a mole or freckle, this is the option of choice where actual content from the image is used as a kind of patch for the flawed area. Large objects can be zapped away with the new content-aware option as shown in Figure 9-14 where we eliminated the cannonballer. Note that you may have to paint over the offending object a couple times to get your desired result. Also, a touch up with the Clone Stamp or other healing tools may be needed.

Istockphoto.com

Figure 9-14: Eliminate cannonballers and other offending objects with the new content-aware option.

Try Proximity Match first, and if it doesn't work, undo it and try Create Texture or Content-Aware.

5. **Choose Sample All Layers to heal an image by using all visible layers.**

   If you leave this check box deselected, you heal from only the active layer.

6. **Click, drag or "paint" over the area you want to fix.**

   We clicked the moles with the Spot Healing Brush. For the wrinkles around the eyes, we broke out the Healing Brush. We needed more control of the sampling source to achieve realistic results as shown in the after image in Figure 9-13.

Lightening and darkening with Dodge and Burn tools

The techniques of dodging and burning originated in the darkroom, where photographers fixed negatives that had overly dark or light areas by adding or subtracting exposure, using holes and paddles as an enlarger made prints. The Dodge and Burn tools are even better than their analog ancestors because they're more flexible and much more precise. You can specify the size and softness of your tool by simply selecting from one of the many brush tips. You can also limit the correction to various tonal ranges in your image — shadows, midtones, or highlights. Finally, you can adjust the amount of correction that's applied by specifying an exposure percentage.

Use these tools only on small areas, such as the girl's face shown in Figure 9-15, and in moderation. You can even make a selection prior to dodging and burning to ensure that the adjustment is applied only to your specific area. Also, keep in mind that you can't add detail that isn't there to begin with. If you try to lighten extremely dark shadows that contain little detail, you get gray areas. If you try to darken overly light highlights, you just end up with white blobs.

Follow these steps to dodge or burn an image:

1. **Choose either the Dodge (to lighten) or Burn (to darken) tool from the Tools panel in Edit Full mode.**

   Press Shift+O to cycle through the Dodge, Burn, and Sponge tools.

2. **Select a brush from the Brush Preset Picker drop-down panel and also adjust the brush size, if necessary.**

   Larger, softer brushes spread the dodging or burning effect over a larger area, making blending with the surrounding area easier.

Figure 9-15: Use the Dodge and Burn tools to lighten and darken small areas.

3. **From the Range pop-up list, select Shadows, Midtones, or Highlights.**

   Select Shadows to darken or lighten the darker areas of your image. Select Midtones to adjust the tones of average darkness. Select Highlights to make the light areas lighter or darker.

   In Figure 9-15, the original image had mostly dark areas, so we dodged the shadows.

4. **Choose the amount of correction you want to apply with each stroke by adjusting the Exposure setting on the Options bar.**

   Start with a lower percentage to better control the amount of darkening or lightening. Exposure is similar to the opacity setting that you use with the regular Brush tool. We used a setting of 10 percent.

5. **Paint over the areas you want to lighten or darken.**

   If you don't like the results, press Ctrl+Z (⌘+Z on the Mac) to undo.

Smudging away rough spots

The Smudge tool, one of the focus tools, pushes your pixels around using the color that's under the cursor when you start to drag. Think of it as dragging a brush through wet paint. You can use this tool to create a variety of effects. When it's used to the extreme, you can create a warped effect. When it's used more subtly, you can soften the edges of objects in a more natural fashion than you can with the Blur tool. Or you can create images that take on a painterly effect, as shown in Figure 9-16. Keep an eye on your image while you paint, however, because you can start to eliminate detail and wreak havoc if you're not careful with the Smudge tool.

PhotoSpin

Figure 9-16: The Smudge tool can make your images appear to be painted.

To use the Smudge tool, follow these steps:

1. **Choose the Smudge tool from the Tools panel in Edit Full mode.**

   Press Shift+R to cycle through the Smudge, Blur, and Sharpen tools.

2. **Select a brush from the Brushes Preset Picker drop-down panel.**

   Use a small brush for smudging tiny areas, such as edges. Larger brushes produce more extreme effects.

3. **Select a blending mode from the Mode pop-up menu.**

4. **Choose the strength of the smudging effect with the Strength slider or text box.**

   The lower the value, the lighter the effect.

5. **If your image has multiple layers, select Sample All Layers to make Elements use pixels from all the visible layers when it produces the effect.**

   The smudge still appears on only the active layer, but the look is a bit different, depending on the colors of the underlying layers.

6. **Use the Finger Painting option to begin the smudge by using the foreground color.**

Rather than use the color under your cursor, this option smears your foreground color at the start of each stroke. If you want the best of both worlds, you can quickly switch into Finger Painting mode by pressing the Alt key while you drag. Release Alt to go back to Normal mode.

7. **Paint over the areas you want to smudge.**

   Pay attention to your strokes because this tool can radically change your image. If you don't like the results, press Ctrl+Z (⌘+Z on the Mac) to undo the changes and then lower the Strength percentage (discussed in Step 4) even more.

Softening with the Blur tool

The Blur tool can be used for both repair and more artistic endeavors. You can use the Blur tool to soften a small flaw or part of a rough edge. You can add a little blur to an element to make it appear as though it was moving when photographed. You can also blur portions of your image to emphasize the focal point, as shown in Figure 9-17, where we blurred everything except the girl's face. The Blur tool works by decreasing the contrast among adjacent pixels in the blurred area.

PhotoSpin

Figure 9-17: The Blur tool can be used to emphasize a focal point.

The mechanics of using the Blur tool and its options are similar to those of the Smudge tool, as we describe in the preceding section. When you use the Blur tool, be sure to use a small brush for smaller areas of blur.

Focusing with the Sharpen tool

If the Blur tool is yin, the Sharpen tool is yang. The Sharpen tool increases the contrast among adjacent pixels to give the illusion that things are sharper. This tool needs to be used with restraint, however. Sharpen can quickly give way to overly grainy and noisy images if you're not cautious.

Use a light hand and keep the areas you sharpen small. Sometimes, the eyes in a soft portrait can benefit from a little sharpening, as shown in Figure 9-18. You can also slightly sharpen an area to emphasize it against a less-than-sharp background.

PhotoSpin

Figure 9-18: Reserve the Sharpen tool for small areas, such as eyes.

To use the Sharpen tool, grab the tool from the Tools panel and follow the steps provided for the Smudge tool in the section "Smudging away rough spots," earlier in this chapter. In addition, here are some tips for using the Sharpen tool:

- Use a low value, around 25 percent or less.

- Remember that you want to gradually sharpen your element to avoid the nasty, noisy grain that can occur from oversharpening.

- Because sharpening increases contrast, if you use other contrast adjustments, such as Levels, you boost the contrast of the sharpened area even more.

If you need to sharpen your overall image, try choosing either Enhance⇨Unsharp Mask or Enhance⇨Adjust Sharpness instead. These features offer more options and better control.

Sponging color on and off

The Sponge tool soaks up color or squeezes it out. In more technical terms, this tool reduces or increases the intensity, or *saturation,* of color in both color and grayscale images. Yes, the Sponge tool also works in Grayscale mode by darkening or lightening the brightness value of those pixels.

Like with the Blur and Sharpen tools, you can use the Sponge tool to reduce or increase the saturation in selected areas in order to draw attention to or away from those areas.

Follow these steps to sponge color on or off your image:

1. **Choose the Sponge tool from the Tools panel in Edit Full mode.**

    Press Shift+O to cycle through the Sponge, Dodge, and Burn tools.

2. **Select a brush from the Brushes Preset Picker drop-down panel.**

    Use large, soft brushes to saturate or desaturate a larger area.

3. **Choose either Desaturate or Saturate from the Mode pop-up menu to decrease or increase color intensity, respectively.**

4. **Choose a flow rate with the Flow slider or text box.**

    The *flow rate* is the speed with which the saturation or desaturation effect builds while you paint.

5. **Paint carefully over the areas you want to saturate or desaturate with color.**

    In the example shown in Figure 9-19, we saturated one of the women to make her more of a focal point and desaturated the others.

Replacing one color with another

The Color Replacement tool allows you to replace the original color of an image with the foreground color. You can use this tool in a multitude of ways:

- Colorize a grayscale image to create the look of a hand-painted photo.

- Completely change the color of an element, or elements, in your image, as shown in Figure 9-20.

- Eliminate red-eye (or yellow-eye in animals) if other, more automated methods don't work to your satisfaction.

PhotoSpin

Figure 9-19: The Sponge tool increases or decreases the intensity of the color in your image.

What we particularly like about the Color Replacement tool is that it preserves all the tones in the image. The color that's applied isn't like the opaque paint that's applied when you paint with the Brush tool. When you're replacing color, the midtones, shadows, and highlights are retained. The Color Replacement tool works by first sampling the original colors in the image and then replacing those colors with the foreground color. By specifying different sampling methods, limits, and tolerance settings, you can control the range of colors that Elements replaces.

PhotoSpin

Figure 9-20: The Color Replacement tool replaces the color in your image with the foreground color.

Follow these steps to replace existing color with your foreground color:

1. **Select the Color Replacement tool from the Tools panel in Edit Full mode.**

   This tool shares a flyout menu with the Brush and Pencil tools. Press Shift+B to cycle through the tools.

2. **Specify your desired brush tip diameter and hardness from the Brush Preset Picker drop-down panel.**

3. **Choose your desired blend mode.**

   Here's a brief rundown of each one:

   - *Color:* The default, this mode works well for most jobs. This mode works great for eliminating red-eye.

   - *Hue:* Similar to color, this mode is less intense and provides a subtler effect.

   - *Saturation:* This mode is the one to use to convert the color in your image to grayscale. Set your foreground color to Black on the Tools panel.

   - *Luminosity:* This mode, the opposite of Color, doesn't provide much of an effect.

4. **Select your Limits mode.**

   You have these options:

   - *Contiguous:* Replaces the color of adjacent pixels containing the sampled color.

   - *Discontiguous:* Replaces the color of the pixels containing the sampled color, whether or not they're adjacent.

5. **Set your Tolerance percentage.**

   Tolerance refers to a range of color. The higher the value, the broader the range of color that's sampled, and vice versa.

6. **Select the Anti-Alias option.**

   Anti-aliasing slightly softens the edges of the sampled areas.

7. **Click or drag your image.**

   The foreground color replaces the original colors of the sampled areas. In our example (refer to Figure 9-20), we used a black foreground color.

If you want to be very precise, make a selection before you replace your color. We did this with the girl in our figure so we could avoid "coloring outside the lines."

Correcting Contrast, Color, and Clarity

In This Chapter

▶ Correcting shadows, highlights, and contrast

▶ Removing colorcasts and adjusting hue and saturation

▶ Adjusting skin tones

▶ Working with color variations

▶ Removing noise and artifacts and repairing dust and scratches

▶ Sharpening and blurring your image

▶ Working with the Smart Brush tools

*I*f you've tried the quick and easy automatic fixes on your images and they didn't quite do the job, you've come to the right place. The great thing about Elements is that it offers multiple ways and multiple levels of repairing and enhancing your images. If an auto fix doesn't cut it, move on to a manual fix. If you're still not happy, you can consider shooting in Camera Raw format, as long as your camera can do so. Elements has wonderful Camera Raw support, enabling you to process your images to your exact specifications (as we explain in Chapter 4). Chances are good that if you can't find the tools to correct and repair your images in Elements, those images are probably beyond salvaging.

This chapter covers the manual fixes you can make to your photos to correct lighting, contrast, color casts, artifacts, dust, scratches, sharpening, and blurring. We also cover using the Smart Brush tools to selectively apply an image adjustment.

Editing Your Photos Using a Logical Workflow

With information in Chapter 9 (where we explain those quick fixes) and this chapter at your fingertips, try to employ some kind of logical workflow when you tackle the correction and repair of your images. By performing steps in a particular order, you will be less likely to exacerbate the flaws and able to accentuate what's good. For example, we use the following workflow when editing photos:

1. Crop, straighten, and resize your images, if necessary.

2. After you have the images in their proper physical state, correct the lighting and establish good tonal range for your shadows, highlights, and midtones in order to display the greatest detail possible.

   Often, just correcting the lighting solves minor color problems. If not, move on to adjusting the color balance.

3. Eliminate any colorcasts and adjust the saturation, if necessary.

4. Grab the retouching tools, such as the healing tools and filters, to retouch any flaws.

5. Sharpen your image if you feel that it could use a boost in clarity and sharpness.

6. Apply any enhancements or special effects, if so desired.

By following these steps and allocating a few minutes of your time, you can get all your images in shape to print, post, and share with family and friends.

Adjusting Lighting

Elements has several simple, manual tools you can use to fix lighting if the Auto tools that we describe in Chapter 9 didn't work or were just too, well, automatic for you. The manual tools offer more control over adjusting overall contrast, as well as bringing out details in shadow, midtones, and highlight areas of your images. Note that all lighting adjustments can be found in both Edit Full and Edit Quick modes.

Fixing lighting with Shadows/Highlights

The Shadows/Highlights command offers a quick and easy method of correcting over- and underexposed areas. This feature works especially well with images shot in bright, overhead light or in light coming from the back (backlit). These images usually suffer from having the subject partially or completely surrounded in shadows, such as the original image (left) in Figure 10-1.

Before

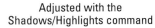
Adjusted with the
Shadows/Highlights command

Figure 10-1: Correct the lighting in your images with the Shadows/Highlights adjustment.

To use the Shadows/Highlights adjustment, follow these steps:

1. **In Edit Full or Edit Quick mode, choose Enhance⇨Adjust Lighting⇨ Shadows/Highlights and make sure the Preview check box is selected.**

   When the dialog box appears, the default correction is automatically applied in your preview.

2. **If the default adjustment doesn't quite do the job, move the sliders (or enter a value) to adjust the amount of correction for your shadows (dark areas), highlights (light areas), and midtones (middle-toned areas).**

   You want to try to reveal more detail in the dark and light areas of your image. If, after you do so, your image still looks like it needs more correction, add or delete contrast in your midtone areas.

3. **Click OK to apply the adjustment and close the dialog box.**

   If you want to start over, press Alt (Option on the Mac) and click the
   Reset button (previously the Cancel button).

Using Brightness/Contrast

Despite its aptly descriptive moniker, the Brightness/Contrast command
doesn't do a great job of brightening (making an image darker or lighter)
or adding or deleting contrast. Initially, users tend to be drawn to this command because of its appropriate name and ease of use. But after users realize its limitations, they move on to better tools with more control, such as
Shadows/Highlights and Levels.

The problem with the Brightness/Contrast command is that it applies the
adjustment equally to all areas of your image. For example, a photo's highlights may need darkening, but all the midtones and shadows are perfect. The
Brightness slider isn't smart enough to recognize that, so when you darken
the highlights in your image, the midtones and shadows also become darker.
To compensate for the unwanted darkening, you try to adjust the Contrast,
which doesn't fix the problem.

The moral is, if you want to use the Brightness/Contrast command, select
only the areas that need the correction, as shown in Figure 10-2. (For
more on selections, see Chapter 7.) After you make your selection, choose
Enhance⇨Adjust Lighting⇨Brightness/Contrast.

Figure 10-2: The Brightness/Contrast adjustment is best reserved for correcting selected
areas (left) rather than the entire image (right).

Pinpointing proper contrast with Levels

If you want real horsepower when it comes to correcting the brightness and
contrast (and even the color) in your image, look no further than the Levels
command. Granted, the dialog box is a tad more complex than what you find

with the other lighting and color adjustment commands, but when you understand how it works, it can be downright user-friendly.

You can get a taste of what Levels can do by using Auto Levels, detailed in Chapter 9. The Levels command, its manual cousin, offers much more control. And unlike the primitive Brightness/Contrast control, Levels enables you to darken or lighten 256 different tones. Keep in mind that Levels can be used on your entire image, a single layer, or a selected area. You can also apply the Levels command by using an adjustment layer, as we describe in Chapter 8.

If you're serious about image editing, the Levels command is one tool you want to know how to use. Here's how it works:

1. **In Edit Full or Edit Quick mode, choose Enhance⇨Adjust Lighting⇨ Levels.**

   We recommend using Edit Full mode for this command, where you'll have access to the Info panel in Step 2.

   The Levels dialog box appears, displaying a *histogram*. This graph displays how the pixels of the image are distributed at each of the 256 available brightness levels. Shadows are shown on the left side of the histogram, midtones are in the middle, and highlights are on the right. Note that, in addition to viewing the histogram of the composite RGB channel (the entire image), you can view the histogram of just the Red, Green, or Blue channel by selecting one of them from the Channel panel menu.

   Although you generally make changes to the entire document by using the RGB channel, you can apply changes to any one of an image's component color channels by selecting the specific channel from the Channel panel menu. You can also make adjustments to just selected areas, which can be helpful when one area of your image needs adjusting and others don't.

2. **In Edit Full mode, choose Window⇨Info to open the Info panel.**

3. **Set the black and white points manually by using the eyedroppers in the dialog box; first select the White Eyedropper tool and then move the cursor over the image.**

4. **Look at the Info panel, try to find the lightest white in the image, and then select that point by clicking it.**

   The lightest white has the highest RGB values.

5. **Repeat Steps 3 and 4, using the Black Eyedropper tool and trying to find the darkest black in the image.**

   The darkest black has the lowest RGB values.

When you set the pure black and pure white points, the remaining pixels are redistributed between those two points.

You can also reset the white and black points by moving the position of the white and black triangles on the input sliders (just below the histogram). Or you can enter values in the Input Levels boxes. The three boxes represent the black, gray, and white triangles, respectively. Use the numbers 0 to 255 in the white and black boxes.

6. **Use the Gray Eyedropper tool to remove any colorcasts by selecting a neutral gray portion of your image, one in which the Info panel shows equal values of red, green, and blue.**

If your image is grayscale, you can't use the Gray Eyedropper tool.

If you're not sure where there's a neutral gray, you can also remove a colorcast by choosing a color channel from the Channel pop-up menu and doing one of the following:

- Choose the Red channel and drag the midtone slider to the right to add cyan or to the left to add red.

- Choose the Green channel and drag the midtone slider to the right to add magenta or to the left to add green.

- Choose the Blue channel and drag the midtone slider to the right to add yellow or to the left to add blue.

7. **If your image requires it, adjust the output sliders at the bottom of the Levels dialog box.**

Moving the black triangle to the right reduces the contrast in the shadows and lightens the image. Moving the white triangle to the left reduces the contrast in the highlights and darkens the image.

8. **Adjust the midtones (or *gamma values*) with the gray triangle input slider.**

The default value for gamma is 1.0. Drag the triangle to the left to lighten midtones and drag to the right to darken them. You can also enter a value.

9. **Click OK to apply your settings and close the dialog box.**

Your image should be greatly improved, as shown in Figure 10-3.

When you click the Auto button, Elements applies the same adjustments as the Auto Levels command, as we explain in Chapter 9. Note the changes and subsequent pixel redistribution made to the histogram after you click this button.

Figure 10-3: Improve the contrast of an image with the intelligent Levels command.

Adjusting Color

Getting the color you want can seem about as attainable as winning the state lottery. Sometimes, an unexpected *colorcast* (a shift in color) can be avoided at the shooting stage, for example, by using (or not using, in some cases) a flash or lens filter or by setting the camera's white balance for lighting condiditons that aren't present. After the fact, you can usually do a pretty good job of correcting the color with one of the many Elements adjustments. Occasionally, you may want to change the color of your image to create a special effect. Conversely, you also may want to strip out an image's color altogether to create a vintage feel. Remember that all these color adjustments can be applied to your entire image, a single layer, or just a selection. Whatever your color needs are, they'll no doubt be met in Elements.

All color adjustments can be found in either Edit Full or Edit Quick mode, except for Defringe Layers, which is reserved for Edit Full mode only.

If you shoot your photos in the Camera Raw file format, you can open and fix your files in the Camera Raw dialog box. Remember that Camera Raw files haven't been processed by your camera. You're in total control of the color and the exposure. For more on Camera Raw, see Chapter 4.

Removing colorcasts automatically

If you ever took a photo in an office or classroom and got a funky green tinge in your image, it was probably the result of the overhead fluorescent lighting. To eliminate this green colorcast, you can apply the Remove Color Cast command. This feature is designed to adjust the image's overall color and remove the cast.

Follow these short steps to correct your image:

1. **Choose Enhance⇨Adjust Color⇨Remove Color Cast in either Edit Full or Edit Quick mode.**

   The Remove Color Cast dialog box appears. Move the dialog box to better view your image. Note that this command is also available in Guided mode.

2. **Click an area in your photo that should be white, black, or neutral gray, as shown in Figure 10-4.**

Figure 10-4: Get rid of nasty color shifts with the Remove Color Cast command.

In our example, we clicked the sky in the image on the left.

The colors in the image are adjusted according to the color you choose. Which color should you choose? The answer depends on the subject matter of your image. Feel free to experiment. Your adjustment is merely a preview at this point and isn't applied until you click OK. If you goof up, click the Reset button, and your image reverts to its unadjusted state.

3. **If you're satisfied with the adjustment, click OK to accept it and close the dialog box.**

 If the Remove Color Cast command doesn't cut it, try using the Color Variations commands or applying a photo filter (as we describe in the section "Adjusting color temperature with photo filters," later in this chapter). For example, if your photo has too much green, try applying a magenta filter.

Adjusting with Hue/Saturation

The Hue/Saturation command enables you to adjust the colors in your image based on their hue, saturation, and lightness. *Hue* is the color in your image. *Saturation* is the intensity, or richness, of that color. And *lightness* controls the brightness value.

Follow these steps to adjust color by using the Hue/Saturation command:

1. **In either Edit Full or Edit Quick mode, choose Enhance⇨Adjust Color⇨Adjust Hue/Saturation.**

   The Hue/Saturation dialog box appears. Be sure to select the Preview check box so that you can view your adjustments. Note that this command is also available in Guided mode.

2. **Select all the colors (Master) from the Edit drop-down menu or choose one color to adjust.**

3. **Drag the slider for one or more of the following attributes to adjust the colors as described:**

   - *Hue:* Shifts all the colors clockwise (drag right) or counterclockwise (drag left) around the color wheel.

   - *Saturation:* Increases (drag right) or decreases (drag left) the richness of the colors. Note that dragging all the way to the left gives the photo the appearance of a grayscale image.

   - *Lightness:* Increases the brightness values by adding white (drag right) or decreases the brightness values by adding black (drag left).

   The top color bar at the bottom of the dialog box represents the colors in their order on the color wheel before you make any changes. The lower color bar displays the colors after you make your adjustments.

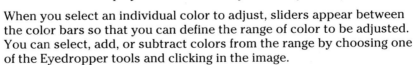 When you select an individual color to adjust, sliders appear between the color bars so that you can define the range of color to be adjusted. You can select, add, or subtract colors from the range by choosing one of the Eyedropper tools and clicking in the image.

The Hue/Saturation dialog box also lets you colorize images, a useful option for creating sepia-colored images.

4. **(Optional) Select the Colorize option to change the colors in your image to a new, single color. Drag the Hue slider to change the color to your desired hue.**

   The pure white and black pixels remain unchanged, and the intermediate gray pixels are colorized.

Use the Hue/Saturation command, with the Colorize option, to create tinted photos, such as the one shown in Figure 10-5. You can also make selections in a grayscale image and apply a different tint to each selection. This can be especially fun with portraits. Tinted images can create vintage or moody feels, and they can transform even mediocre photos into something special.

Eliminating color with Remove Color

Despite all the talk in this chapter about color, we realize that there may be times when you don't want *any* color. With the Remove Color command, you can easily eliminate all the color from an image, layer, or selection. To use this one-step command, simply choose Enhance⇨Adjust Color⇨Remove Color.

PhotoDisc/Getty Images

Figure 10-5: Adjust the color, intensity, or brightness of your image with the Hue/Saturation command.

Sometimes, stripping away color with this command can leave your image *flat,* or low in contrast. If this is the case, adjust the contrast by using one of Element's many lighting fixes, such as Auto Levels, Auto Contrast, or Levels.

The Enhance⇨Convert to Black and White command, shown in Figure 10-6, enables you to convert a selection, a layer, or an entire image to grayscale. But, rather than just arbitrarily strip color like the Remove Color command does, the Convert to Black and White command enables you to select a conversion method by first choosing an image style. To further tweak the results, you can add or subtract colors (Red, Green, or Blue) or contrast by moving the Intensity sliders until your grayscale image looks the way you want. Note that you aren't really adding color; you're simply altering the amount of data in the color channels. For more information on channels, see Chapter 2.

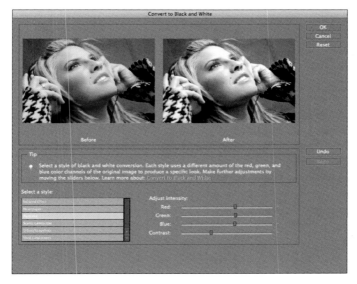

www.istockphoto.com

Figure 10-6: Wash away color with the Convert to Black and White command.

Switching colors with Replace Color

The Replace Color command enables you to replace designated colors in your image with other colors. You first select the colors you want to replace by creating a *mask,* which is a selection made by designating white (selected), black (unselected), and gray (partially selected) areas. See Chapter 8 for more details on masks. You can then adjust the hue and/or saturation of those selected colors.

Follow these steps to get on your way to replacing color:

1. **In Edit Full or Edit Quick mode, choose Enhance⇨Adjust Color⇨ Replace Color.**

   The Replace Color dialog box appears. Make sure to select the Preview check box.

2. **Choose either Selection or Image:**

   • *Selection:* Shows the mask in the Preview area. The deselected areas are black, partially selected areas are gray, and selected areas are white.

   • *Image:* Shows the actual image in the Preview area.

3. **Click the colors you want to select in either the image or the Preview area.**

4. **Shift-click or use the plus sign (+) Eyedropper tool to add more colors.**

5. **Press the Alt (Option on the Mac) key or use the minus sign (–) Eyedropper tool to delete colors.**

6. **To add colors similar to the ones you select, use the Fuzziness slider to fine-tune your selection, adding or deleting from the selection based on the Fuzziness value.**

   If you can't quite get the selection you want with the Fuzziness slider, try selecting the Localized Color Clusters option. This option enables you to select multiple clusters, or areas, of color and can assist in getting a cleaner, more precise selection, *especially when trying to select more than one color.*

7. **Move the Hue and/or Saturation sliders to change the color or color richness, respectively. Move the Lightness slider to lighten or darken the image.**

   Be careful to use a light hand (no pun intended) with the Lightness slider. You can reduce the tonal range too much and end up with a mess.

8. **View the result in the image window.**

9. **If you're satisfied, click OK to apply the settings and close the dialog box.**

   Figure 10-7 shows how we substituted the color of our tulips to change them from orange to yellow.

Corbis Digital Stock

Figure 10-7: The Replace Color command enables you to replace one color with another.

Correcting with Color Curves

Elements borrowed a much-used feature from Photoshop named Curves. However, it added the word *Color* and took away some of its sophistication. Nevertheless, the Color Curves adjustment attempts to improve the tonal range in color images by making adjustments to highlights, shadows, and midtones in each color channel. (For more on channels, see Chapter 2.) Try using this command on images in which the foreground elements appear overly dark due to backlighting. Conversely, the adjustment is also designed to correct images that appear overexposed and washed out.

Here's how to use this great adjustment on a selection, a layer, or an entire image:

1. **In Edit Full or Edit Quick mode, choose Enhance⇨Adjust Color⇨ Adjust Color Curves.**

   The Adjust Color Curves dialog box appears. Make sure to select the Preview check box. Move the dialog box to the side so that you can view the image window while making adjustments.

2. **Various curve adjustments appear in the Select a Style area. Select a style to make your desired adjustments while viewing your image in the After window.**

3. **If you need greater precision, use the highlight, brightness, contrast, and shadow adjustment sliders, as shown in Figure 10-8, and then adjust the sliders as desired.**

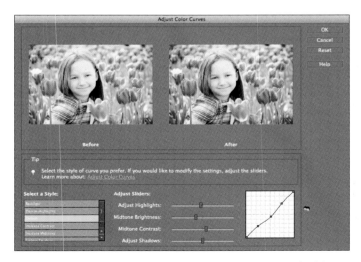

www.istockphoto.com

Figure 10-8: The Color Curves adjustment provides both basic and advanced adjustment controls.

The graph on the right represents the distribution of tones in your image. When you first access the Color Curves dialog box, the tonal range of your image is represented by a straight line. While you drag the sliders, the straight line is altered, and the tonal range is adjusted accordingly.

4. **Click OK when you've adjusted the image satisfactorily.**

5. **To start over, click the Reset button.**

Check out Figure 10-9 for another before-and-after image.

Original After the Color Curves adjustment

Figure 10-9: Color Curves improves tonal range in color images.

Adjusting skin tones

Occasionally, you may find that the loved ones in your photos have taken on a rather sickly shade of green, red, or some other non-flesh-colored tone. To rectify that problem, Elements has a command specifically designed to adjust the overall color in the image and get skin tones back to a natural shade.

Here's how to use this feature:

1. **Open your image in Edit Full or Edit Quick mode, select the Preview check box, and do one or both of the following:**

   • *Select the layer that needs to be adjusted.* If you don't have any layers, your entire image is adjusted.

   • *Select the areas of skin that need to be adjusted.* Only the selected areas are adjusted. This is a good way to go if you're happy with the color of your other elements and just want to tweak the skin tones. For more on selection techniques, see Chapter 7.

2. **Choose Enhance⇨Adjust Color⇨Adjust Color for Skin Tone.**

   The Adjust Color for Skin Tone dialog box appears. This command is also found in Guided mode.

3. **In the image window, click the portion of skin that needs to be corrected.**

   The command adjusts the color of the skin tone, as well as the color in the overall image, layer, or selection, depending on what you selected in Step 1.

4. **If you're not satisfied with the results, click another area or fiddle with the Skin and Ambient Light sliders:**

   - *Tan:* Adds or removes the amount of brown in the skin.

   - *Blush:* Adds or removes the amount of red in the skin.

   - *Temperature:* Adjusts the overall color of the skin, making it warmer (right toward red) or cooler (left toward blue).

5. **When you're happy with the correction, click OK to apply the adjustment and close the dialog box.**

   The newly toned skin appears, as shown in Figure 10-10.

   To start anew, click the Reset button. And, of course, to bail out completely, click Cancel.

PhotoSpin

Figure 10-10: Give your friends and family a complexion makeover with the Adjust Color for Skin Tone command.

Defringing layers

A telltale sign of haphazardly composited images is selections with fringe. We don't mean the cute kind hanging from your leather jacket or upholstery; we mean the unattractive kind that consists of background pixels that surround the edges of your selections, as shown in Figure 10-11.

Inevitably, when you move or paste a selection, some background pixels are bound to go along for the ride. These pixels are referred to as a *fringe* or *halo*. Luckily, the Defringe command replaces the color of the fringe pixels with the colors of neighboring pixels that don't contain the background color. In our example, we plucked the toy boat out of a white studio background and placed it on an image of water. Some of the background pixels were included in our selection and appear as a white fringe. When we apply the Defringe command, those white fringe pixels are changed to colors of nearby pixels, such as blue or red, as shown in Figure 10-11.

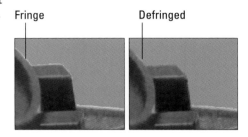

Fringe   Defringed

PhotoSpin

Figure 10-11: Remove the colored halo around your selections with the Defringe command.

Follow these steps to defringe your selection:

1. **In Edit Full or Edit Quick mode, copy and paste a selection onto a new or existing layer, or drag and drop a selection onto a new document.**

   For more on selections, see Chapter 7.

2. **Choose Enhance⇨Adjust Color⇨Defringe Layer.**

   The Defringe dialog box appears.

3. **Enter a value for the number of pixels that needs to be converted.**

   Try entering 1 or 2 first to see whether that does the trick. If not, you may need to enter a slightly higher value.

4. **Click OK to accept the value and close the dialog box.**

Correcting with Color Variations

Although we give you several ways in this chapter to eliminate colorcasts in an image, here's one more. The Color Variations command is a digital color-correction feature that's been around for years and is largely unchanged. That's probably because it's one of those great features that's easy to use and easy to understand, and it works. The command enables you to make corrections by visually comparing thumbnails of color variations of your image. You may use this command when you're not quite sure what's wrong with the color or what kind of colorcast your image has.

Here's how to use the Color Variations command:

1. **Choose Enhance⇨ Adjust Color⇨Color Variations in Edit Full or Edit Quick mode.**

   The Color Variations dialog box appears, displaying a preview of your original image (before) and the corrected image (after), as shown in Figure 10-12.

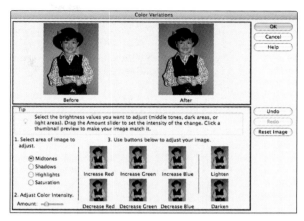

PhotoSpin

Figure 10-12: Color Variations enables you to visually correct your images by comparing thumbnails.

2. **Select a tonal range or color richness (if you're unsure which range to select, start with the Midtones):**

   - *Shadows, Midtones, Highlights:* Adjusts the dark, middle, or light areas in the image, respectively.

   - *Saturation:* Adjusts the color intensity or richness, making colors more intense *(saturated)* or less intense *(desaturated).* If your image is faded from time, be sure to increase the saturation after you correct any colorcast issues.

   Usually, just correcting the midtones is enough to get your image's color in order, but if it's not, you can always adjust the shadows and highlights, as well.

3. **Specify how much adjustment you want with the Adjust Color Intensity slider.**

   Drag left to decrease the amount of adjustment and drag right to increase the amount.

4. **If you selected Midtones, Shadows, or Highlights in Step 2, adjust the color by clicking the various Increase or Decrease Color buttons.**

   Click more than once if your initial application wasn't sufficient to correct the problem.

   Be sure to keep an eye on the After thumbnail, which reflects your corrections while you make them.

5. **Click the Darken or Lighten buttons to make the colors a little darker or lighter, respectively.**

6. **If you selected Saturation in Step 2, click the Less Saturation or More Saturation buttons.**

7. **If you make a mistake — or several mistakes, for that matter — click the Undo button.**

   The Color Variations dialog box supports multiple levels of undo. If you botch something, you can always click the Reset Image button to start again. Keep in mind that you can't undo the Reset Image command after you click it. Click Cancel to bail entirely.

8. **To apply your color adjustments and close the dialog box, click OK.**

The Color Variations command is a great tool to correct those old, faded, green- (or some other unwanted color) tinted circa yesteryear photos. The Color Variations command allows you to easily correct the color and saturation of these precious, but damaged, images. Remember to either decrease the offending color or add the color that's the opposite of the cast in the image. If it's too red, add cyan and vice versa.

Adjusting color temperature with photo filters

Light has its own color temperature. A photo shot in a higher color temperature of light makes an image blue. Conversely, an image shot in a lower color temperature makes a photo yellow. In the old days, photographers used to place colored glass filters in front of their camera lenses to adjust the color temperature of the light. They did this to either warm up or cool down photos, or to just add a hint of color for subtle special effects. Elements gives you the digital version of these filters with the Photo Filter command.

To apply the Photo Filter adjustment, follow these steps:

1. **In Edit Full or Edit Quick mode, choose Filter⇨Adjustments⇨Photo Filter.**

   The Photo Filter dialog box appears.

   Note that you can also apply the photo filter to an individual layer by creating a photo-filter adjustment layer. For details, see Chapter 8.

2. **In the dialog box, select Filter to choose a preset filter from the drop-down menu, or select Color to select your own filter color from the Color Picker.**

Here's a brief description of each of the preset filters:

- *Warming Filter (85), (81), and (LBA):* Adjust the white balance in an image to make the colors warmer, or more yellow. Filter (81) is like (85) and (LBA), but it's best used for minor adjustments.

- *Cooling Filter (80), (82), and (LBB):* Also adjust the white balance that's shown, but instead of making the colors warmer, they make the colors cooler, or bluer. Filter (82) is like (80) and (LBB), but it's designed for slight adjustments.

- *Red, Orange, Yellow, and so on:* The various color filters adjust the hue, or color, of a photo. Choose a color filter to try to eliminate a colorcast or to apply a special effect.

3. **Adjust the Density option to specify the amount of color applied to your image.**

4. **Select the Preserve Luminosity option to prevent the photo filter from darkening your image.**

5. **Click OK to apply your filter and close the dialog box.**

One one way to minimize the need for color adjustments is to be sure you set your camera's white balance for your existing lighting conditions before shooting your photo.

Mapping your colors

Elements provides color mapper commands that change the colors in your image by mapping them to other values. You find the color mappers on the Filter⇨Adjustments submenu. Figure 10-13 shows an example of each command, all of which are also briefly described in the following list:

- **Equalize:** This mapper first locates the lightest and darkest pixels in the image and assigns them values of white and black. It then redistributes all the remaining pixels among the grayscale values. The exact effect depends on your individual image.

- **Gradient Map:** This command maps the tonal range of an image to the colors of your chosen gradient. For example, colors (such as orange, green, and purple) are mapped to the shadow, highlight, and midtone areas.

- **Invert:** This command reverses all the colors in your image, creating a kind of negative. Black reverses to white, and colors convert to their complementary hues. (Blue goes to yellow, red goes to cyan, and so on.)

Equalize

Gradient Map

Invert

Threshold

Posterize

Figure 10-13: Change the colors in your image by remapping them to other values.

- **Posterize:** This command reduces the number of colors in your image. Choose a value between 2 and 255 colors. Lower values create an illustrative, poster look, and higher values produce a more photo-realistic image.

- **Threshold:** Threshold makes your image black and white, with all pixels that are brighter than a value you specify represented as white, and all pixels that are darker than that value as black. You can change the threshold level to achieve different high-contrast effects.

Adjusting Clarity

After your image has the right contrast and color, and you fix any flaws (as we describe in Chapter 9), you're ready to work on the overall clarity of that image. Although you may have fixed the nitpicky little blemishes with the healing tools, if your image suffers from an overall problem, like dust, scratches, or *artifacts* (blocky pixels or halos), you may need to employ the help of a filter. After you totally clean up your image, your last chore is to give it a good sharpening. Why wait until the bitter end to do so? Sometimes, while you're improving the contrast and color and getting rid of flaws, you can reduce the clarity and sharpness of an image. So, you want to be sure that your image is as soft as it's going to get before you tackle your sharpening tasks. On the other hand, also be aware that sharpening increases contrast, so depending on how much of your image you're sharpening, you may need to go back and fine-tune it by using the lighting adjustments described in the section "Adjusting Lighting," earlier in this chapter.

Finally, with all this talk about sharpening, we know that you may find it strange when we say that you may also need to occasionally blur your image. You can use blurring to eliminate unpleasant patterns that occur during scanning, soften distracting backgrounds to give a better focal point, or even to create the illusion of motion.

Removing noise, artifacts, dust, and scratches

Surprisingly, the tools you want to use to eliminate junk from your images are found on the Filter⇨Noise submenu in Edit Full or Edit Quick mode. With the exception of the Add Noise filter, the others help to hide noise, dust, scratches, and artifacts. Here's the list of junk removers:

- **Despeckle:** Decreases the contrast, without affecting the edges, to make the dust in your image less pronounced. You may notice a slight blurring of your image (that's what's hiding the junk), but hopefully the edges are still sharp.

- **Dust & Scratches:** Like its name says, hides dust and scratches by blurring those areas of your image that contain the nastiness. (It looks for harsh transitions in tone.) Specify your desired Radius value, which is the size of the area to be blurred. Also, specify the Threshold value, which determines how much contrast between pixels must be present before they're blurred.

  Use this filter with restraint because it can obliterate detail and make your image go from bad to worse.

- **Median:** Reduces contrast around dust spots. The process the filter goes through is rather technical, so suffice it to say that the light spots darken, the dark spots lighten, and the rest of the image isn't changed. Specify your desired radius, which is the size of the area to be adjusted.

- **Reduce Noise:** Designed to remove luminance noise and artifacts from your images. We used this filter to correct the original image (on the left) in Figure 10-14. *Luminance noise* is grayscale noise that makes images look overly grainy. Specify these options to reduce the noise in your image:

- *Strength:* Specify the amount of noise reduction.

- *Preserve Details:* A higher percentage preserves edges and details but reduces the amount of noise that's removed.

- *Reduce Color Noise:* Remove random colored pixels.

- *Remove JPEG Artifact:* Remove the blocks and halos that can occur from low-quality JPEG compression.

Figure 10-14: Use the Reduce Noise filter to remove noise and artifacts.

Blurring when you need to

It may sound odd that anyone would intentionally want to blur an image. But, if your photo is overly grainy or suffers from a nasty moiré (wavy) pattern (described in the following list), you may need to blur the image to correct the problem. And often, you may even want to blur the background of an image to deemphasize distractions, or to make the foreground elements appear sharper and provide a better focal point.

All the blurring tools are found on the Filter⇨Blur menu in Edit Full or Edit Quick mode, with the exception of the Blur tool, which is explained in Chapter 9:

- **Average:** This one-step filter calculates the average value of the image or selection and fills the area with that average value. You can use it for smoothing overly noisy areas in your image.

- **Blur:** Another one-step filter, this one applies a fixed amount of blurring to the whole image.

- **Blur More:** This one-step blur filter gives the same effect as Blur, but more intensely.

- **Gaussian Blur:** This blur filter is probably the one you'll use most often. It offers a Radius setting to let you adjust the amount of blurring you desire.

Use the Gaussian Blur filter to camouflage moiré patterns on scanned images. A *moiré pattern* is caused when you scan halftone images. A *halftone* is created when a continuous tone image, such as a photo, is digitized and converted into a screen pattern of repeating lines (usually between 85 and 150 lines per inch) and then printed. When you then scan that halftone, a second pattern results and is overlaid on the original pattern. These two different patterns bump heads and create a nasty moiré pattern. The Gaussian Blur filter doesn't eliminate the moiré — it simply merges the dots and reduces the appearance of the pattern. Play with the Radius slider until you get an acceptable trade-off between less moiré and less focus. If you happen to have a descreen filter built into your scanning software, you can use that, as well, during the scanning of the halftone image.

- **Motion Blur:** This filter mimics the blur given off by moving objects. Specify the angle of motion and the distance of the blur. Make sure to select the Preview check box to see the effect while you enter your values.

- **Radial Blur:** Need to simulate a moving Ferris wheel or some other round object? This filter produces a circular blur effect. Specify the amount of blur you want. Choose the Spin method to blur along concentric circular lines, as shown in the thumbnail. Or, choose Zoom to blur along radial lines and mimic the effect of zooming in to your image. Specify your desired Quality level. Because the Radial Blur filter is notoriously slow, Elements gives you the option of Draft (fast but grainy), Good, or Best (slow but smooth). The difference between Good and Best is evident only on large, high-resolution images. Finally, indicate where you want the center of your blur by moving the blur diagram thumbnail.

- **Smart Blur:** This filter provides several options to enable you to specify how the blur is applied. Specify a value for the radius and threshold, both defined in the following section. Start with a lower value for both and adjust from there. Choose a quality setting from the pop-up menu. Choose a mode setting. Normal blurs the entire image or selection. Edge Only blurs only the edges of your elements and uses black and white in the blurred pixels. Overlay Edge also blurs just the edges, but it applies only white to the blurred pixels.

- **Surface Blur:** This filter blurs the surface or interior of the image, instead of the edges. If you want to retain your edge details, but blur everything else, use this filter.

Sharpening for better focus

Of course, if your images don't need any contrast, color, and flaw fixing, feel free to jump right into sharpening. Sometimes, images captured by a scanner or a digital camera are a little soft, and it's not due to any tonal adjustments. Occasionally, you may even want to sharpen a selected area in your image just so that it stands out more.

First, let us say that you can't really improve the focus of an image after it's captured. But you can do a pretty good job of faking it. All sharpening tools work by increasing the contrast between adjacent pixels. This increased contrast causes the edges to appear more distinct, thereby giving the illusion that the focus is improved, as shown in Figure 10-15. Remember that you can also use the Sharpen tool for small areas, as described in Chapter 9. Here's a description of the two sharpening commands:

Figure 10-15: Sharpening mimics an increase in focus by increasing contrast between adjacent pixels.

✓ **Unsharp Mask:** Unsharp Mask, on the Enhance menu in Edit Full or Edit Quick mode, which gets its odd name from a darkroom technique, is the sharpening tool of choice. It gives you several options that enable you to control the amount of sharpening and the width of the areas to be sharpened. Use them to pinpoint your desired sharpening:

   • *Amount:* Specify an amount (from 1 to 500 percent) of edge sharpening. The higher the value, the more contrast between pixels around the edges. Start with a value of 100 percent (or less), which usually gives good contrast without appearing overly grainy.

   • *Radius:* Specify the width (from 0.1 to 250 pixels) of the edges that the filter will sharpen. The higher the value, the wider the edge. The value you use is largely based on the resolution of your image. Low-resolution images require a smaller radius value. High-resolution images require a higher value.

Be warned that specifying a value that's too high overemphasizes the edges of your image and makes it appear too "contrasty" or even "goopy" around the edges.

A good guideline in selecting a starting radius value is to divide your image's resolution by 150. For example, if you have a 300 ppi image, set the radius at 2 and then use your eye to adjust from there.

- *Threshold:* Specify the difference in brightness (from 0 to 255) that must be present between adjacent pixels before the edge is sharpened. A lower value sharpens edges with very little contrast difference. Higher values sharpen only when adjacent pixels are very different in contrast. We recommend leaving Threshold set at 0 unless your image is very grainy. Increasing the value too high can cause unnatural transitions between sharpened and unsharpened areas.

Occasionally, the values you enter for Amount and Radius may sharpen the image effectively but in turn create excess *grain,* or noise, in your image. You can sometimes reduce this noise by increasing the Threshold value.

✔ **Adjust Sharpness:** When you're looking for precision in your image sharpening, Unsharp Mask is one option. The Adjust Sharpness command, as shown in Figure 10-16, is the other. This feature enables you to control the amount of sharpening applied to shadow and highlight areas. It also allows you to select from various sharpening algorithms.

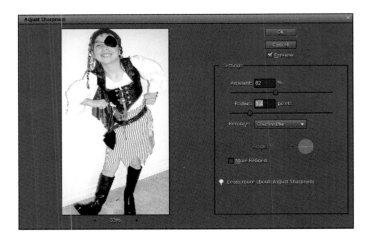

Figure 10-16: The Adjust Sharpness command.

Here are the various options you can specify:

- *Amount and Radius:* See the two descriptions in the preceding Unsharp Mask bullet list.

- *Remove:* Choose your sharpening algorithm. Gaussian Blur is the algorithm used for the Unsharp Mask command. Lens Blur detects detail in the image and attempts to respect the details while reducing the nasty halos that can occur with sharpening. Motion Blur tries to sharpen the blurring that occurs when you move the camera (or if your subject doesn't sit still).

- *Angle:* Specify the direction of motion for the Motion Blur algorithm, described in the preceding bullet.

- *More Refined:* Runs the algorithm more slowly than the default speed for better accuracy.

Working Intelligently with the Smart Brush Tools

The Smart Brush and Detail Smart Brush tools enable you to selectively apply an image adjustment or special effects that appear on all or part of your image. What's even more exciting is that these adjustments and effects are applied via an adjustment layer, meaning that they hover over your layers and don't permanently alter the pixels in your image. It also means that the adjustments can be flexibly edited and deleted, if so desired.

Follow these steps to use the Smart Brush tool:

1. **Select the Smart Brush tool from the toolbar in Edit Full mode.**

   The tool icon looks like a house paint brush with an adjacent gear. You can also press F, or Shift+F, if the Detail Smart Brush tool is visible.

2. **Choose your desired brush attributes, such as diameter and hardness, from the Brush Picker drop-down panel.**

   For more on working with brushes, see Chapter 12.

3. **Select an adjustment category and then your particular preset adjustment from the Smart Paint drop-down menu on the Options bar, as shown in Figure 10-17.**

   Note that you can tear off this panel from its place by grabbing the grip area in the upper-left corner of the panel and dragging it anywhere in your application window (Windows) or on your screen (Mac). In the Smart Paint menu, you can find adjustments ranging from photographic effects, such as a vintage Yellowed Photo, to nature effects, such as Sunset (which gives a warm, orange glow to your image).

4. **Paint an adjustment on the desired layer in your image.**

   Note that while you paint, the Smart Brush tool attempts to detect edges in your image and snaps to those edges. In addition, while you brush, a selection border appears.

   A new adjustment layer is automatically created with your first paint stroke. The accompanying layer mask also appears on that adjustment layer. For more on adjustment layers, see Chapter 8.

Figure 10-17: The Smart Brush enables you to paint on adjustments.

5. **Using the Add and Subtract Smart Brush modes, fine-tune your adjusted area by adding and subtracting from it.**

   When you add and subtract from your adjusted area, you're essentially modifying your layer mask. Adding to your adjusted area adds white to your layer mask, and subtracting from your adjusted area adds black to your layer mask. For more on layer masks, see Chapter 8.

6. **Select a different preset adjustment for your selected area, if you want.**

   In fact, try them all out before you settle on your final choice.

7. **If you feel you need to refine your selected area, select the Refine Edge option on the Options bar.**

   For more on Refine Edge, see Chapter 7.

   If you'd rather apply the adjustment to your unselected area, select the Inverse option on the Options bar.

Using touch screen monitors

Elements now supports touch screen capability on both Windows and Mac platforms. Not only can you browse through images in the Organizer by flicking with your fingers, you can even retouch and enhance your images using all of the tools in your Tools panel with your fingers! The following figure shows how you can use an ELO touch monitor to edit a photo. Talk about digital finger painting!

If you want to modify your adjustment, double-click the Adjustment Layer pin on your image. The pin is annotated by a small, square, black and red gear icon. After you double-click the pin, the dialog box corresponding to your particular adjustment appears. For example, if you double-click the Shoebox photo adjustment (under Photographic), you access the Hue/Saturation dialog box.

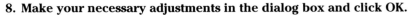

8. **Make your necessary adjustments in the dialog box and click OK.**

   You can also right-click (Right-click or Control-click on the Mac if you're using a one-button mouse) and select Change Adjustment Settings from the contextual menu that appears. Or you can select Delete Adjustment and Hide Selection from the same menu.

9. **After you finish, simply deselect your selection by choosing Select⇨ Deselect.**

You can add multiple Smart Brush adjustments. After you apply one effect, reset the Smart Brush tool and apply additional adjustments.

Follow these steps to work with the Detail Smart Brush tool:

1. **Select the Detail Smart Brush tool in the toolbar in Edit Full mode.**

   This tool shares the flyout menu with the Smart Brush tool. The tool icon looks like an art paint brush with an adjacent gear. You can also press F, or Shift+F, if the Smart Brush tool is visible.

2. **Choose a brush tip preset and brush size, and attributes from the Brushes drop-down panel.**

   Feel free to change your brush tip and size as needed for your desired effect. For more on working with brushes, see Chapter 12. For better accessibility, you can tear off this panel (and the Smart Paint panel in Step 3) by grabbing the grip area in the upper-left corner of the panel and dragging it anywhere in your application window.

3. **Select your desired adjustment category and then your particular preset adjustment from the Smart Paint drop-down menu in the Options bar.**

   Several of the Special Effect adjustments are shown in Figure 10-18.

4. **Paint an adjustment on the desired layer in your image.**

   A new adjustment layer is automatically created with your first paint stroke, along with an accompanying layer mask. For details on adjustment layers and layer masks, see Chapter 8.

5. **Follow Steps 5 through 8 in the preceding list for the Smart Brush tool.**

Figure 10-18: The Detail Smart Brush lets you paint on a variety of special effects.

Part IV
Exploring Your Inner Artist

The 5th Wave   By Rich Tennant

©RICHTENNANT

Jeez. — that's impressive! Let's see that airbrush effect again.

In this part . . .

Delve into the world of the Photoshop Elements artist, where you can use tools to draw and paint on existing photos, or create new, blank documents and create your own drawings. The tools rival an artist's analog tools, and Photoshop Elements capabilities are limited only by your imagination. In this part, you can find out how to apply different artistic effects by using many tools and customizing them for your own use, and you find tips for creating some dazzling images.

In addition to describing the artistic effects you can apply to your photos, this part tells you how to handle working with text. When it comes time for creating a poster, an advertisement, or some Web icons, the text features in Elements offer you many options for creating headline type, body copy, and special type effects.

11

Playing with Filters, Effects, Styles, and More

In This Chapter

- ▶ Fooling with filters
- ▶ Getting familiar with the Filter Gallery
- ▶ Making digital taffy with Liquify
- ▶ Fixing camera distortion
- ▶ Enhancing with effects
- ▶ Using layer styles
- ▶ Changing colors with blend modes
- ▶ Compositing images with Photomerge

After giving your images a makeover — edges cropped, color corrected, flaws repaired, focus sharpened — you may want to get them all gussied up for a night out on the town. You can do just that with filters, effects, layer styles, and blend modes. These features enable you to add that touch of emphasis, drama, whimsy, or just plain goofy fun. We're the first to admit that often the simplest art (and that includes photographs) is the best. That gorgeous landscape or the portrait that perfectly captures the expression on a child's happy face is something you may want to leave unembellished. But for the times when a little artistic experimentation is in order, turn to this chapter as your guide.

Having Fun with Filters

Filters have been around since the early days of digital imaging, when Photoshop was just a little bitty program. *Filters,* also called *plug-ins* because they can be installed or removed independently, change the look of your image in a variety of ways, as shown in Figure 11-1. They can correct less-than-perfect images by making them appear sharper or by covering up flaws, as we describe in Chapter 10. Or they can enhance your images by making them appear as though they're painted, tiled, photocopied, or lit by spotlights. Just make sure to create a backup of your original image if you plan on saving your filtered one. The following sections give you the basics on how to apply a filter and they give you a few filtering tips.

Original   Unsharp Mask filter   Water Paper filter

Figure 11-1: Use filters to correct image imperfections or to completely transform images.

Applying filters

You can apply a filter in three ways:

- **In either Edit Full or Edit Quick mode:** From the Filter menu, choose your desired filter category and then select a specific filter.

- **In Edit Full mode only:** Choose Window⇨Effects to open the panel. Click the Filters button at the top of the panel. Select your filter category from the drop-down menu to the right of the buttons. Double-click the thumbnail of your desired filter or drag the filter onto your image window.

✔ **In either Edit Full or Edit Quick mode:** Choose Filter⇨Filter Gallery to apply one or more filters in a flexible editing environment. The Filter Gallery is described in the section "Working in the Filter Gallery," later in this chapter.

Even when you're using the Filter Gallery, make a backup copy of your image (or at least create a duplicate layer) before you apply filters. Filters change the pixels of an image permanently, and when you exit the Filter Gallery, the filters you apply can't be removed.

You can't apply filters to images that are in Bitmap or Index Color mode. And some filters don't work on images in Grayscale mode. For a refresher on color modes, see Chapter 3.

Corrective or destructive filters

Although there are no hard and fast rules, most digital-imaging folks classify filters into two basic categories, *corrective* and *destructive:*

✔ **Corrective filters** usually fix some kind of image problem. They adjust color, improve focus, remove dust or artifacts, and so on. Don't get us wrong — pixels are still modified. It's just that the basic appearance of the image remains the same, albeit hopefully improved. Two of the most popular corrective filters, Sharpen and Blur, are covered in Chapter 10.

✔ **Destructive filters** are used to create some kind of special effect. Pixels are also modified, but the image may look quite a bit different from its original. These kinds of filters create effects, such as textures, brush strokes, mosaics, lights, and clouds. They can also distort an image with waves, spheres, and ripples.

One-step or multistep filters

All corrective and destructive filters are one or the other:

✔ **One-step filters** have no options and no dialog boxes; select the filter and watch the magic happen.

✔ **Multistep filters** act almost like mini-applications.

Choose the filter to open a dialog box that has options for you to specify. The options vary widely depending on the filter, but most come equipped with at least one option to control the intensity of the filter. A multistep filter appears on the menu with an ellipsis following its name, indicating that a dialog box opens when you choose the command.

Fading a filter

Sometimes, you don't want the full effect of a filter applied to your image. Sometimes, fading a filter a bit softens the effect and makes it look less "computerish." Here's what you can do:

1. **Choose Layer⇨Duplicate Layer.**

   The Duplicate Layer dialog box appears.

2. **Click OK.**

3. **Apply your desired filter to the duplicate layer.**

4. **Use the blend modes and opacity settings located on the Layers panel to merge the filtered layer with the original unfiltered image.**

5. **(Optional) With the Eraser tool, selectively erase portions of your filtered image to enable the unfiltered image to show through.**

   For example, if you applied a Gaussian Blur filter to soften a harshly lit portrait, try erasing the blurred portion that covers the subject's eyes to let the unblurred eyes of the layer below show through. The sharply focused eyes provide a natural focal point.

Instead of erasing, you can also apply a layer mask to selectively show and hide portions of your filtered image. For details on layer masks, see Chapter 8.

Selectively applying a filter

Up to this point in the book, we refer to applying filters to your *images*. But we use this word rather loosely. You don't necessarily have to apply filters to your entire image. You can apply filters to individual layers or even to selections. You can often get better effects when you apply a filter just to a portion of an image or layer. For example, you can blur a distracting background so that the person in your image gets due attention. Or, as shown in Figure 11-2, you can apply an Ocean Ripple or Wave filter to the ocean, leaving your surfer unfiltered to avoid that overly Photoshopped effect.

Exercising a little restraint in applying filters usually produces a more attractive image.

Corbis Digital Stock

Figure 11-2: Selectively applying a filter can prevent an image from looking overly manipulated.

Working in the Filter Gallery

When you apply a filter, don't be surprised if you're presented with a gargantuan dialog box. This *editing window,* as it's officially called, is the Filter Gallery. You can also access it by choosing Filter⇨Filter Gallery. In the flexible Filter Gallery, you can apply multiple filters, tweak their order, as well as edit them *ad nauseum.*

Follow these steps to work in the Filter Gallery:

1. **Choose Filter⇨Filter Gallery in either Edit Full or Edit Quick mode.**

   The Filter Gallery editing window appears, as shown in Figure 11-3.

Show/hide applied filter

Filter category folder   New effect layer

Delete effect layer

istockphoto.com

Figure 11-3: Apply and edit multiple filters in the Filter Gallery.

 2. **In the center of the editing window, click your desired filter category folder.**

 The folder expands and shows the filters in that category. A thumbnail displays each filter's effect.

 3. **Select your desired filter.**

 You get a large, dynamic preview of your image on the left side of the dialog box. To preview a different filter, just select it. Use the magnification controls to zoom in and out of the preview. To hide the Filter menu and get a larger preview box, click the arrow to the left of the OK button.

 4. **Specify any settings associated with the filter.**

 The preview is updated accordingly.

5. **When you're happy with the results, click OK to apply the filter and close the editing window.**

6. **If you want to apply another filter, click the New Effect Layer button at the bottom of the editing window.**

   This step duplicates the existing filter.

7. **Choose your desired new filter, which then replaces the duplicate in the Applied Filters area of the dialog box.**

   Each filter you apply is displayed in the lower-right area of the Filter Gallery dialog box. To delete a filter, select it and click the Delete Effect Layer button. To edit a filter's settings, select it from the list and make any changes. Keep in mind that when you edit a filter's settings, the edit may affect the look of any subsequent filters you've applied. Finally, you can rearrange the order of the applied filters. Doing so changes the overall effect, however.

8. **When you're completely done, click OK to apply the filters and close the editing window.**

Distorting with the Liquify Filter

The Liquify filter is really much more than a filter. It's a distortion that allows you to manipulate an image as though it were warm taffy. You can interactively twist, pull, twirl, pinch, and bloat parts of your image. You can even put your image on a diet, as we did in Figure 11-4. In fact, most ads and magazine covers feature models and celebrities whose photos have "visited" the Liquify filter once or twice. You can apply this distortion filter on the entire image, on a layer, or on a selection. This _überfilter_ comes equipped with a mega dialog box that has its own set of tools (on the left) and options (on the right), as shown in Figure 11-4.

Follow these steps to turn your image into a melted Dalí-esque wannabe:

1. **Choose Filter⇨Distort⇨Liquify in either Edit Full or Edit Quick mode.**

   Your image appears in the preview area.

2. **Choose your distortion weapon of choice.**

   You also have a number of tools to help zoom and navigate around your image window.

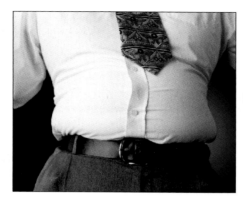

Pre Nip/Tuck

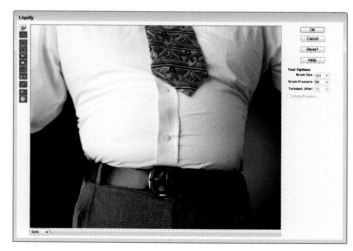

Post Nip/Tuck

PhotoSpin

Figure 11-4: The Liquify filter enables you to interactively distort your image.

Here's a description of each tool to help you decide which to use. (The letter in parentheses is the keyboard shortcut.)

- *Warp (W):* This tool pushes pixels forward while you drag, creating a stretched effect. Use short strokes or long pushes.

- *Turbulence (T):* Drag to randomly jumble your pixels. Use this tool to re-create maelstroms of air, fire, and water with clouds, flames, and waves. Adjust how smooth the effect is by dragging the Turbulent Jitter slider in the Tool Options area. The higher the value, the smoother the effect.

- *Twirl Clockwise (R) and Twirl Counterclockwise (L):* These options rotate pixels either clockwise or counterclockwise. Place the cursor in one spot, hold down the mouse button, and watch the pixels under your brush rotate; or drag the cursor to create a moving twirl effect.

- *Pucker (P):* Click and hold or drag to pinch your pixels toward the center of the area covered by the brush. To reverse the pucker direction *(bloat),* press the Alt (Option on the Mac) key while you hold or drag.

- *Bloat (B):* Click and hold or drag to push pixels toward the edge of the brush area. To reverse the bloat direction *(pucker),* press the Alt (Option on the Mac) key while you hold or drag.

- *Shift Pixels (S):* This tool moves pixels to the left when you drag the tool straight up. Drag down to move pixels to the right. Drag clockwise to increase the size of the object being distorted. Drag counterclockwise to decrease the size. To reverse any direction, press the Alt (Option on the Mac) key while you hold or drag.

- *Reflection (M):* This tool drags a reversed image of your pixels at a 90-degree angle to the motion of the brush. Hold down the Alt (Option on the Mac) key to force the reflection in the direction opposite the motion of the brush. This tool works well for making reflections on water.

- *Resconstruct (E):* See Step 4 for an explanation of this tool's function.

- *Zoom (Z):* This tool, which works like the Zoom tool on the Elements Tools panel, zooms you in and out so that you can better see your distortions.

  You can zoom out by holding down the Alt (Option on the Mac) key when you press Z. You can also zoom by selecting a magnification percentage from the pop-up list in the lower-left corner of the dialog box.

- *Hand (H):* This tool works like the Hand tool on the Elements Tools panel. Drag with the Hand tool to move the image around the preview window.

3. **Specify your options in the Tool Options area:**

- *Brush Size:* Drag the pop-up slider or enter a value from 1 to 600 pixels to specify the width of your brush.

- *Brush Pressure:* Drag the pop-up slider or enter a value from 1 to 100 to change the pressure. The higher the pressure, the faster the distortion effect is applied.

- *Turbulent Jitter:* Drag the pop-up slider or enter a value from 1 to 100 to adjust the smoothness when you're using the Turbulence tool.

- *Stylus Pressure:* If you're lucky enough to have a graphics tablet and stylus, click this option to select the pressure of your stylus.

4. **(Optional) If you get a little carried away, select the Reconstruct tool, and then hold down or drag the mouse on the distorted portion of the image that you want to reverse or reconstruct.**

   Note that the reconstruction occurs faster at the center of the brush's diameter. To partially reconstruct your image, set a low brush pressure and watch closely while your mouse drags across the distorted areas.

5. **Click OK to apply the distortions and close the dialog box.**

   However, if you mucked up things and want to start again, click the Revert button to get your original, unaltered image back. This action also resets the tools to their previous settings.

Correcting Camera Distortion

If you've ever tried to capture a looming skyscraper or cathedral in the lens of your camera, you know that it often involves tilting your camera and putting your neck in an unnatural position. And then, after all that, what you end up with is a distorted view of what was an impressive building in real life, as shown with the before image on the left in Figure 11-5. That's not a problem with Elements — now. The Correct Camera Distortion filter fixes the distorted perspective created by both vertical and horizontal tilting of the camera. As a bonus, this filter also corrects other kinds of distortions caused by lens snafus.

Here's how to fix all:

1. **Choose Filter⇨Correct Camera Distortion in either Edit Full or Edit Quick mode.**

2. **In the Correct Camera Distortion dialog box, be sure to select the Preview option.**

3. **Specify your correction options:**

   - *Remove Distortion:* Corrects *lens barrel,* which causes your images to appear spherized or bloated. This distortion can occur when you're using wide-angle lenses. It also corrects *pincushion* distortion, which creates images that appear to be pinched in at the center, a flaw that's found when using telephoto or zoom lenses. Slide the slider while keeping an eye on the preview. Use the handy grid as your guide for proper alignment.

 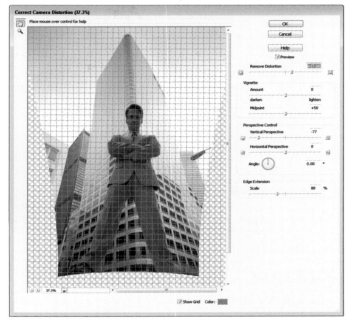

istockphoto.com

Figure 11-5: The Correct Camera Distortion filter fixes distortions caused by camera tilt and lens flaws.

- *Vignette Amount:* Adjusts the amount of lightening or darkening around the edges of your photo that you can get sometimes from incorrect lens shading. Change the width of the adjustment by specifying a midpoint value. A lower midpoint value affects more of the image. Then, move the Amount slider while viewing the preview.

- *Vertical Perspective:* Corrects the distorted perspective created by tilting the camera up or down. Again, use the grid to assist in your correction. We used the vertical perspective to correct the building and man shown in Figure 11-5. Even though this image was intentionally shot like this, we thought the perspective was a little too extreme and wanted to tone it down a bit.

- *Horizontal Perspective:* Corrects halos and blurs caused by moving the camera (or a subject who can't sit still). For better results, set the angle of movement under the Angle option.

- *Angle:* Enables you to rotate the image to compensate for tilting the camera. You may also need to tweak the angle slightly after correcting the vertical or horizontal perspective.

- *Edge Extension Scale:* When you correct the perspective on your image, you may be left with blank areas on your canvas. You can scale your image up or down to crop into the image and eliminate these holes. Note that scaling up results in interpolating your image up to its original pixel dimensions. Therefore, if you do this, be sure to start with an image that has a high-enough pixel dimension, or resolution, to avoid severe degradation. For more on resolution and interpolation, see Chapter 3.

- *Show Grid:* Shows and hides the grid, as needed. Choose the color of your grid lines.

- *Zoom Tool:* Zooms in and out for your desired view. You can also use plus and minus icons and the zoom pop-up menu in the bottom left of the window.

- *Hand Tool:* Moves you around the image window when you are zoomed in.

4. **Click OK to apply the correction and close the dialog box.**

Dressing Up with Photo and Text Effects

In addition to the multitude of filters at your disposal, Elements also provides a lot of effects that you can apply to enhance your photos. Note that some effects automatically create a duplicate of the selected layer, whereas other effects can work only on flattened images. (See Chapter 8 for details on layers.) Finally, unlike with filters, you can't preview how the effect will look on your image or type, nor do you have any options to specify.

Here are the short steps to follow to apply an effect:

1. **Select your desired image layer in the Layers panel.**

   Or, if you're applying the effect to just a selection, make the selection before applying the effect.

2. **Choose Window⇨Effects.**

3. **Select the Photo Effects button at the top of the panel.**

4. **Select your desired category of photo effects from the drop-down menu in the upper-right area of the panel:**

   - *Frame:* Includes effects that enhance the edges of the layer or selection, as shown in Figure 11-6.

   - *Faded Photo, Monotone Color, Old Photo, and Vintage Photo:* This group of effects makes your image fade from color to grayscale, appear as a single color, or look like an old pencil sketch or a photo on old paper.

PhotoSpin

Figure 11-6: Enhance your images by adding effects to your image and type layers.

- *Misc Effects:* Includes a wide variety of effects to make your image appear as though it's snowing, made of lizard skin or neon tubes, or painted with oil pastels.

- *Show All:* Shows all the effects described in this list.

5. **On the Effects panel, double-click your desired effect or drag the effect onto the image.**

   Note that you can view your styles and effects by thumbnails or by list. To change the view, click More in the upper-right corner of the panel.

You can also apply an effect to type. Select your type layer and follow Steps 2–5 in the preceding list. Note that a dialog box alerts you that the type layer must be simplified before the effect can be applied. Simplifying the layer, of course, means you lose any text editability.

Adding Shadows, Glows, and More

Layer styles go hand in hand with filters and photo effects. Also designed to enhance your image and type layers, layer styles range from simple shadows and bevels to the more complex styles, such as buttons and patterns. The wonderful thing about layer styles is that they're completely nondestructive. Unlike filters, layer styles don't change your pixel data. You can edit them or even delete them if you're unhappy with the results.

Here are some important facts about layer styles:

- **Layer styles can be applied only to layers.** If your image is just a background, convert it to a layer first.

- **Layer styles are dynamically linked to the contents of a layer.** If you move or edit the contents of the layers, the results are updated.

- **When you apply a layer style to a layer, an fx symbol appears next to the layer's name on the Layers panel.** Double-click the fx to bring up the Style Settings dialog box and perform any editing that's necessary to get the look you want.

Applying layer styles

Layer styles are stored in a few different libraries. You can add shadows, glows, beveled and embossed edges, and more complex styles, such as neon, plastic, chrome, and various other image effects. A sampling of styles is shown in Figure 11-7.

Drop Shadow   Inner Shadow   Bevel

istockphoto.com

Figure 11-7: Add dimension by applying shadows and bevels to your object or type.

Here are the steps to apply a style and a description of each of the style libraries:

1. **Select your desired image or type layer on the Layers panel.**

2. **Choose Window⇨Effects.**

3. **Select the Layer Styles button at the top of the Effects panel.**

4. **Select your desired library of styles from the drop-down menu in the upper-right area of the panel:**

   • *Bevels:* Bevels add a three-dimensional edge on the outside or inside edges of the contents of a layer, giving the element some dimension. Emboss styles make elements appear as though they're raised off or punched into the page. You can change the appearance of these styles, depending on the type of bevel chosen. Adjust parameters, such as the lighting angle, distance (how close the shadow is to the layer contents), size, bevel direction, and opacity.

   • *Drop and Inner Shadows:* Add a soft drop or inner shadow to a layer. Choose from the garden-variety shadow or one that includes noise, neon, or outlines. You can adjust the lighting angle, distance, size, and opacity, as desired.

   • *Outer and Inner Glows:* Add a soft halo that appears on the outside or inside edges of your layer contents. Adjust the appearance of the glow by changing the lighting angle, size, and opacity of the glow.

   • *Visibility:* Click Show, Hide, or Ghosted to display, hide, or partially show the layer contents. The Layer Style remains fully displayed.

   • *Complex and others:* The remaining layer styles are a cornucopia of different effects ranging from simple glass buttons to the more exotic effects, such as Groovy and Rose Impressions. You can customize all these layer styles to a certain extent by adjusting the various settings, which are similar to those for other styles in this list.

5. **On the Layer Styles panel, double-click your desired effect or drag the effect onto the image.**

   The style, with its default settings, is applied to the layer. Note that layer styles are cumulative. You can apply multiple styles — specifically, one style from each library — to a single layer.

   To edit the style's settings, either double-click the fx on the Layers panel or choose Layer⇨Layer Style⇨Style Settings.

   You can also apply layer styles to type layers, and the type layer doesn't need to be simplified.

Working with layer styles

Here are a few last tips for working with layer styles:

- **Delete a layer style or styles.** Choose Layer⇨Layer Style⇨Clear Layer Style or drag the fx icon on the Layers panel to the trash can icon.

- **Copy and paste layer styles onto other layers.** Select the layer containing the layer style and choose Layer⇨Layer Style⇨Copy Layer Style. Select the layer(s) on which you want to apply the effect and choose Layer⇨Layer Style⇨Paste Layer Style. If it's easier, you can also just drag and drop an effect from one layer to another while holding down the Alt (Option on the Mac) key.

- **Hide or show layer styles.** Choose Layer⇨Layer Style⇨Hide All Effects or Show All Effects.

- **Scale a layer style.** Choose Layer⇨Layer Style⇨Scale Effects. Select Preview and enter a value between 1 and 1,000 percent. This action allows you to scale the style without scaling the element.

Mixing It Up with Blend Modes

Elements sports a whopping 25 blend modes. *Blend modes* affect how colors interact between layers and also how colors interact when you apply paint to a layer. Not only do blend modes create interesting effects, but you can also easily apply, edit, or remove blend modes without touching your image pixels.

The various blend modes are located on a drop-down menu at the top of your Layers panel in Edit Full mode. The best way to get a feel for the effect of blend modes is not to memorize the descriptions we give you in the following sections. Instead, grab an image with some layers and apply each of the blend modes to one or more of the layers to see what happens. The exact result varies, depending on the colors in your image layers.

General blend modes

The Normal blend mode needs no introduction. It's the one you probably use the most. Dissolve is the next one on the list and, ironically, is probably the one you use the least. (Both blend modes are illustrated in Figure 11-8.)

- **Normal:** The default mode displays each pixel unadjusted.

- **Dissolve:** This mode can be seen only on a layer with an opacity setting of less than 100 percent. It allows some pixels from lower layers, which are randomized, to show through the target (selected) layer.

Darken blend modes

These blend modes produce effects that darken your image in various ways, as shown in Figure 11-9.

Normal   Dissolve

Corbis Digital Stock

Figure 11-8: The Dissolve blend mode allows pixels from one layer to peek randomly through another.

- ✐ **Darken:** Turns lighter pixels transparent if the pixels on the target layer are lighter than those below. If the pixels are darker, they're unchanged.

- ✐ **Multiply:** Burns the target layer onto the layers underneath, thereby darkening all colors where they mix. When you're painting with the Brush or Pencil tool, each stroke creates a darker color, as though you're drawing with markers.

- ✐ **Color Burn:** Darkens the layers underneath the target layer and burns them with color, creating a contrast effect, like applying a dark dye to your image.

- ✐ **Linear Burn:** Darkens the layers underneath the target layer by decreasing the brightness. This effect is similar to Multiply but often makes parts of your image black.

- ✐ **Darker Color:** When blending two layers, the darker color of the two colors is visible.

Darken   Multiply   Color Burn   Linear Burn   Darker Color

Corbis Digital Stock

Figure 11-9: These blend modes darken your image layers.

Lighten blend modes

The lighten blend modes are the opposite of the darken blend modes. All these blend modes create lightening effects on your image, as shown in Figure 11-10.

- **Lighten:** Turns darker pixels transparent if the pixels on the target layer are darker than those below. If the pixels are lighter, they're unchanged. This effect is the opposite of Darken.

- **Screen:** Lightens the target layer where it mixes with the layers underneath. This effect is the opposite of Multiply.

- **Color Dodge:** Lightens the pixels in the layers underneath the target layer and infuses them with colors from the top layer. This effect is similar to applying a bleach to your image.

- **Linear Dodge:** Lightens the layers underneath the target layer by increasing the brightness. This effect is similar to Screen but often makes parts of your image white.

- **Lighter Color:** When blending two layers, the lighter color of the two colors is visible.

Lighten	Screen	Color Dodge	Linear Dodge	Lighter Color

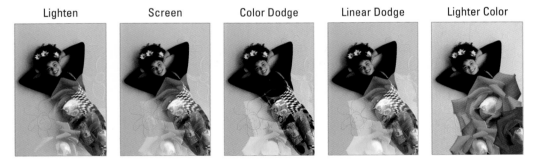

Corbis Digital Stock

Figure 11-10: These blend modes lighten your image layers.

Lighting blend modes

This group of blend modes plays with the lighting in your layers, as shown in Figure 11-11.

- **Overlay:** Overlay multiplies the dark pixels in the target layer and screens the light pixels in the underlying layers. It also enhances the contrast and saturation of colors.

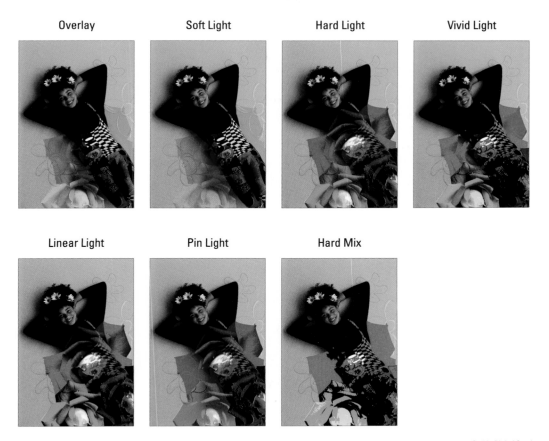

Corbis Digital Stock

Figure 11-11: Some blend modes adjust the lighting between your image layers.

- **Soft Light:** This mode darkens the dark (greater than 50 percent gray) pixels and lightens the light (less than 50 percent gray) pixels. The effect is like shining a soft spotlight on the image.

- **Hard Light:** This mode multiplies the dark (greater than 50 percent gray) pixels and screens the light (less than 50 percent gray) pixels. The effect is similar to shining a bright, hard spotlight on the image.

- **Vivid Light:** If the pixels on the top layer are darker than 50 percent gray, this mode darkens the colors by increasing the contrast. If the pixels on the top layer are lighter than 50 percent gray, the mode lightens the colors by decreasing the contrast.

✔ **Linear Light:** If the pixels on the top layer are darker than 50 percent gray, the mode darkens the colors by decreasing the brightness. If the pixels on the top layer are lighter than 50 percent gray, the mode lightens the colors by increasing the brightness.

✔ **Pin Light:** If the pixels on the top layer are darker than 50 percent gray, the mode replaces pixels darker than those on the top layer and doesn't change lighter pixels. If the pixels on the top layer are lighter than 50 percent gray, the mode replaces the pixels lighter than those on the top layer and doesn't change pixels that are darker. The mode is usually reserved for special effects.

✔ **Hard Mix:** This mode is similar to Vivid Light but reduces the colors to a total of eight — cyan, magenta, yellow, black, red, green, blue, and white. This mode creates a posterized effect.

Inverter blend modes

The Inverter blend modes invert your colors and tend to produce some radical effects, as shown in Figure 11-12.

Difference   Exclusion

Corbis Digital Stock

Figure 11-12: Difference and Exclusion blend modes invert colors.

✔ **Difference:** Produces a negative effect according to the brightness values on the top layers. If the pixels on the top layer are black, no change occurs in the underlying layers. If the pixels on the top layer are white, the mode inverts the colors of the underlying layers.

✔ **Exclusion:** Like Difference, but with less contrast and saturation. If the pixels on the top layer are black, no change occurs in the underlying layers. If the pixels on the top layer are white, this mode inverts the colors of the underlying layers. Medium colors blend to create shades of gray.

HSL blend modes

These blend modes use the HSL (hue, saturation, lightness) color model to mix colors, as shown in Figure 11-13.

- **Hue:** Blends the *luminance* (brightness) and *saturation* (intensity of the color) of the underlying layers with the *hue* (color) of the top layer.

- **Saturation:** Blends the luminance and hue of the underlying layers with the saturation of the top layer.

- **Color:** Blends the luminance of the underlying layers with the saturation and hue of the top layer. This mode enables you to paint color while preserving the shadows, highlights, and details of the underlying layers.

The Color mode is a great tool for colorizing images. If you've ever admired those hand-tinted black-and-white photos used in greeting cards and posters, you can create the same effect fairly easily. First, make sure that your black-and-white image is in RGB (red, green, blue) mode so that it can accept color. Create a new layer on the Layers panel and set it to the Color blend mode. Grab the Brush tool (with a soft-edged tip), choose your desired color, and paint over your image. Adjust your opacity to less than 100 percent to create a softer effect.

- **Luminosity:** The opposite of Color, this mode blends the hue and saturation of the underlying layers with the luminance of the top layer. This mode also preserves the shadows, highlights, and details from the top layer and mixes them with the colors of the underlying layers.

| Hue | Saturation | Color | Luminosity |

Corbis Digital Stock

Figure 11-13: Some blend modes mix colors based on the actual hue, richness, and brightness of color.

Using Photomerge

The awesome Photomerge features help you to create fabulous composites from multiple images. Whether it's creating the perfect shot of a group of friends or of your favorite vacation spot (without the passing cars and people), the Photomerge feature is the go-to tool to get it done. The following sections tell you how the Photomerge commands help to create the special type of composite image you need.

Note that all Photomerge commands can be accessed in all three Edit Modes or in the Organizer.

Photomerge Panorama

The Photomerge Panorama command enables you to combine multiple images into a single panoramic image. From skylines to mountain ranges, you can take several overlapping shots and stitch them together into one. To be successful at merging photos into a panorama, you need to start with good source files. First of all, make sure that when you shoot your photos, you overlap your individual images by 15 to 40 percent, but no more than 50 percent. Then, avoid using distortion lenses (such as fish-eye) and your camera's zoom setting. Also, try to keep the same exposure settings for even lighting. Lastly, try to stay in the same position and keep your camera at the same level for each photo. If possible, using a tripod and moving both the tripod and camera along a level surface, taking the photos from the same distance and angle is best. However, if conditions don't allow for this, using a tripod and just rotating the head is the next best method.

Follow these steps to create a Photomerge Panorama image:

1. **Choose File⇨New⇨Photomerge Panorama in Edit Full mode.**

   The first Photomerge dialog box opens.

2. **Select Files or Folder from the Use drop-down menu.**

3. **Click Add Open Files to use all open files, or click the Browse button and navigate to where your files or folder are located.**

4. **Choose your desired mode under Layout.**

   Here's a brief description of each mode:

   - *Auto:* Elements analyzes your images.

   - *Perspective:* If you shot your images with perspective or at extreme angles, this is your mode. Try this mode if you shot your images with a tripod and rotating head.

- *Cylindrical:* If you shot your images with a wide-angle lens or you have those 360-degree, full panoramic shots, this is a good mode.

- *Reposition Only:* Elements doesn't take any distortion into account; it simply scans the images and positions them best.

If you choose any of the preceding modes, Elements opens and automatically assembles the source files to create the composite panorama in the work area of the dialog box. If it looks good, skip to Step 7.

Elements alerts you if it can't automatically composite your source files. You then have to assemble the images manually.

- *Interactive Layout:* This option opens the work area pane, as shown in Figure 11-14. Elements tries to align and stitch the images the best it can, but you may have to manually complete or adjust the panorama.

Note that with any of the modes, Elements leaves your merged image in layers. You'll also notice that a layer mask has been added to each layer to better blend your panoramic image. For more on layer masks, see Chapter 8.

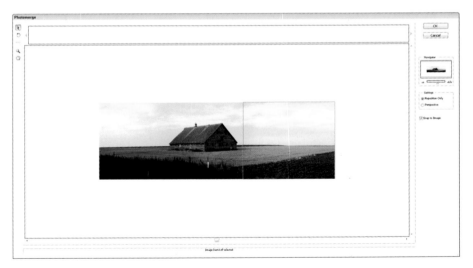

PhotoSpin

Figure 11-14: Combine multiple images into a single panorama with Photomerge.

5. **If Elements hasn't already, drag the image thumbnails from the light-box area (the small white area at the top) onto the work area with the Select Image tool (the arrow).**

   Or you can simply double-click the lightbox thumbnail to add it to the composition.

6. **Arrange and position your images:**

   - *Select Image tool:* Positions the images.

   - *Rotate Image tool:* Makes rotations.

   - *Zoom and Move View tools:* Helps view and navigate around your panorama.

   - *Navigator view box:* Zooms into and out of your composition when you drag the slider.

   - *Snap to Image option:* Enables overlapping images to automatically snap into place.

7. **To adjust the Vanishing Point, first select the Perspective option in the Settings area and click your desired image with the Set Vanishing Point tool.**

   Elements changes the perspective of the composition. By default, Elements selects the center image as the vanishing point. If necessary, you can move the other images.

   Note that when you select the Perspective setting, Elements links non–Vanishing Point images to the Vanishing Point image. To break the link, click the Normal Setting button or separate the images in the work area.

8. **Click OK to create the panorama.**

   The file opens as a new, unsaved file in Elements. Note that you can also click the Save Composition button to save the file as a Photomerge Composition (.pmg) file. We would avoid this, however, because the file format isn't very compatibility friendly.

Photomerge Group Shot

We all know how hard it is to get a group of people to all look great in one shot. Well, Photomerge Group Shot lets you take multiple group photos and merge the best of them to get that perfect shot.

Here are the steps to create a Photomerge Group Shot image:

1. **Select two or more photos from your Project Bin.**

2. **Choose File⇨New⇨Photomerge Group Shot in any of the Edit modes.**

3. **Take your best overall group shot and drag it from the Project Bin onto the Final window.**

4. **Select one of your other photos in the Project Bin to use as your source image. Drag it to the Source window.**

5. **With the Pencil tool, draw a line around the portions of the Source photo you want to merge into your Final photo, as shown in Figure 11-15.**

   You can choose to show your pencil strokes and/or show your regions, which will be highlighted with an overlay.

Figure 11-15: Get the perfect group shot from several images.

6. **Repeat Steps 4 and 5 with any remaining photos.**

   If your photos aren't aligned, you can use the Alignment tool under the Advanced Options.

7. **With the Alignment tool, click your source image and position the three target markers on three key locations. Do the same on the final image and choose similar locations.**

8. **Click the Align Photos button.**

   As with Photomerge Panorama, the more alike in framing, size, and so on, that your source and final images are, the better the merged result.

   Note that if you see any noticeable seams on your final image around the copied area, click the Pixel Blending button to help smooth over those flaws.

9. **(Optional) If you make a mess of things, click the Reset button.**

10. **When you're satisfied with the result, click Done.**

    The file opens as a new file in Elements.

Photomerge Scene Cleaner

Photomerge Scene Cleaner (see Figure 11-16) sounds like a tool you might see in an episode of CSI to mop up a crime scene, but it isn't quite that gory. This recent addition to the Photomerge commands family enables you to create the optimum image by allowing you to eliminate annoying distractions, such as cars, passersby, and so on.

To get the best Source images for a clean scene, be sure to take multiple shots of your scene from the same angle and distance. It also works best when the elements you want to eliminate are moving.

Follow these steps to create a Photomerge Scene Cleaner composite:

1. **Select two or more photos from your Project Bin.**

2. **Choose File⇨New⇨Photomerge Scene Cleaner in any of the Edit modes.**

   Elements attempts to auto-align your images the best it can.

3. **Take your best overall shot of the scene and drag it from the Project Bin onto the Final window.**

4. **Select one of your other photos in the Project Bin to use as your source image. Drag it to the Source window.**

5. **With the Pencil tool, draw a line around the elements in the final photo that you want to be replaced by content from the source photo.**

6. **Repeat Steps 4 and 5 with the remaining shots of the scene.**

   If your photos aren't aligned, you can use the Alignment tool under the Advanced Options.

7. **With the Alignment tool, click your source image and position the three target markers on three key locations.**

   Do the same on the final image, choosing similar locations.

8. **Click the Align Photos button, as shown in Figure 11-16.**

   Again, as with the other Photomerge commands, the more similar your starting source images are (framing, angle), the better the merged result.

   If you see any noticeable seams on your final image around the copied area, click the Pixel Blending button to help smooth over those flaws.

9. **If you make a mess of things, click the Reset button.**

10. **When you're satisfied with the result, click Done.**

    The resulting image opens as a new file in Elements.

Figure 11-16: Eliminate annoying distractions with Photomerge Scene Cleaner.

Photomerge Faces

Photomerge Faces, more of a fun than useful tool, lets you blend features from multiple faces to get a kind of hybrid face. To create a hybrid human by using the Photomerge Faces feature, select two or more photos from your Project Bin and choose File➪New➪Photomerge Faces in any of the Edit modes. Use the Alignment and Pencil tools to choose how you'd like to merge the photos, similar to the steps described in the section "Photomerge Group Shot."

Photomerge Exposure

Sometimes you need to capture a shot that poses an exposure challenge — your foreground and background require different exposure settings. This dilemma often occurs in shots that are backlit. For example, you have a person in front of an indoor window in the day or someone in front of a lit nighttime cityscape. With the Photomerge Exposure, you can take shots with two different exposure settings and let the command blend them together for the perfect shot.

You can shoot your initial images using *exposure bracketing* (shooting at consecutive exposure camera settings) or with a flash and then without. Elements will be able to detect all of these camera settings. We recommend that you use a tripod, if possible, to keep your shots aligned. This will help the blending algorithm do its job.

Here's how to use this great new command:

1. **Select two or more photos from your Project Bin.**

2. **Choose File➪New➪Photomerge Exposure in any of the Edit modes.**

3. **If you have done a good job keeping your shots aligned, leave the mode on Automatic.**

   Select the quickie Simple Blending option and Elements automatically blends the two images. Select the Smart Blending option to access sliders to adjust the Highlights, Shadows, and Saturation settings for finer tuning of the resulting images. If you muck things up, click the Reset button.

4. **If you feel the need for even more control, click the Manual mode tab.**

5. **In Manual mode, choose your first shot from the Project Bin and drag it to the Final window. If your other image isn't already the source image, drag it from the Project Bin to the Source window.**

6. **With the Pencil tool, draw over the well-exposed areas you want to retain in the source image. As you draw, your final image will show the incorporation of those drawn areas, as shown in Figure 11-17.**

Figure 11-17: Copy a style from one image to another.

7. **If you mistakenly draw over something you don't want, grab the Eraser tool and erase the Pencil tool marks.**

   Choose the appropriate option to have your preview show strokes or regions.

8. **You can further control the blending by dragging the Transparency slider.**

   Dragging to the right will blend less of the source areas into the final image. Check the Edge Blending option to get an even better blend of the two images.

9. **If your photos aren't aligning correctly, grab the Alignment Tool under Advanced Options.**

   With the Alignment tool, click your source image and position the three target markers on three key locations.

   Do the same on the final image, choosing similar locations.

10. **Click the Align Photos button.**

    Again, as with the other Photomerge commands, the more similar your starting source images are (framing, angle), the better the merged result.

11. **Again, if you make a mess of things, click the Reset button.**

12. **When you're satisfied with the result, click Done.**

    The image opens as a new, layered file in Elements. The blended image will appear on Layer 1. The background will be your starting Final image. You can either flatten the layered file which keeps the appearance of Layer 1 or you can double-click your background to convert it to a layer and then delete it by dragging it to the trash icon in the Layers panel.

Photomerge Style Match

You can now match or apply the style of one image onto another image. It is hard to explain exactly what Adobe defines as "style," but basically tonal properties are transferred from one image to another. But rather than read a definition of the feature, it's best to spend a couple minutes trying it.

Here are the steps to transfer a style from one image onto another:

1. **Select a photo from your Project Bin onto which you would like to transfer a style.**

2. **Choose File⇨New⇨Photomerge Style Match in any of the Edit modes.**

3. **Your selected photo appears in the right window as your source (After) image.**

4. **Drag an image from the Style Bin to the left window to act as your sample (Style) image from which your desired style will be transferred.**

    To add more images to the Style Bin, click the green plus sign and choose to add sample images from either the Organizer or from your hard drive.

5. **Adjust the following sliders, as shown in Figure 11-18:**

    • *Style Intensity:* Specifies the intensity or strength of the style transfer. Keep the number low to blend more of the original image with the styled image.

    • *Style Clarity:* Specifies how clearly the style transfer appears.

    • *Style Details:* Enhances or decreases details in the styled image.

       Note that the results really depend on your chosen images, so be sure and experiment with above options to get your desired result.

6. **Further define the styled image by adjusting the following options under Basic mode:**

- *Style Eraser:* Paint with this tool to erase the style from areas on your source image.

- *Style Painter:* Paint with this tool to add the style to areas on your source image.

- *Soften Stroke Edges:* Drag the slider to clean up your image and remove any seams between the styled and original image areas.

- *Transfer Tones:* Select the check box to transfer the tonal values of the source image onto the styled image.

7. **You can use more than one image as your sample image. To do so, simply repeat Steps 4 through 6.**

8. **Again, if you make a mess of things, click the Reset button.**

9. **When you're satisfied with the result, click Done.**

   The file opens as a new file in Elements.

Figure 11-18: Copy a style from one image to another.

Drawing and Painting

*E*lements is such a deluxe, full-service image-editing program that it doesn't just stop at giving you tools to select, repair, organize, and share your images. It figures that you may need to add a swash of color, either freeform with a brush or pencil, or in the form of a geometric or organic shape. Don't worry: This drawing and painting business isn't just for those with innate artistic talent. In fact, Elements gives you plenty of preset brushes and shapes that you can use. If you can pick a tool and drag your mouse, you can draw and paint.

Choosing Color

Before you start drawing or painting, you may want to change your color to something other than the default black. If you read the earlier chapters in this book, you may have checked out the Elements Tools panel and noticed the two overlapping color swatches at the bottom of the panel. These two swatches represent two categories of color: *foreground* and *background.* Here's a quick look at how they work with different tools:

 ✔ When you add type, paint with the Brush tool, or create a shape, you're using the foreground color.

 ✔ On the background layer of an image, when you use the Eraser tool, or when you increase the size of your canvas, you're accessing the background color.

 ✔ When you drag with the Gradient tool, so long as your gradient is set to the default, you're laying down a blend of color from the foreground to the background.

Elements gives you three ways to choose your foreground and background colors: the Color Picker; the color swatches; and the Eyedropper tool, which samples color in an image. In the following sections, we explore each one.

Working with the Color Picker

By default, Elements uses a black foreground color and a white background color. If you're experimenting with color and want to go back to the default color, press the D key. If you want to swap between foreground and background colors, press the X key. If you want any other color of the rainbow, click your desired swatch to change either the foreground or background color. This action transports you to the Color Picker, as shown in Figure 12-1.

Here are the steps to choose your color via the Color Picker:

1. **Click either the foreground or background color swatch on the Tools panel.**

   The Color Picker appears.

2. **Drag the color slider or click the color bar to get close to the general color you desire.**

3. **Choose the exact color you want by clicking in the large square, or *color field,* on the left.**

   The circle cursor targets your selected color. The two swatches in the upper-right corner of the dialog box represent your newly selected color and the original foreground or background color.

   The numeric values on the right side of the dialog box also change according to the color you selected. If you happen to know the values of your desired color, you may also enter them in the text boxes. RGB (red, green, blue) values are based on brightness levels, from 0 (black) to 255 (white). You can also enter HSB (hue, saturation, brightness) values, or the hexadecimal formula for Web colors.

4. **When you're happy with your color, click OK.**

New color

Original color

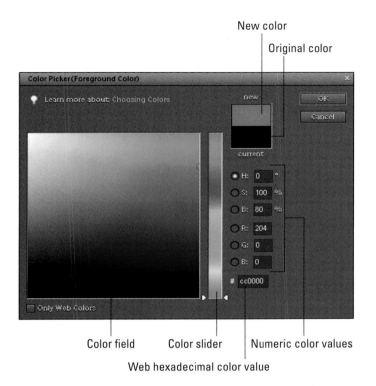

Color field   Color slider   Numeric color values

Web hexadecimal color value

Figure 12-1: Choose your desired color from the Color Picker.

Dipping into the Color Swatches panel

Another way Elements enables you to choose a foreground or background color is by selecting a color on the Color Swatches panel. The Color Swatches panel is a digital version of the artist's paint pal-
ette. In addition to preset colors, you can mix and store your own colors for use now and later. You can have palettes for certain types of projects or images. For example, you may want a palette of skin tones for retouching portraits. Choose Window⇨Color Swatches to bring up the panel, as shown in Figure 12-2.

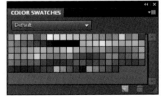

Figure 12-2: Choose and store colors in the Color Swatches panel.

To grab a color from the Color Swatches panel, click the color swatch you want. By the way, it doesn't matter which tool you have. As soon as you move the tool over the panel, it temporarily converts to an eyedropper that samples the color and makes it your new foreground or background color.

Although the Color Swatches panel is a breeze to use, here are a few tips to help you along:

- **Change the background color.** Either first select the background swatch on the Tools panel or Ctrl-click (⌘-click on the Mac) a swatch.

- **Use preset colors.** To load a particular preset swatch library, select it from the Color Swatches panel menu. Elements offers libraries specific to Web graphics, photo filters, and Windows and Mac OS systems.

- **Add a color to the Color Swatches panel.** Choose New Swatch from the panel menu. You can also simply click an empty portion of the panel. Name your swatch and click OK.

- **Save swatches.** Choose Save Swatches from the panel menu in the upper-right corner of the panel. We recommend saving the swatch library in the default Color Swatches folder in the Presets folder. If by chance this folder doesn't come up by default, just navigate to the Color Swatches folder by following this partial path: `Adobe\Photoshop Elements 9.0\Presets\Color Swatches` (**Win**) or `Adobe\Adobe Photoshop Elements 9\Presets\Color Swatches` (**Mac**).

- **Save swatches for Exchange.** Choose this command to save your swatches for use in another Adobe program. Name the swatch set, and save it in the same folder listed in the above bullet.

- **Load swatches.** If you want to load a custom library created by you or someone else, choose Load Swatches from the panel menu. In the dialog box, select your desired library from the Color Swatches folder. The new library is added to your current library.

  You can also work with swatches by using the Preset Manager. For more on the Preset Manager, see Chapter 2.

- **Delete swatches.** To delete a swatch, drag it to the trash can at the bottom of the panel or Alt-click (Option-click on the Mac) the swatch.

- **Change the panel's appearance.** Click the panel menu in the upper-right corner to choose from Small or Large Thumbnail (swatch squares) or Small or Large List (swatch squares with a name).

- **Replace your current swatch library with a different library.** Choose Replace Swatches from the panel menu. Choose a library from the Color Swatches folder.

Sampling with the Eyedropper tool

Another way that Elements enables you to choose color is via the Eyedropper tool. The Eyedropper tool comes in handy when you want to sample an existing color in an image and use it for another element. For example, you may want your text to be the same color as the green background in the image shown in Figure 12-3. Grab the Eyedropper tool (or press I) and click a shade of green in the background. The tool samples the color and makes it your new foreground color. You can then create the type with your new foreground color.

Corbis Digital Stock

Figure 12-3: The Eyedropper tool enables you to sample color from your image to use with other elements, such as type.

Here are a few things to remember when you're using the Eyedropper tool:

- **Sample a new foreground or background color.** Obviously, you can select either the foreground or background swatch on the Tools panel before you sample a color. But if the foreground color swatch is active, holding down the Alt key (Option key on the Mac) samples a new background color, and vice versa.

- **Choose a color from any open image.** If you have multiple images open, you can even sample a color from an image that you're not working on!

- **Choose your sample size on the Options bar.** You can select the color of just the single pixel you click (Point Sample), or Elements can average the colors of the pixels in a 3-x-3- or 5-x-5-pixel area.

- **Make colors Web safe.** If you right-click your image to bring up the context menu, you have a hidden option: Copy Color as HTML. This option provides the Web hexadecimal color formula for that sampled color and copies it to the Clipboard. You can then paste that formula into an HTML file or grab the Type tool and choose Edit⇨Paste to view the formula in your image.

✔ **Toggle between the Eyedropper and other tools.** Elements, multitasker that it is, enables you to temporarily access the Eyedropper tool when you're using the Brush, Pencil, Color Replacement, Gradient, Paint Bucket, Cookie Cutter, or Shape tool. Simply press the Alt (Option on the Mac) key to access the Eyedropper. Release the Alt (Option on the Mac) key to go back to your original tool.

Getting Artsy with the Pencil and Brush Tools

You want to find out how to paint and draw with a color you've chosen. The Pencil and Brush tools give you the power to put your creative abilities to work, and the following sections show you how.

When you use these two tools, you benefit immensely from the use of a pressure-sensitive digital drawing tablet. The awkwardness of trying to draw or paint with a mouse disappears and leaves you with tools that behave much closer to their analog ancestors.

Drawing with the Pencil tool

Drawing with the Pencil tool creates hard edges. You can't get the soft, feathery edges that you can with the Brush tool. In fact, the edges of a pencil stroke can't even be *anti-aliased*. (For more on anti-aliasing, see the following section.) Keep in mind that if you draw anything other than vertical or horizontal lines, your lines will have some jaggies when they're viewed up close. But hey, don't diss the Pencil just yet. Those hard-edged strokes can be perfect for Web graphics. What's more, the Pencil tool can erase itself, and it's great for digital sketches, as shown in Figure 12-4.

Follow these steps to become familiar with the Pencil tool:

1. **Select the Pencil tool from the Tools panel.**

   You can also press the N key. By default, the Pencil tool's brush tip is the 1-pixel brush. Yes, even though the Pencil tip is hard edged, we still refer to it as a brush.

Illustration by Chris Blair

Figure 12-4: The Pencil tool can be used for digital drawings.

2. **On the Options bar, choose your desired pencil options, beginning with a brush preset. Click the arrow and select your desired brush from the Brush Preset Picker drop-down panel.**

   To load another preset library, click the Brushes menu at the top of the panel.

   Remember that you aren't limited to the standard old brush strokes. Check out the Assorted and Special Effects brushes found in the Brushes drop-down menu on the Brushes panel. You'll be surprised by the interesting brushes lurking on these panels. Use them to create standalone images or to enhance your photographic creations.

   Access the menu on the Brushes panel to save, rename, or delete individual brushes and also save, load, and reset brush libraries. For more on these operations, see the following section.

3. **Choose your brush size.**

   A preset brush's pixel diameter is shown as text below a thumbnail image of the brush shape. If you want to change the size of that brush tip, drag the Size slider or enter a value.

4. **Select a blending mode.**

   Blend modes alter the way the color you're applying interacts with the color on your canvas. You can find more about blend modes in Chapter 11.

5. **If you want the background to show through your strokes, adjust the opacity by dragging the slider or entering an opacity percentage less than 100 percent.**

   The lower the percentage, the more the background images show through.

   Your strokes must be on a separate layer above your images for you to be able to adjust the opacity and blend modes after you draw them. For more on layers, see Chapter 8.

6. **(Optional) Select Auto Erase if you want to enable that option.**

   This option removes portions of your pencil strokes. For example, say that your foreground color is black and your background color is white, and you apply some black strokes. With Auto Erase enabled, you apply white if you drag back over the black strokes. If you drag over the white background, you apply black.

7. **Click and drag with the mouse to create your freeform lines.**

   To draw straight lines, click at a starting point, release the mouse button, and then Shift-click at a second point.

Painting with the Brush tool

The Brush tool creates soft-edged strokes. How soft those strokes are depends on which brush you use. By default, even the hardest brush has a slightly soft edge because it's anti-aliased. *Anti-aliasing* creates a single row of partially filled pixels along the edges to produce the illusion of a smooth edge. You can also get even softer brushes, which employ feathering. For details on feathering, see Chapter 7.

The Brush tool shares most of the options found in the Pencil tool, except that the Auto Erase feature isn't available. Here's the lowdown on the unique Brush options:

- **Airbrush:** Click the Airbrush button on the Options bar to apply the Airbrush mode. In this mode, the longer you hold down the mouse button, the more paint the Brush pumps out and the wider the airbrush effect spreads.

- **Tablet Options:** Click the down-pointing arrow between the airbrush button and the brush icon. If you're using a pressure-sensitive digital drawing tablet, check the settings you want the tablet to control, including size, scatter, opacity, roundness, and hue jitter. The harder you press with the stylus, the greater the effect of these options.

- **More Options:** Click the brush icon to access additional brush options. These options, referred to as brush *dynamics,* change while you apply your stroke. See Figure 12-5 for an example of each one. These options include:

  - *Fade:* The lower the value, the quicker the stroke fades. However, 0 creates no fade.

  - *Hue Jitter:* Vary the stroke between the foreground and background colors. The higher the value, the more frequent the variation.

  - *Scatter:* The higher the value, the higher the number of brush marks and the farther apart they are.

  - *Spacing:* The higher the number, the more space between marks.

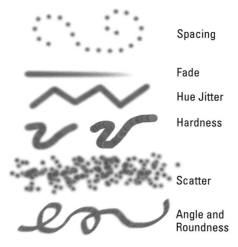

Figure 12-5: Change brush options to create a custom brush.

- *Hardness:* The higher the value, the harder the brush.

- *Angle:* If you create an oval brush by adjusting the roundness (see the following bullet), this option controls the angle of that oval brush stroke. It's so much easier to drag the points and the arrow on the diagram than to guesstimate values in the text boxes.

- *Roundness:* A setting of 100 percent is totally circular. The lower the percentage, the more elliptical your brush becomes.

You can lock in these brush dynamics by selecting the Keep These Settings For All Brushes check box, ensuring that every brush you select adopts these settings.

Like the Pencil tool, additional features for the Brush tool appear in the menu on the Brush Preset Picker drop-down panel. Here's a quick description of each:

- ✔ **Save Brush:** Allows you to save a custom brush as a preset. See the following section for details.

- ✔ **Rename Brush:** Don't like your brush's moniker? Change it with this option.

- ✔ **Delete Brush:** Don't like your entire brush? Eliminate it with this option.

- ✔ **The display options:** Not a single command, rather a set of commands that enable you to change the way your brush tips are displayed. The default view is Stroke Thumbnail, which displays the appearance of the stroke. These commands include Text Only, Small and Large Thumbnail, and Small and Large List.

- ✔ **Reset Brushes:** Reverts your current brush library to the default.

- ✔ **Save Brushes:** Saves custom brushes in a separate library.

- ✔ **Load Brushes:** Loads a preset or custom brush library.

You can also manage brush tip libraries by using the Preset Manager. See Chapter 2 for information on using the Preset Manager.

Creating your own brush

After playing with all the various options, if you really like the Franken-brush you've created, feel free to save it as a preset that you can access in the future. Choose Save Brush from the panel menu on the Brush Preset Picker panel. Name the brush and click OK. Your new custom brush shows up at the bottom of the Brush Preset Picker drop-down panel.

There's one additional way to create a brush. Elements allows you to create a brush from all or part of your image. The image can be a photograph or something you've painted or drawn.

Here's how to create a brush from your image:

1. **Select part of your image with any of the selection tools.**

   If you want to use the entire image or entire layer, deselect everything.

   For more on selections, see Chapter 7.

2. **Choose Edit⇨Define Brush or Edit⇨Define Brush from Selection.**

   You see one command or the other, depending on what you do in Step 1.

3. **Name the brush and click OK.**

   The new brush shows up at the bottom of your Brush Preset Picker drop-down panel. Note that your brush is only a grayscale version of your image. When you use the brush, it automatically applies the color you've selected as your foreground color, as shown in Figure 12-6.

Digital Vision

Figure 12-6: Create a custom brush from a portion of your image.

Using the Impressionist Brush

In this section, we introduce the Impressionist Brush. This tool is designed to paint over your photos in a way that makes them look like fine art paintings. You can set various options that change the style of the brush strokes.

Here's how to use this artistic brush:

1. **Select the Impressionist Brush from the Tools panel.**

   It looks like a brush with a curlicue next to it. You can also press B, or Shift+B, to cycle through the brushes.

2. Set your brush options.

The Brushes presets (Size, Mode, and Opacity options) are identical to those found with the Brush tool, described in the section "Painting with the Brush tool," earlier in this chapter. You can also find some unique options on the More Options panel, displayed by clicking the Impressionist Brush icon on the Options bar:

- *Style:* This drop-down menu contains various brush stroke styles, such as Dab and Tight Curl.

- *Area:* Controls the size of your brush stroke. The larger the value, the larger the area covered.

- *Tolerance:* Controls how similar color pixels have to be before they're changed by the brush stroke.

Corbis Digital Stock

Figure 12-7: The Impressionist Brush turns your photo into a painting.

3. Drag on your image and paint with your brush strokes, as shown in Figure 12-7.

The best way to get a feel for what this tool does is to open your favorite image, grab the tool, and take it for a test drive.

Filling and Outlining Selections

There may be times when you want to create an element on your canvas that can't quite be created with a brush or pencil stroke. Maybe it's a perfect circle or a five-point star. If you have a selection, you can fill or stroke that selection to create that element, rather than draw or paint it on. The Fill command adds a color or a pattern to the entire selection, whereas the Stroke command applies the color to only the edge of the selection border.

Fill 'er up

You won't find a Fill tool on the Tools panel. Elements decided to avoid the over-populated panel and placed the Fill and Stroke commands on the Edit menu.

Here are the simple steps to fill a selection:

1. **Grab the selection tool of your choice and create your selection on a new layer.**

   Although you don't have to create a new layer to make a selection to fill, we recommend it. That way, if you don't like the filled selection, you can delete the layer, and your image or background below it remains safe. See Chapter 7 for more on selections and Chapter 8 for details on working with layers.

2. **Select either the foreground or background color and then choose a fill color.**

   See "Choosing Color," earlier in this chapter, if you need a refresher.

3. **Choose Edit➪Fill Selection.**

   The Fill Layer dialog box, shown in Figure 12-8, appears.

   If you want to bypass the Fill Layer dialog box (and the rest of these steps), you can use these handy keyboard shortcuts instead:

   • *To fill the selection with the foreground color:* Press Alt+Backspace (Option+Delete on the Mac).

   • *To fill it with the background color:* Press Ctrl+Backspace (⌘+ Delete on the Mac).

Figure 12-8: Fill your selection or layer with color or a pattern.

4. **Choose your desired fill from the Use pop-up menu.**

   You can select whether to fill with the foreground or background color. You also can choose Color, Black, 50% Gray, White, or Pattern. If you select Color, you're transported to the Color Picker. If you choose Pattern, you must then choose a pattern from the Custom Pattern drop-down panel. For more on patterns, see the section "Working with Patterns," later in this chapter.

   If you don't have an active selection border in your image, the command says Fill Layer and your entire layer is filled with your color or pattern.

5. **In the blending area, you can specify whether to preserve transparency, which enables you to fill only the portions of the selection that contain pixels (the nontransparent areas).**

Although you can also choose a *blend mode* (how the fill color interacts with colors below it) and opacity percentage, we urge you not to adjust your blend mode and opacity in the Fill Layer dialog box. Make those adjustments on your layer later, by using the Layer panel commands, where you have more flexibility for editing.

6. **Click OK.**

   The color or pattern fills the selection.

Outlining with the Stroke command

Stroking a selection enables you to create colored outlines, or *borders,* of selections or layers. You can put this border inside or outside the selection border or centered on it. Here are the steps to stroke a selection:

1. **Choose a foreground color and create a selection.**

2. **Choose Edit⇨Stroke (Outline) Selection.**

   The Stroke dialog box opens.

3. **Select your desired settings.**

   Many settings are the same as those found in the Fill Layer dialog box, as we explain in the preceding section. Here's a brief rundown of the options that are unique to strokes:

   - *Width:* Enter a width of 1 to 250 pixels for the stroke.

   - *Location:* Specify how Elements should apply the stroke: outside the selection, inside the selection, or centered on the selection.

4. **Click OK to apply the stroke.**

   We gave a 30-pixel centered stroke to our selection, as shown in Figure 12-9.

Figure 12-9: Stroke a selection to create a colored border.

Splashing On Color with the Paint Bucket Tool

The Paint Bucket tool has been a longtime occupant of the Tools panel. This tool, whose icon looks just like a bucket, behaves like a combination of the Fill command and the Magic Wand tool. It makes a selection based on similarly colored pixels and then immediately fills that selection with color or a pattern. Just like the Magic Wand tool, this tool is the most successful when you have a limited number of colors, as shown in Figure 12-10.

To use the Paint Bucket tool, simply click inside the selection you want to fill. Before you click, however, specify your options:

- ✔ **Color:** Choose between a fill of the foreground color or a pattern. If you want to use the foreground color, leave Pattern deselected.

- ✔ **Pattern:** If you select Pattern, choose a preset pattern from the drop-down panel. For more details on patterns, see the section "Working with Patterns," later in this chapter.

- ✔ **Mode:** Select a blending mode to change how your fill color interacts with the color below it.

Corbis Digital Stock

Figure 12-10: The Paint Bucket tool makes a selection and fills it at the same time.

- ✔ **Opacity:** Adjust the opacity to make your fill more or less transparent.

- ✔ **Tolerance:** Choose a tolerance level that specifies how similar in color a pixel must be before it's selected and then filled. The lower the value, the more similar the color must be. For more on tolerance, see the section on the Magic Wand in Chapter 7.

- ✔ **Anti-alias:** Choose this option to smooth the edges between the filled and unfilled areas.

- ✔ **Contiguous:** If selected, this option selects and fills only pixels that are touching within your selection. If the option is deselected, pixels are selected and filled wherever they lie within your selection.

- ✔ **All Layers:** This option selects and fills pixels within the selection in all layers that are within your tolerance level.

Working with Multicolored Gradients

If one color isn't enough for you, you'll be pleased to know that Elements enables you to fill a selection or layer with a gradient. A *gradient* is a blend of two or more colors that gradually dissolve from one to another. Elements provides a whole slew of preset gradients. But creating your own custom gradient is also fun and easy.

Applying a preset gradient

Similar to colors, patterns, and brushes, gradients have a whole group of presets that you can apply to your selection and layers. You can also load other libraries of gradients from the Gradient panel pop-up menu.

Here's how to apply a preset gradient:

1. **Make the selection you want to fill with a gradient.**

   We recommend making the selection on a new layer so that you can edit the gradient later without harming the underlying image.

   If you don't make a selection, the gradient is applied to the entire layer or background.

2. **Select the Gradient tool from the Tools panel or press the G key.**

3. **On the Options bar, click the down-pointing arrow on the gradient swatch to display the Gradient Picker drop-down panel and choose a preset gradient.**

   Remember that you can choose other preset libraries from the panel menu. Libraries, such as Color Harmonies and Metals, contain interesting presets.

4. **Choose your desired gradient type by clicking one of the icons.**

   See Figure 12-11 for an example of each type.

5. **Choose from the following options on the Options bar:**

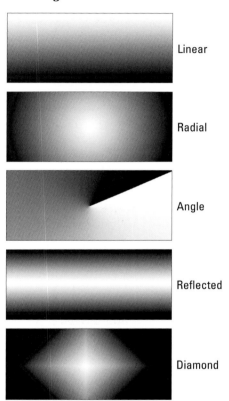

Figure 12-11: Choose from one of five gradient types.

- *Mode:* Select a blending mode to change how the color of the gradient interacts with the colors below it.

- *Opacity:* Specify how opaque or transparent the gradient is.

- *Reverse:* Reverse the order in which the colors are applied.

- *Dither:* Add *noise,* or random information, to produce a smoother gradient that prints with less *banding* (weird stripes caused by printing limitations).

- *Transparency:* Deselect this option to make Elements ignore any transparent areas in the gradient, making them opaque instead.

6. **Position your gradient cursor at your desired starting point within your selection or layer.**

7. Drag in any direction to your desired end point for the gradient.

Longer drags result in a subtler transition between colors, whereas shorter drags result in a more abrupt transition. Hold down the Shift key to restrain the direction of the gradient to multiples of a 45-degree angle.

8. Release the mouse button to apply the gradient.

We applied an Orange Yellow radial gradient from the Color Harmonies 2 preset library to a selection of a sun in Figure 12-12. We selected the Reverse option and dragged from the center of the sun to the tip of the top ray.

Figure 12-12: We filled our sun selection with a radial Orange Yellow gradient.

Customizing gradients

If you can't find the exact gradient you need, you can easily create your own. The Gradient Editor lets you create your own custom gradient using as many colors as you want. After you create a custom gradient, you can save it as a preset to reuse in the future.

Follow these steps to create a custom gradient:

1. Select the Gradient tool from the Tools panel.

2. Click the Edit button (which looks like a gradient swatch) on the Options bar.

The Gradient Editor dialog box opens, as shown in Figure 12-13.

3. Pick an existing preset to use as the basis for your new gradient.

4. Choose your gradient type, either Solid or Noise, from the pop-up menu.

A Noise gradient contains random colors. Interestingly, each time you create a Noise gradient, the result is different.

Note that as soon as you start to edit the existing gradient, the name of the gradient changes to Custom.

5. Choose your options for either a Solid or Noise gradient, depending on what you chose in Step 4:

• *If you chose Solid:* Adjust the Smoothness percentage to determine how smoothly one color blends into another.

● *If you chose Noise:* You can choose which Color Model to use to set the color range. You can also adjust the Roughness, which affects how smoothly or abruptly the color transitions from one to another. Click Restrict Colors to avoid oversaturated colors. The Add Transparency option adds transparency to random colors. Click the Randomize button to randomly generate a new gradient. You can then skip to Step 15 to finish the gradient-making process.

6. **If you're creating a solid gradient, begin choosing the first color of your gradient by clicking the left color stop under the gradient bar. (Refer to Figure 12-13.)**

The triangle on top of the stop turns black to indicate that you're working with the starting point of the gradient.

7. **Choose the starting color by double-clicking the left color stop and selecting a color from the Color Picker that appears.**

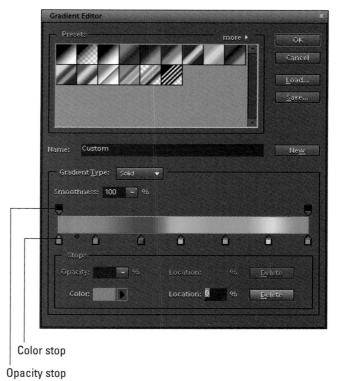

Color stop

Opacity stop

Figure 12-13: Use the Gradient Editor to edit and customize gradients.

In the Stops area, you can also click the color swatch or choose Foreground, Background, or User Color from the Color pop-up menu. If you select Color with the Foreground or Background option when you change either of those colors, the color in the gradient changes automatically for gradients you make. However, when you open the Gradient Editor again, you can revert to your original foreground or background color by selecting the User Color option.

8. **Select the ending color by clicking the right color stop. Repeat Step 7 to define the color.**

9. **Change the percentage of one color versus the other by moving the starting or ending point's color stop to the left or right. Drag the midpoint slider (a diamond icon) to where the colors mix equally, 50-50.**

   You can also change the position of the midpoint by typing a value in the Location box.

10. **To add another color, click below the gradient bar at the position you want to add the color. Define a color in the same way you did in Steps 7–9.**

11. **Repeat Step 10 to add colors.**

12. **To add transparency to your gradient, select an opacity stop (refer to Figure 12-13) and adjust the Opacity slider to specify the amount of transparency you desire.**

    By default, a gradient has colors that are 100-percent opaque. You can fade a gradient to transparency so that the portion of the image under the gradient shows through.

    You can also add opacity stops in the same way you add color stops.

13. **Adjust your color and opacity stops and their midpoint sliders to vary the percentages of each color.**

14. **You can also redefine any of the colors. To delete a color stop, drag it up or down off the gradient bar.**

15. **When you're done, name your gradient and click the New button.**

    Your gradient is added to the Presets menu.

After all that work, you may want to consider saving your gradients for later use. To save a gradient, click the Save button in the Gradient Editor dialog box. Save the current presets, with your new gradient, under the current library's name or a new name altogether. You can later load that preset library. You can also manage your gradient presets with the Preset Manager, as we explain in Chapter 2.

Working with Patterns

If you've ever seen someone wearing leopard-print pants with an argyle sweater and a plaid blazer, you're familiar with patterns. Not always pretty when used without restraint, patterns can be used to occasionally fill selections or layers. You can also stamp your image by using the Pattern Stamp tool. You can even retouch by using a pattern with the Healing Brush tool. Elements offers a lot of preset patterns to keep you happy. And, if you're not happy with Elements' selection, you can create your own, of course.

Applying a preset pattern

Although you can apply patterns by using many different tools, this chapter sticks with applying patterns as fills. To fill a layer or selection with a preset pattern, follow these steps:

1. **Choose the layer or selection you want to fill with a pattern.**

   Again, we recommend making your selection on a new layer above your image for more flexible editing later on.

2. **Choose Edit⇔Fill Selection or Fill Layer and choose Pattern from the Use drop-down menu.**

3. **Click the down-pointing arrow and select a pattern from the Custom Pattern drop-down panel, as shown in Figure 12-14.**

   If you don't see a pattern to your liking, choose another preset library by clicking the panel pop-up menu and choosing another preset library at the bottom of the submenu.

4. **Choose any other fill options you want to apply, such as Mode, Opacity, or Preserve Transparency.**

   Figure 12-14: Fill your selection with one of the many Elements preset patterns.

   For details on these options, see the section "Filling and Outlining Selections," earlier in this chapter.

5. **Click OK to fill the layer or selection with the chosen pattern.**

Creating a new pattern

You may someday want to create your own pattern. Patterns can be easily created from any existing photo or painting you create in Elements. You can even scan your signature or logo, define it as a pattern, and use it with the Pattern Stamp tool to sign all your work.

To create your own pattern, follow these steps:

1. **Open the photographic, painted, or scanned image that contains the area you want to use as a pattern.**

2. **Use the Rectangular Marquee tool to select the area you want to convert into a pattern.**

   Make sure that your Feather option is set to 0 or the pattern command won't be available.

   If you don't make a selection, Elements uses your entire layer as a basis for the pattern.

3. **Choose Edit➪Define Pattern from Selection or Edit➪Define Pattern.**

   The Pattern Name dialog box appears.

4. **Enter a name for your pattern.**

   Your new pattern now appears in every Pattern panel, wherever it may lurk in Elements.

In addition to filling your selection with a pattern, you can stamp on a pattern with the Pattern Stamp tool. For details, see Chapter 9.

Creating Shapes of All Sorts

In this section, we leave the land of pixels and head into uncharted territory — Vectorville. Before we discuss the ins and outs of creating shapes, here's a little overview that explains the difference between pixels and vectors:

- **Pixel images describe a shape in terms of a grid of pixels.** When you increase the size of a pixel-based image, it loses quality and begins to look blocky, mushy, and otherwise nasty. For more details on resizing pixel-based images and the ramifications of doing so, see Chapter 3.

- **Vectors describe a shape mathematically.** The shapes comprise paths made up of lines, curves, and anchor points. Because vector shapes are math-based, you can resize them without any loss of quality whatsoever.

Figure 12-15: Elements images can be vector based (top) or pixel based (bottom).

In Figure 12-15, you can see both types of images.

When you create a shape in Elements, you're creating a vector-based element. Shapes reside on a special kind of layer called, not surprisingly, a *shape layer*. Use shapes to create simple logos, Web buttons, and other small spot illustrations.

Drawing a shape

Elements offers an assortment of shape tools for you to choose from. Follow these steps to draw a shape in your document:

1. **Choose your desired shape tool from the Tools panel.**

   You can also press Shift+U to cycle through the shape tools. All the following tools have associated Geometry options, which are described in the section "Specifying Geometry options," later in this chapter. Here are the available tools:

   - *Rectangle and Ellipse:* As with their Marquee counterparts, you can hold down the Shift key while dragging to produce a square or circle; hold down the Alt (Option on the Mac) key to draw the shape from the center outward.

   - *Rounded Rectangle:* This tool works like the regular Rectangle but with the addition of a radius value used to round off the corners of the rectangle.

   - *Polygon:* This tool creates a polygon or star with a specified number of sides, from 3 to 100.

   - *Line:* This tool draws a line with a width from 1 to 1,000 pixels. You can also add arrowheads at either end.

   - *Custom:* Custom is the most varied shape tool. You have numerous preset custom shapes to choose from. As with any shape, hold down Shift to constrain proportions or the Alt (Option on the Mac) key to draw from the center out.

2. **In the Options bar, click the down-pointing arrow just to the right of the Shape tool icon to specify your Geometry options.**

   For detailed explanations on the various Geometry options, see the upcoming sections.

   If you chose the Custom Shape tool in Step 1, click the down-pointing arrow to access the drop-down Shapes panel and choose your desired shape. You can access more preset shape libraries via the pop-up menu at the top of the panel.

3. **Select your desired color from the Color drop-down panel on the Options bar.**

   Click the More Colors button (the down-pointing arrow) to access the Color Picker for additional color choices.

4. **Select a style from the Style drop-down panel.**

   To jazz up the shape with bevels and other fancy edges, choose a style from the panel. For more on styles, see Chapter 11.

5. Drag in the document to draw the shape you defined.

The shape appears in the image window on its own shape layer. Check out the Layers panel to see this phenomenon. Figure 12-16 shows our shape, a Japanese hairstyle, which we add to in the following section.

Drawing multiple shapes

After you create a shape layer, you can draw additional shapes on that layer. You can add, subtract, overlap, and intersect shapes in exactly the same way you do with selections. (See Chapter 7.) Just follow these steps:

Figure 12-16: Custom shapes run the gamut from the ordinary to the exotic, such as this hairstyle.

1. Select your desired state button on the Options bar.

You can choose from the following options:

- *New Shape Layer:* Creates your initial shape layer.

- *Add to Shape Area:* Combines and joins two or more shapes.

- *Subtract from Shape Area:* Subtracts one shape from another shape.

- *Intersect Shape Areas:* Creates a shape from only the areas that overlap.

- *Exclude Overlapping Shape Areas:* Creates a shape from only the areas that don't overlap.

2. Choose your desired Shape tool and draw the next shape.

We completed the shape by adding the face, as shown in Figure 12-17.

Figure 12-17: Add to your shape layer.

Specifying Geometry options

Geometry options help define how your shapes look. Click the down-pointing arrow on the Options bar to access the Geometry options described in the sections that follow.

Rectangle and Rounded Rectangle Geometry options

Here are the Geometry options for the Rectangle and Rounded Rectangle shapes:

- ✔ **Unconstrained:** Enables you to have free rein to draw a rectangle at any size or shape.

- ✔ **Square:** Constrains the shape to a perfect square.

- ✔ **Fixed Size:** Lets you draw rectangles in fixed sizes, as specified by your width and height values.

- ✔ **Proportional:** Allows you to define a proportion for the rectangle. For example, specifying 2W and 1H makes a rectangle twice as wide as it is high.

- ✔ **From Center:** Enables you to draw from the center out.

- ✔ **Snap to Pixels:** Aligns the shape to the pixels on your screen.

- ✔ **Radius:** For Rounded Rectangles, applies the radius of a circle used to round off the corners. Note that this option is found on the Options bar itself, not in the Geometry options drop-down menu.

Ellipse geometry options

The Ellipse shape has the same options that are available for rectangles, except for the Snap to Pixels option. The only difference is that, instead of being able to create a perfect square, you can create a perfect circle with the Circle option.

Polygon Geometry options

The Geometry options for the Polygon shape are as follows:

- ✔ **Radius:** Enter the radius of a circle used to round off the corners of a polygon when you have the Smooth Corners option selected.

- ✔ **Smooth Corners:** Round off the corners.

- ✔ **Star:** Create an inward-pointing polygon called a star.

- ✔ **Indent Sides By:** Determine the amount that the sides indent inward.

- ✔ **Smooth Indents:** Round off the inner corners of indented sides.

- ✔ **Sides:** Specify the number of sides for your polygon or the number of points for your star.

Line Geometry options

The line's Geometry settings include whether to put arrowheads at the start or end of the line. You can also adjust the width, length, and concavity settings to change the arrowhead shapes.

Custom Shape Geometry options

The Custom Shape options are similar to those you find for the other shapes, but with a couple of unique options:

- **Defined Proportions:** Draws a shape based on the original proportions you used when you created it.

- **Defined Size:** Draws a shape based on its original size when you created it.

Editing shapes

You can edit shapes that you create by using a variety of tools and techniques. Here's a list of the things you can do to modify your shapes:

- **Select:** Choose the Shape Selection tool to move one or more shapes in their layers. This tool shares a flyout menu with the Shapes tools.

- **Move:** Choose the Move tool (press V) to move the entire contents of the shape layer.

- **Delete:** Select a shape with the Shape Selection tool and press Delete to remove it.

- **Transform shapes:** Choose the Shape Selection tool and select your shape. Choose Image⇨Transform Shape and choose your desired transformation.

- **Change the color:** Double-click the thumbnail of the shape layer on the Layers panel. This action transports you to the Color Picker, where you can choose a new color.

- **Clone a shape:** Hold down the Alt (Option on the Mac) key and move the shape with the Move tool.

To convert your vector-based shape into a pixel-based shape, click the Simplify button on the Options bar or choose Layer⇨Simplify Layer. Note that you can't edit a shape after you simplify it, except to modify the pixels. But you can now apply filters to the layer. See Chapter 11 for more on fun with filters.

13

Working with Type

*A*lthough we spout on in this book about how a picture says a thousand words, we would be terribly negligent if we didn't at least give a nod to the power of the written word, as well. You may find that you never need to go near the type tools. That's fine. We won't be offended if you skip right past this chapter.

Then again, you may have an occasional need to add a caption, a headline, or maybe even a short paragraph to an image. Although it's by no means a word-processing or even page-layout program, Elements does give you ample tools for creating, editing, stylizing, and even distorting type.

Understanding Type Basics

Elements has four type tools. Two of them are for entering horizontally oriented type, and two are for entering vertically oriented type. Don't worry about the vertical type tools. Although you can use them, they're really designed for the Asian market, to enter Chinese and Japanese characters. The horizontal and vertical type tools are identical in their attributes, so we just cover the two horizontal type tools from here on, and for the sake of simplicity, we just call them the Type and Type Mask tools:

✔ **Type:** Use this tool to enter type. This type is created on its own type layer, except when used in Bitmap mode or Indexed Color mode, neither of which supports layers.

 We refer to layers a lot in this chapter, so if your layer knowledge is rusty, check out Chapter 8.

 ✔ **Type Mask:** This tool doesn't create actual type; instead, it creates a selection border in the shape of the type you want to enter. The selection border is added to the active layer. You can do anything with a type selection that you can do with any other selection.

 We also talk more about selections in this chapter; for even more detail on selections, see Chapter 7.

You can enter text in Elements in two different modes: point type and paragraph type. Both the Type and Type Mask tools can enter either one. Here's a brief description of each one (for the step-by-step process of creating the text, see the following sections):

 ✔ **Point:** Use this mode if you want to enter only a few words or so. To create point type, select the Type tool, click in your image, and, well, type. The text appears while you type and continues to grow. In fact, it even continues past the boundary of your image!

 Remember that point type *never* wraps around to a new line. To wrap to the next line, you must press Enter (Return on a Mac).

 ✔ **Paragraph:** Use this mode to enter longer chunks (or constrained blocks) of text on an image. To create paragraph type, click and drag your type tool to create a text bounding box, and then type. All the text is entered in this resizable bounding box. If a line of text is too long, Elements automatically wraps it around to the next line.

Elements is capable of displaying and printing type in two different formats. Each format has its pros and cons, and which format you use depends on your needs. Here's the lowdown on each one:

 ✔ **Vector:** All text in Elements is initially created as vector type. *Vector* type provides scalable outlines that you can resize without producing jaggy edges in the diagonal strokes. Vector type remains fully editable and always prints with optimum quality, appearing crisp and clean. Vector type is the default type format in Elements.

 ✔ **Raster:** When Elements converts vector type into pixels, the text is *rasterized.* Elements refers to this rasterization process as simplifying. When text is *simplified,* it's no longer editable as text but is converted into a raster image. You usually simplify your vector type when you want to apply filters to the type to produce a special effect or when you want to merge the type with the image. You can't resize simplified type without losing some quality or risking jagged edges. For more details, see the section, "Simplifying Type," later in this chapter.

Creating Point Type

The majority of your type entry will most likely be in point type mode. Point type is useful for short chunks of text, such as headlines, labels, logos, and headings for Web pages.

Point type is so called because it contains a single *anchor point,* which marks the starting point of the line of the type. Remember that point-type lines don't wrap automatically, as shown in Figure 13-1.

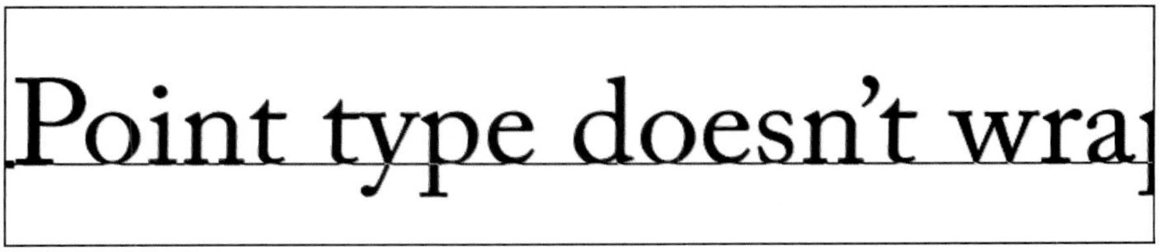

Point type doesn't wra|

Figure 13-1: Point type doesn't wrap automatically, but instead can run off your image into a type Neverland.

Follow these steps to create point type:

1. **Open the Editor and choose Edit Full mode.**

2. **Open an image or create a new, blank Elements file (File⇨New).**

3. **Select the Type tool from the Tools panel.**

   You can also press the T key.

4. **On the image, click where you want to insert your text.**

   Your cursor is called an *I-beam.* When you click, you make an insertion point.

   A small, horizontal line about one-third of the way up the I-beam shows the *baseline* (the line on which the text sits) for horizontal type.

5. **Specify your type options from the Options bar.**

   All the options are described in detail in the section, "Specifying Type Options," later in this chapter.

6. **Type your text and press Enter (Return on a Mac) to begin a new line.**

   When you press Enter (or Return), you insert a hard return that doesn't move.

7. **When you finish entering the text, click the Commit button (the check mark icon) on the Options bar.**

   You can also commit the type by pressing Enter on the numeric keypad or by clicking any other tool on the Tools panel. A new type layer with your text is created. Type layers appear on your Layers panel and are indicated by the T icon.

Creating Paragraph Type

If you have larger chunks of text, it's usually more practical to enter the text as paragraph type. Entering paragraph type is similar to entering text in a word-processing or page-layout program, except that text is contained inside a bounding box. When you type and come to the end of the bounding box, Elements automatically wraps the text to the next line.

To enter paragraph type, follow these steps:

1. **Open the Editor and choose Edit Full mode.**

2. **Open an image or create a new, blank Elements file.**

3. **Select the Type tool from the Tools panel or press the T key.**

4. **On the image, insert and size the bounding box by using one of two methods:**

   • *Drag to create a bounding box close to your desired size.* After you release the mouse button, you can drag any of the handles at the corners and sides of the box to resize the box.

   • *Hold down the Alt (Option on the Mac) key and click the image.* The Paragraph Text Size dialog box appears. Enter the exact dimensions of your desired bounding box. When you click OK, your specified box appears, complete with handles for resizing later.

5. **Specify your type options from the Options bar.**

   Options are described in detail in the following section.

6. **Enter your text; to start a new paragraph, press Enter (Return on a Mac).**

   Each line wraps around to fit inside the bounding box, as shown in Figure 13-2.

   If you type more text than can squeeze into the text box, an overflow icon appears. Just resize the text box by dragging a bounding box handle.

7. **Click the Commit button (the check mark icon) on the Options bar or press Enter on the numeric keypad.**

   Elements creates a new type layer.

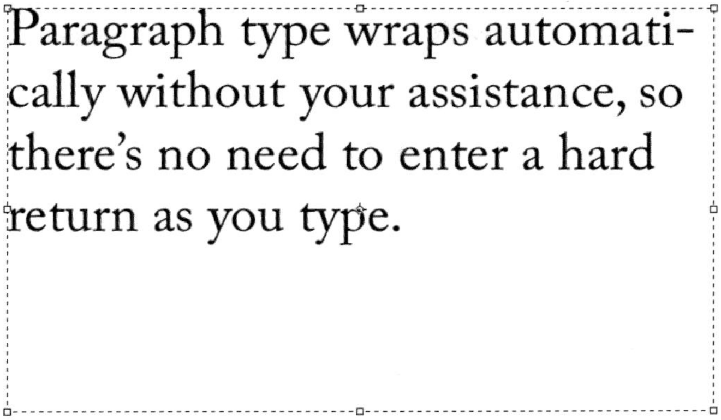

Paragraph type wraps automatically without your assistance, so
there's no need to enter a hard
return as you type.

Figure 13-2: Paragraph type automatically wraps to fit within your
bounding box.

Specifying Type Options

You can find several character and paragraph type settings on the Options
bar, as shown in Figure 13-3. These options enable you to specify your type
to your liking and pair it with your images.

Figure 13-3: Specify your type options, such as font family and size,
before you type.

Here's an explanation of each available option on the Options bar, from left
to right:

✔ **Font Family:** Select the font you want from the drop-down menu.
   Elements provides a WYSIWYG (What You See Is What You Get) font
   menu. After each font name, the word *Sample* is rendered in the actual
   font — no more selecting a font without knowing what it really looks
   like. You also find one of these abbreviations before each font name to
   let you know what type of font it is:

   • *a:* Adobe Type 1 (PostScript) fonts

   • *TT:* TrueType fonts

   • *O:* OpenType fonts

   Fonts with no abbreviation are bitmapped fonts.

- **Font Style:** Some font families have additional styles, such as light or condensed. Only the styles available for a particular font appear in the list. This is also a WYSIWYG menu.

- **Font Size:** Select your type size from the drop-down list or just type a size in the text box. Note that type size is most commonly measured in points (72 points equals about 1 inch at a resolution of 72 ppi). You can switch to millimeters or pixels by choosing Edit⇨Preferences⇨Units and Rulers (or on the Mac, Photoshop Elements⇨Preferences⇨Units and Rulers).

- **Anti-Aliased:** Select Anti-Aliased to slightly smooth out the edges of your text. Anti-aliasing softens that edge by 1 pixel, as shown in Figure 13-4. For the most part, you want to keep this option turned on. The one occasion in which you may want it turned off is when you're creating small type to be displayed onscreen, such as on Web pages. The soft edges can sometimes be tough to read.

- **Faux Bold:** Use this option to create a fake bold style when a real bold style (which you'd choose under Font Style) doesn't exist. Be warned that although the sky won't fall, applying faux styles can distort the proportions of a font. You should use fonts with real styles, and if they don't exist, oh well.

- **Faux Italic:** This option creates a phony oblique style and carries the same warning as the Faux Bold option.

Figure 13-4: Anti-aliasing softens the edges of your type.

- **Underline:** This setting obviously underlines your type, like <u>this</u>.

- **Strikethrough:** Choose this option to apply a ~~strikethrough~~ style to your text.

- **Text Alignment:** These three options align your horizontal text on the left or right, or in the center. If you happen to have vertical text, these options rotate 90 degrees clockwise and change into top, bottom, and center vertical settings.

- **Leading:** Leading (pronounced *LED-ing*) is the amount of space between the baselines of lines of type. A *baseline* is the imaginary line on which a line of type sits. You can choose Auto Leading or specify the amount of leading to apply. When you choose Auto Leading, Elements uses a value of 120 percent of your type point size. Therefore, 10-point type gets 12 points of leading. Elements adds that extra 20 percent so that the bottoms of the lowest letters don't crash into the tops of the tallest letters on the line below them.

- **Text Color:** Click the color swatch to select a color for your type from the Color Picker. You can also choose a color from the Swatches panel.

- **Style:** Click this option to access a drop-down panel of preset styles that you can apply to your type. For more on this option and the Create Warped Text option (described in the following bullet), see "Stylizing and Warping Type," later in this chapter.

- **Create Warped Text:** This fun option lets you distort type in more than a dozen ways.

- **Change the Text Orientation:** Select your type layer and then click this option to switch between vertical and horizontal type orientations.

- **Cancel:** Click this button (or press Esc) to cancel and keep the type from being entered. Use this option or the Commit option only after you click the Type tool on your canvas.

- **Commit:** Click this button to apply the type to your canvas.

Editing Text

Remember that you can apply type settings either before or after you enter your text. To correct typos, add and delete type, or change any of the type options, simply follow these steps:

1. **Select the Type tool from the Tools panel.**

2. **Select your desired type layer on the Layers panel or click within the text to automatically select the type layer.**

3. **Do one of the following:**

- *To change the font family, size, color, or other type option:* If you want to change all the text, simply select that type layer on the Layers panel. To select only portions of the text, highlight the text by dragging across it with the I-beam of the Type tool.

- *To delete text:* Highlight the text by dragging across it with the I-beam of the Type tool. Then press the Backspace key (Delete on the Mac).

- *To add text:* Make an insertion point by clicking your I-beam within the line of text. Then, type your new text.

4. **When you're done editing your text, click the Commit button.**

You may also occasionally need to transform your text. To do so, make sure that the type layer is selected on the Layers panel. Then, choose Image⇨Transform⇨Free Transform. Grab a handle on the bounding box and drag to rotate or scale. Press Ctrl (⌘ on the Mac) and drag a handle to distort. When you're done, double-click inside the bounding box to commit the transformation. For more details on transformations, see Chapter 9.

Simplifying Type

As we explain in the section, "Understanding Type Basics," earlier in this chapter, Elements can display and print type in two different formats: vector and raster. Remember that as long as you keep type in a vector format in a type layer, you can edit and resize that type all day long.

Occasionally, however, you may find the need to *simplify* your type — to convert your type into pixels. After it's simplified, you can apply filters, paint on the type, and apply gradients and patterns. If you're working with layers and *flatten* your image (merge your layers into a single background image), your type layer is also simplified and merged with the other pixels in your image. By the way, if you try to apply a filter to a type layer, Elements barks at you that the type layer must be simplified before proceeding and gives you the opportunity to click OK (if you want to simplify) or Cancel.

To simplify your type, select the type layer on the Layers panel and choose Layer⇨Simplify Layer. Your type layer is then converted (the T icon disappears) into a regular layer on which your type is now displayed as pixels against a transparent background, as shown in Figure 13-5.

To avoid re-creating your type from scratch, make all necessary edits before simplifying. This includes sizing your text. After you simplify your type, you can't resize your text without risking the dreaded jaggies. The other downside to remember about simplified type is that although it looks identical to vector type onscreen, it never prints as crisply and cleanly as vector type. Even at higher-resolution settings, a slight jagged edge always appears on simplified type. So, if you're experimenting with painting or filters on your type, just make a duplicate of your type layer before simplifying it and then hide that layer.

Masking with Type

Using the Type Mask tool epitomizes the combination of type and image. Unlike its conventional cousin, the Type Mask tool doesn't create a new layer. Instead, it creates a selection on the active layer. This is the tool of choice for filling text with an image or cutting text out of an image so that the background shows through, as shown in Figure 13-6.

Vector type

Simplified rastor type

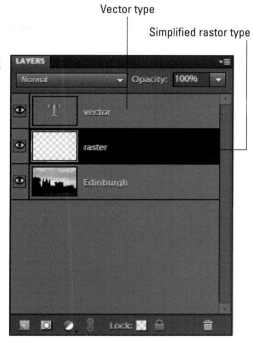

Figure 13-5: Simplifying your type layer converts vector type into pixels.

A selection is a selection, no matter how it was created. So, even though they look like letters, they act like selections. You can move, modify, and save them.

Here are the steps to create a type mask:

1. **In Edit Full mode, open the image of your choice.**

   We selected a stone texture.

2. **Convert your background into a layer by double-clicking the word *Background* on the Layers panel; and then click OK.**

   This step enables you to jazz up the type with styles later on.

3. **Choose the Horizontal Type Mask tool from the Tools panel.**

4. **Specify your type options (such as font family, style, and size) on the Options bar.**

5. **Click the image and type your desired text. When you're done, click the Commit button on the Options bar.**

   A selection border in the shape of your type appears on your image.

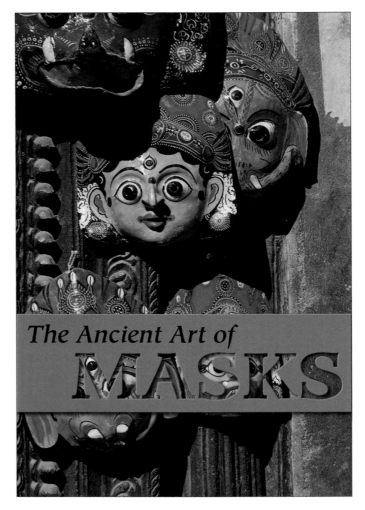

Corbis Digital Stock

Figure 13-6: The Type Mask tool enables you to cut type out of solid color or image layers.

6. **Choose Select↪Inverse, which deselects your letter selections and selects everything else.**

7. **Press the Backspace (Delete on a Mac) key to delete everything outside your selection border.**

Your type is now filled with your image.

8. **Choose Select➪Deselect.**

9. **Experiment with applying layer styles to your type.**

   If the Effects panel isn't visible, choose Window➪Effects. Select the Layer Styles button (second from the left) located in the Effects panel. Select the type of Layer Styles you desire from the drop-down menu on the panel, such as Drop Shadows or Bevels. Finally, double-click the exact style you want. We used a drop shadow and an inner bevel in Figure 13-7. See Chapter 11 for more about layer styles.

CHISELED IN STONE

Corbis Digital Stock

Figure 13-7: Fill type with imagery by using the Type Mask tool.

If you want to admire your type against a solid background, as we did, create a new layer and then choose Edit➪Fill Layer and choose your desired color from the Use drop-down menu.

Stylizing and Warping Type

If you've tried your hand at creating a type mask, you know that Elements is capable of much more than just throwing a few black letters at the bottom of your image. With a few clicks here and there, you can warp, distort, enhance, and stylize your type. If you're not careful, your creative typography can outshine your image.

Adjusting type opacity

If you checked out Chapter 8 before reading this chapter, you know that *layers* are a digital version of the old analog transparency sheets. You can change element opacity on layers to let the underlying layer show through in varying degrees. This is also possible on a type layer. Peek at Figure 13-8 to see how varying the percentage of opacity of our type layer makes more of the underlying layer (of water) show through.

To change the opacity of a type layer, simply select the layer on the Layers panel, click the arrow to the right of the Opacity percentage, and drag the slider. The lower the percentage, the less opaque the type (and the more the underlying layer shows through).

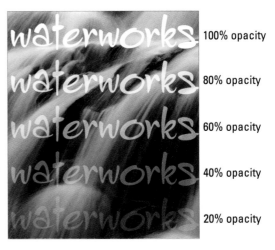

100% opacity

80% opacity

60% opacity

40% opacity

20% opacity

Corbis Digital Stock

Figure 13-8: You can vary the opacity of type layers to allow the underlying layer to peek through.

Applying filters to your type

One of the most interesting things you can do with type in Elements that you can't do in a word-processing or page-layout program is apply special effects, such as filters. You can make type look like it's on fire, underwater, or on the move, as shown in Figure 13-9, where we applied a motion blur.

Corbis Digital Stock

Figure 13-9: Applying a motion blur to type can make it appear as fast as the car.

The only caveat is that type has to be simplified first before a filter can be applied. Be sure to do all your text editing before you get to the filtering stage.

Applying the filter is as easy as selecting the simplified type layer on the Layers panel and choosing a filter from the Filter menu. For more on filters, see Chapter 11.

Painting your type with color and gradients

Changing the color of text is as easy as highlighting it and selecting a color from the Color Picker. But what if you want to do something a little less conventional, such as apply random brush strokes of paint across the type, like we did in the top image shown in Figure 13-10? It's really easier than it looks. Again, as with applying filters to text, the only criterion is that the type has to be simplified first. After that's done, select a color, grab the Brush tool with settings of your choice, and paint. In our example, we used the Granite Flow brush, found in the Special Effect Brushes presets. We used a diameter of 39, 15, and 6 pixels and just swiped our type a few times.

If you want the color or gradient to be confined to the type area, select the text by either Ctrl-clicking (⌘-clicking on a Mac) the layer containing the text or locking the layer's transparency on the Layers panel.

You can also apply a gradient to your type. Here are the steps to follow after simplifying your type:

1. **Select the Gradient tool from the Tools panel.**

2. **On the Options bar, click the down-pointing arrow next to the Gradient Picker to access the Gradient Picker drop-down panel.**

3. **Choose your desired gradient.**

   If you want to create a custom gradient, find out how in Chapter 12.

4. **Position your gradient cursor on the text where you want your gradient to start; drag to where you want your gradient to end.**

   Don't like the results? Drag again until you get the look you want. Remember that you can drag at any angle and to any length, even outside your type. In the bottom image shown in Figure 13-10, we used the copper

Figure 13-10: Bring your type to life with color (top) or a gradient (bottom).

gradient and just dragged from the top of the letters to the bottom. We also locked the transparent pixels on the layer to confine the gradient to just the type area.

Warping your type

If horizontal or vertical text is just way too regimented for you, try the Warp feature. The best part about the distortions you apply is that the text remains fully editable. This feature is fun and easy to use. Click the Create Warped Text button at the far-right end of the Options bar. (It's the T with a curved line below it.) This action opens the Warp Text dialog box, where you find a vast array of distortions on the Style pop-up menu with descriptive names such as Bulge, Inflate, and Squeeze.

After selecting a warp style, you can adjust the orientation, amount of bend, and degree of distortion by dragging the sliders. The Bend setting affects the amount of warp, and the Horizontal and Vertical Distortions apply perspective to that warp. Luckily, you can also view the results while you adjust. We could give you technical explanations of these adjustments, but the best way to see what they do is to just play with them. See Figure 13-11 to get a quick look at a few of the warp styles. The names speak for themselves.

You can also use the Transform command, such as scale and skew, to manipulate text. See Chapter 8 for details on transforming.

Figure 13-11: Text remains fully editable after applying distortions with the Warp command.

Part V
Printing, Creating, and Sharing

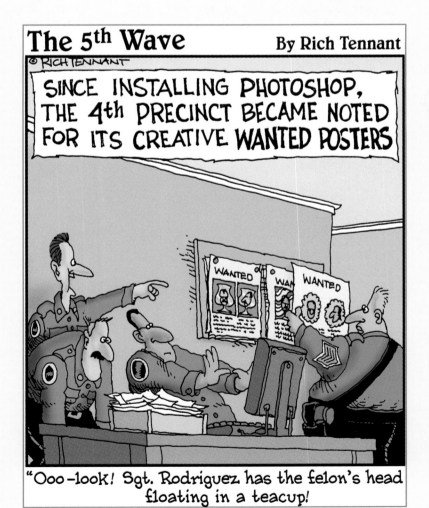

In this part . . .

The focus of this part is photo output and deployment. As is the case with so many other editing features, you have an abundance of opportunities for outputting your files. Beginning with the most familiar method, which is simply printing to your desktop color printer, we talk about how to get the best results on your printed images. We start with printing to your personal desktop printer and then cover issues related to submitting photos to commercial photo labs and service centers.

In addition to printing, you have a number of different options for sharing images, and they're all covered in the final chapters, where you can find out about slide shows and video discs, and about Web hosting, e-mailing, and sharing via online services. The opportunities are enormous, and you may want to look over all that Photoshop Elements has to offer related to photo output and file sharing.

14

Getting It on Paper

*P*erhaps the greatest challenge to individuals using programs like Photoshop Elements (and even the professionals who use its grand-daddy, Adobe Photoshop) is getting what you see on your monitor to render a reasonable facsimile on a printed page. You can find all sorts of books on color printing — how to get color right, how to calibrate your equipment, and how to create and use color profiles — all for the purpose of getting a good match between your computer monitor, your printer, and the paper used to print your output. It's downright discouraging to spend a lot of time tweaking an image so that all the brilliant blue colors jump out on your computer monitor, only to find that all those blues turn to murky purples when the photo is printed.

If you read Chapters 2 and 3, you're ahead of the game because you know a little bit about color management, color profiles, and printer resolutions. After you check out those chapters, your next step is to get to know your printer and understand how to correctly print your pictures.

In this chapter, we talk about options — many options — for setting print attributes for printing to your own color printer. If you need to, reread this chapter a few times just to be certain that you understand the process for printing good-quality images. A little time spent here will, we hope, save you some headaches down the road.

Getting Pictures Ready for Printing

The first step toward getting your photos to your desktop printer is to prepare each image for optimum output. You have several considerations when you're preparing files, including the ones in this list:

- **Set resolution and size.** See your printer's documentation for recommendations for resolution. As a general rule, 200–300 ppi (pixels per inch) works best for most printers printing on high-quality paper. If you print on plain paper, you often find that lower resolutions work just as well or even better. Chapter 3 explains setting size and resolution in detail.

- **Make all brightness and color corrections before printing.** Make sure that your pictures appear their best before sending them off to your printer. If you have your monitor properly calibrated, as we discuss in Chapter 2, you should see a fair representation of what your pictures will look like before you print them. Chapters 9 and 10 cover corrections.

- **Decide how color will be managed before you print.** You can color-manage output to your printer in three ways, as we discuss in the next section. Know your printer's profiles and how to use them before you start to print your files.

- **Get your printer ready.** Finally, when printing to desktop color printers always be certain your ink cartridges have ink and the nozzles are clean. Make sure you use the proper settings for paper and ink when you send a file to your printer. Be sure to review the manual that came with your printer to become aware of how to perform all the steps required to make a quality print.

Working with Color Printer Profiles

In Chapter 2, we talk about creating color profiles for your monitor and selecting a color workspace. The final leg in a color-managed workflow is to convert color from your color workspace profile to your printer's color profile. Basically, this conversion means that the colors you see on your monitor in your current workspace are accurately converted to the color that can be reproduced by your printer. To print accurate color, you need to have a color profile designed for your printer and the paper you use installed on your computer.

You can manage color in Photoshop Elements in three ways when it comes time to print your files:

✔ **Printer Manages Colors:** This method permits your printer to decide which profile is used when your photo is printed to your desktop color printer. Your printer makes this decision according to the paper you select. If you choose Epson Premium Glossy Photo Paper, for example, your printer chooses the profile that goes along with that particular paper. If you choose another paper, your printer chooses a different color profile. This method is all automatic, and color profile selection is made when you print your file.

✔ **Photoshop Elements Manages Color:** When you make this choice, color management is taken out of the hands of your printer and is controlled by Elements. You must choose a color profile after making this choice. If color profiles are installed by your printer, you can choose a color profile from the list of profiles that match your printer and the paper source.

✔ **No Color Management:** You use this choice if you have a color profile embedded in one of your pictures. You'll probably rarely use this option. Unless you know how to embed profiles or receive files with embedded profiles from other users, don't make this choice in the Print dialog box. Because very few Elements users work with files with embedded profiles, we skip coverage on this method of printing your files.

Each of these three options requires you to decide how color is managed. You make choices (as we discuss later in this chapter, when we walk you through the steps for printing) about whether to color-manage your output. These selections are unique to the Print dialog box and more specifically in the More Options dialog box for your individual printer.

Color profiles are also dependent upon the ink being used, and refilling cartridges with generic ink can (in some cases) result in colors shifting. Similarly, if the nozzles aren't clean and delivering ink inconsistently, you may see very strange results.

Printing a photo with the printer managing color

For the following example, we use an Epson printer. If you have a different printer, some of the dialog boxes and terms may appear different. With a little careful examination of the printer driver dialog box, you should be able to apply the following steps for any printer:

1. **Choose File⊅Print with a photo open in Edit Full mode.**

   The Print dialog box that opens contains all the settings you need to print a file as shownin Figure 14-1.

2. **Click Page Setup at the bottom of the Print dialog box and select the orientation of your print. Click OK.**

   Your choices are either Portrait or Landscape. After you click OK, you're returned to the Print dialog box.

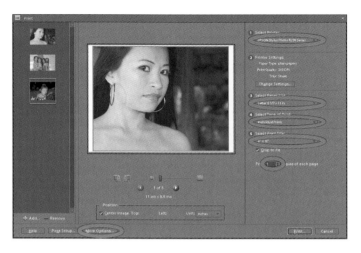

Figure 14-1: Choose File↵Print or press Ctrl+P (⌘+P on the Macintosh).

3. **Choose your printer from the Printer menu.**

4. **Set the print attributes.**

   Select the paper size, type of print, print size, and number of copies you want. (Note the items shown in Figure 14-1.)

5. **Click More Options and choose Color Management in the More Options dialog box.**

   In the Color Management area, shown in Figure 14-2, choose how to manage color when you print files.

6. **From the Color Handling drop-down menu, select Printer Manages Color. Click OK.**

   This choice uses your current workspace color — either sRGB or Adobe RGB (1998) — and later converts the color from your workspace to the printer output file when you open the printer driver dialog box.

7. **Set the printer preferences.**

   • *In Windows,* click Printer Preferences in the More

Figure 14-2: Look over the Color Management area in the More Options dialog box for options on how to manage color.

Options dialog box. The printing preferences dialog box for your printer driver opens as shown in Figure 14-3. Proceed to Step 8. Note that you can also click OK in the More Options dialog box and click Change Settings (item 2 in the right panel of the Print dialog box) to open the same printer preferences dialog box.

Figure 14-3: Click Preferences in the first dialog box that opens, and the selected printer preferences opens.

- *On the Macintosh*, you don't have a Printer Preferences button in the More Options dialog box and there is no button for Change Settings in the Print dialog box. Just set the color settings in the More Options dialog box and click OK, then click Print. The Macintosh OSX System Print dialog box opens. You need to make two choices here. Open the pop-up menu below the Pages item in the Print dialog box and choose Print Settings as shown in Figure 14-4.

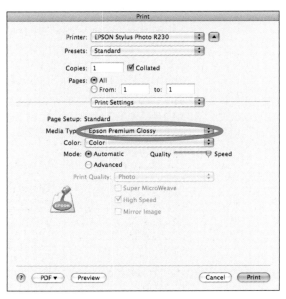

Figure 14-4: Choose Print Settings on the Macintosh and make a choice for the paper you use for the output.

From the Media Type pop-up menu, choose the paper for your output.

The second choice Macintosh users need to make is the selection for Color Management. Open the Print Settings pop-up menu and choose Color Management

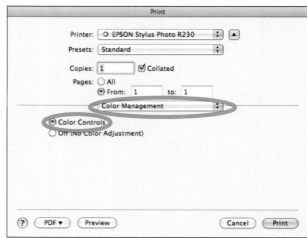

Figure 14-5: Choose Color Management and make sure Color Controls is selected.

as shown in Figure 14-5. Leave the default setting at Color Controls; this setting is used when the printer manages color. Click Print.

8. **Set print attributes (Windows).**

In our Epson example, select a paper type such as Epson Premium Glossy (or another paper from the Type drop-down list that you may be using; refer to Figure 14-3.) and then click the Best Photo radio button.

Now, it's time to color-manage your file. This step is critical in your print-production workflow.

9. **Click the Advanced button and then, in the Warning dialog box that appears, simply click Continue (Windows).**

The printing preferences dialog box opens, displaying advanced settings, as shown in Figure 14-6.

10. **Make your choices in the advanced printing preferences dialog box (Windows).**

Here are the most important choices:

- *Select a paper type.* You selected paper already? The second drop-down menu in the Paper & Quality section of the dialog box determines the application of inks. Choose the same paper here as you did in Step 8.

- *Turn on color management.* Because you're letting the printer driver determine the color, you need to be certain that the Color Controls radio button is active. This setting tells the printer driver to automatically select a printer profile for the paper type you selected.

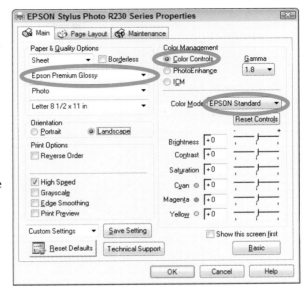

Figure 14-6: Click Advanced and then click Continue to access the advanced settings in the Epson printer driver.

- *Set the color mode.* Don't use Epson Vivid. This choice produces inferior results on photos. Choose Best Photo, the Epson Standard, or Adobe RGB, depending on your printer.

If you frequently print files using the same settings, you can save your settings by clicking the Save Setting button.

11. **To print the photo, click OK and then OK again in the Print dialog box (Windows).**

    Your file is sent to your printer. The color is converted automatically from your source workspace of sRGB or Adobe RGB (1998) to the profile the printer driver automatically selects for you.

Printing a photo with Elements managing color

Another method for managing color when you're printing files is to select a printer profile from the available list of color profiles installed with your printer. Whereas in the preceding section, you used your printer to manage color, this time you let Photoshop Elements manage the color.

The steps in this section are the same as the ones described in the preceding section for printing files for automatic profile selection when you're setting up the page and selecting a printer. Choosing File➪Print opens the Elements Print dialog box. To let Elements handle the color conversion, follow these steps in the Print dialog box:

1. **Choose File➪Print. Click More Options to open the More Options dialog box. Click Color Management in the left pane to display the color management options.**

2. **From the Printer Profile drop-down menu, select the color profile designed for use with the paper you've chosen.**

   In this example, we use a profile designed for a specific printer, as shown in Figure 14-7. (Note that custom color profiles you acquire from a profiling service come with recommended color-rendering intents. For this paper, Relative Colorimetric is recommended and is selected on the Rendering Intent drop-down menu, as you can see in Figure 14-7.)

Figure 14-7: Choose a printer profile that matches the paper you use.

3. **Click Print.**

   The second Print dialog box opens.

4. **Click the Properties button.**

   You arrive at the same dialog box shown in Figure 14-3. On the Macintosh you arrive at the same dialog box shown in Figure 14-4.

5. **Click the Best Photo radio button. From the Type drop-down list, select the recommended paper choice. On the Macintosh you make your paper choice as shown in Figure 14-4.**

   Custom color profiles are also shipped with guidelines for selecting proper paper.

6. **Click Advanced and click Continue to arrive at the same dialog box shown earlier in Figure 14-6. On the Macintosh you choose Color Management from the pop-up menu to arrive at the same dialog box shown in Figure 14-5.**

   The paper choice selection is automatically carried over from the previous Properties dialog box; see Step 2 in the preceding section. The one setting you change is in the Color Management section.

7. **Click the ICM (Image Color Management) radio button and check Off (No Color Adjustment), as shown in Figure 14-8. On the Macintosh, click the Off (No Color Adjustment) radio button. Refer to Figure 14-5.**

Because you selected the color profile in Step 1 and you're letting Elements manage the color, be sure the Color Management feature is turned off. If you don't turn off Color Management, you end up double-profiling your print.

Figure 14-8: Click ICM and choose Off (No Color Adjustment).

 Deciding to manage color or not manage color is simplified in Photoshop Elements. In the Color Management area of the dialog box, a message is reported each time you make a selection from the Color Handling drop-down menu. Right below Rendering Intent, you see a message asking if you remembered to turn color management on or off. Each time you make a selection for the color handling, pause a moment and read the message (shown in Figure 14-7). This is your reminder that you need to follow the recommendation to properly handle color.

Each time you print a file — whether it be a single photo, a contact sheet, a photo package, or other type of print — you use the same steps for color management. In the next section we talk about a number of options you have for printing photos, but remember that you need to manage the color for each type of print you want.

Various sources offer alternatives for purchasing inks. You can purchase third-party inks for your printer, use refillable ink cartridges, or have your printer modified to hold large ink tanks that last much longer than the manufacturer-supplied cartridges. These alternatives provide you with much savings when purchasing inks.

 However, using any inks other than manufacturer recommended inks can produce color problems. Each developer provides printer profiles specific for their recommended inks. With third-party inks you don't have the advantage of using color profiles that have been tested by a printer manufacturer.

If getting the most accurate color on your prints is important to you, use only those inks recommended by your printer manufacturer.

Setting Print Options

You print files from Elements using the File➪Print command. Depending on what workspace you have open, you can set print options in the Print dialog box from the Organizer or from within Edit Full mode. The different modes provide you with some different options, so we want to look at printing from both the Organizer and Edit Full mode.

Printing from the Organizer

You can select one or more images in the Organizer and then choose File➪Print. The images selected when you choose the Print command appear in a scrollable list, as shown in Figure 14-9 (Windows). On the Macintosh when you choose File➪Print in the Organizer, you are switched to the Elements editor, where the Print dialog box opens. Options you have in the Print Photos dialog box (Windows) or Print dialog (Mac) include:

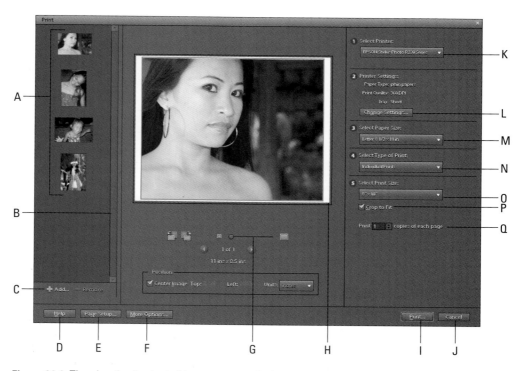

Figure 14-9: Thumbnails of selected images appear in the Print Photos dialog box.

A. **Image Thumbnails:** When you select multiple images in the Organizer, all the selected images appear in a scrollable window on the left side of the dialog box.

B. **Scroll bar:** When so many photos are selected that they all cannot be viewed in the thumbnail list on the left side of the dialog box, you can use the scroll bar to see all images.

C. **Add/Remove:** If the Print Photos dialog box is open and you want to add more photos to print, click the Add (+) icon and the Add Photos dialog box opens. A list of thumbnails appears, showing all photos in the current open catalog. Check the check boxes adjacent to the thumbnails to indicate the photos you want to add to your print queue. You can also choose an entire catalog, albums, photos marked with keyword tags, and photos having a rating.

If you want to remove a photo from the list to be printed, click the photo in the scrollable list in the Print Photos dialog box and click the Remove (-) icon.

D. **Help:** Click the Help button to open help information pertaining to printing photos.

E. **Page Setup:** Click this button to open the Page Setup dialog box. (Refer to Figure 14-1.)

F. **More Options:** Click More Options to open another dialog box where additional options are chosen. (See the section "Using More Options" later in this chapter.)

G. **Scroll Print Preview:** Click the arrows to go through a print preview for all images in the list.

H. **Print Preview:** This image displays a preview of the image to be printed.

I. **Print:** Click Print after making all adjustments in the Print Photos dialog box.

J. **Cancel:** Clicking Cancel dismisses the dialog box without sending a photo to the printer.

K. **Select Printer:** Choose a target printer from the drop-down list.

L. **Printer Settings (Windows only):** Click this button to open properties unique to the selected printer.

M. **Select Paper Size:** Choose from print sizes that your printer supports. This list may change when you choose a different printer from the Select Printer drop-down menu.

N. **Select Type of Prints:** You have three options available — Print Individual Prints, Contact Sheets, or Picture Packages on Windows. On the Macintosh, these options are found as separate menu commands in the File menu in Edit Full mode. For more information on Contact Sheets and Picture Packages, see the section "Exploring Other Print Options," later in this chapter.

O. Select Print Size: Select from the print size options that your printer supports.

P. Crop to Fit: Check this box to crop an image to fit the selected paper size.

Q. Print ___ Copies of Each Page: By default, One Photo Per Page is selected. Remove the check mark and on the same page you can choose a number of prints from the drop-down menu.

Using Page Setup

When you click the Page Setup button in the Print Photos dialog box, the Page Setup dialog box opens; refer to Figure 14-1. In this dialog box, you can select print attributes that may be unique to your printer. However, you can control the options for most desktop printers in the Print Photos dialog box.

Using More Options

When printing photos from the Organizer, click the More Options button in the Print Photos dialog box. The More Options dialog box opens; refer to Figure 14-2.

If you've used Photoshop Elements prior to version 8, notice that the More Options dialog box has changed. As shown in Figure 14-2, you have three categories listed in the left pane. The three items are as follows:

- **Printing Choices:** Similar to what was available in earlier versions of Elements
- **Custom Print Size:** Various settings for the output size
- **Color Management:** Handles color profile selection and color management options

These three items have been moved from the Print dialog box to the More Options dialog box.

When you want to manage color in Elements, as we explain earlier in the section "Working with Color Printer Profiles," you need to open the More Options dialog box.

The default selection is Printing Choices when you open the More Options dialog box. Choices available for printing your photos include

- **Photo Details:** Check the check boxes for the detail items you want printed as labels on your output.
- **Layout:** If you want one photo printed per page, check this box.

- **Flip Image:** This option is used for heat transfer material: Mylar, Lexjet, and other substrates that require *E-down* printing — emulsion-down printing, where the negative and the image are flipped.

- **Border:** Check Add a Border, and you can specify the size and choose a unit of measure in the drop-down list. Click the color swatch to choose a color for the border. Check Include Trim Guideline to print guides for trimming the paper.

- **Print Crop Marks:** Check this box to print crop marks.

Printing from Edit Full mode

If you want to print a photo while in Edit Full mode, choose File⇨Print and the Print dialog box opens. The Print dialog box in Edit Full mode in Elements is identical to the Print dialog box you use when printing from the Organizer.

Exploring Other Print Options

The basic principles of color management are used each time you send a file to your printer. Up to this point, we talk about printing a single photo. Elements provides you with a variety of other choices for printing files without borders, as well as a number of choices for printing photos with decorative frames, picture packages, and contact sheets.

You have choices in the Organizer or Edit Full mode for printing multiple images as either a contact sheet or picture package. From within Edit Full mode, when you choose to print a contact sheet or picture package, Elements switches you to the Organizer view. You then proceed in the Organizer and leave Edit Full mode.

Printing contact sheets

Professional photographers use contact sheets to organize photos and to preview the images before ordering final prints. If you have several shots of a single subject, you may want to see a hard copy of the photos before printing full sizes. Additionally, you can print contact sheets to keep albums of thumbnail images organized in a book without having to preview images in the Organizer.

To print a contact sheet, do the following:

1. **Open the Organizer.**

2. **In the Organizer, select photos you want to print on a contact sheet.**

   Ctrl-click (⌘-click on the Macintosh) to choose multiple photos in a noncontiguous selection. You can also sort photos by keyword tags, albums, dates, and so on. You then select all the sorted photos by pressing Ctrl+A (⌘+A). For more information on sorting files, see Chapter 5. For more information on creating albums and using keyword tags, see Chapter 6.

3. **Choose File➪Print or press Ctrl+P (⌘+P on the Macintosh).**

   The Print Photos dialog box opens. In the dialog box select the printer you want to use from the Select Printer drop-down menu.

4. **Choose Contact Sheet from the Select Type of Print drop-down menu.**

   The Prints dialog box refreshes to show your contact sheet options, as shown in Figure 14-10.

5. **Select a layout.**

   Choose the number of columns you want for the contact sheet. If you specify fewer columns, the images appear larger; as more columns are selected, the images appear smaller. Choose a size according to the number of columns that you want to print.

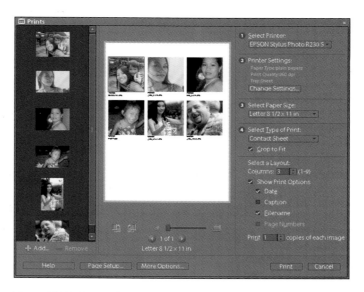

Figure 14-10: Choose Contact Sheet and select a layout for the number of columns.

6. **Check the boxes for the items you want included in the captions.**

   If you want print options to be shown on your prints, check the Show Print Options check box, and the list of options are displayed below the check box. Caption items can include the date, a text line for the caption, filename, and page numbers.

7. **Click More Options in the bottom left of the dialog box.**

8. **Choose a color profile from the Print Space drop-down menu.**

   For more on printing with color profiles, see the section "Working with Color Printer Profiles" earlier in this chapter.

9. **Click OK in the More Options dialog box.**

10. **Click Print (back in the Print Photos dialog box) to print your contact sheet.**

Printing picture packages

Another option you have for printing multiple photos is picture packages. This feature prints multiple copies of the same photo or multiple copies of many photos.

A picture package is typically a single sheet of paper with the same photo printed at different sizes — something like your graduation photos or prom photos. You can print a single picture package from one photo selected in the Organizer, or you can select multiple photos and print them all as multiple picture packages.

To create a picture package, do the following:

1. **Open the Organizer.**

2. **In the Organizer, select a single photo or multiple photos that you want to print.**

3. **Choose File⇨Print or press Ctrl+P (⌘+P on the Macintosh).**

   The Print Photos dialog box opens. In the dialog box, select the printer you want to use for your output from the Select Printer drop-down menu.

4. **Choose Picture Package from the Select Type of Print drop-down menu.**

   The Print Photos dialog box refreshes to show your picture package options.

5. **Choose a layout.**

   Choose a layout from the Select a Layout drop-down menu.

6. **(Optional) Choose a frame.**

If you like you can also choose a frame from the Select a Frame drop-down menu. As you make layout selections, you see a dynamic preview of the picture package as shown in Figure 14-11. Select different layouts to examine the results and choose the layout you want for your picture package.

Figure 14-11: Choose Picture Package and select a layout for the package.

Using Online Printing Services

Photoshop Elements supports the Adobe Photoshop Services program, which is a joint effort between Adobe Systems and Adobe Partners. The Adobe Photoshop Services program offers online ordering of prints and sharing of photos and projects, and it has a huge array of different print products for consumers and professionals.

To use a sharing service do the following:

1. **Select files in the Organizer much as you'd select files for printing.**

2. **In either editing mode or the Organizer, choose File⇨Order Prints. From the submenu you can choose Order Shutterfly Prints or Order Kodak Prints. Alternatively, you can click the Share tab in the Panel Bin and click the Order Prints button.**

In our example we chose Shutterfly. The first screen you see using either service is a log-on screen. Here you can create a new account or log on with your existing account's log-on information. Click Next and the Shutterfly Wizard order screen opens, as shown in Figure 14-12.

Figure 14-12: Choose File⇨Order Prints⇨Order Shutterfly Prints to open the Shutterfly Wizard.

If you try to place an order from your office where the IT department prevents you from connecting to some external sources, you may need to have your firewall settings adjusted. Talk to someone in your IT department to help you make a connection.

3. **If you haven't set up an account already, fill in the information and step through the wizard by clicking the Next button on each page. If you have set up an account, supply your log-on information.**

   The selected files in the Organizer are automatically loaded in Step 1 of the wizard's order page.

4. **You can modify your order by deleting files from the order and specifying different print sizes and quantities.**

One nice feature in the service is the option to send duplicate prints to another party. You can keep an address book on the provider's Web site and specify whom should receive an order. This feature is helpful if you're away spending your children's inheritance on a Caribbean cruise and want to send photos of the great time you're having to all of them. Just pop open your laptop on the pool deck, load the digital camera images, and connect via a wireless connection. Before you return to Buffalo in midwinter with a suntan, your kids will frown as they fan through the prints they received a week earlier.

5. **Continue stepping through the wizard to upload your files and confirm your order; click the Finish button on the last pane to complete your order.**

Showing It Onscreen

*E*lements is a great packaging tool that can deploy your photos and projects for screen viewing. And that's not just your computer monitor. You can edit photos or assemble creations that are exported for Web viewing, too, and you can even prepare files to show on your television.

In Chapter 3, you can find out about resolutions and color modes. The output requirements for printing files, which we cover in Chapter 14, are much different from what you use for screen viewing.

In this chapter, we cover the options for Web and screen viewing that get you started with basics, including saving images for the Web (or for screen viewing), setting up a slide show, and burning your images on CDs or DVDs.

Getting Familiar with the Elements Sharing Options

Before you delve into making creations for screen viewing, you should be familiar with your available options for not only screen images, but also sharing — particularly online sharing services. You also need to be familiar with the acceptable standards for online hosts, where you eventually expect to send your creations, and the kinds of devices people are likely to use to view your creations.

Planning ahead

A few questions need to be answered before you choose a sharing activity and ultimately begin work on a creation. The questions include

✔ **What device(s) are going to display my creations?** When it comes to viewing photos and movies you have choices between computers (including desktops, notebooks, and netbooks), handheld devices such as mobile photos, tablets such as the Apple iPad, and TVs. If you want your creations viewed on all devices, then the Elements tools you use and the file format are different than the tools and file formats you might use for showing creations exclusively on a TV or on a computer.

Issues you need to understand regarding devices and viewing your creations include

- **Adobe Flash.** Some hosts convert your video uploads to Adobe Flash. If you want to share photos with iPhone/iPod/iPad users (more than one hundred million and counting), then stay away from any host that supports Flash-only conversions.

- **Storage space.** Hosts vary greatly in terms of space allocated for storing content. If you want to share large video files, be certain the storage host you choose allocates enough storage space to permit you to upload your files.

✔ **What storage hosts are the most popular?** From within Photoshop Elements you can export directly to Podbean, Kodak Easy Share Gallery, Adobe Photoshop Showcase, SmugMug Gallery, and Flickr. Some of these providers may be new to you. Just be aware that they all perform a similar kind of service where photos are uploaded and people you invite to see your creations can access them. The most popular online sharing services include:

- **Facebook.** Facebook is a private online service that's clearly among the most popular worldwide for sharing photos. Facebook offers you up to 200 photos maximum per album, up to 1024MB for each video, and unlimited space for total albums and videos. When you submit videos to Facebook, the videos are transcoded to Adobe Flash for viewing on computers but also contains coding for viewing on iPhone/iPod/iPad; see Figure 15-1. This is all transparent to the user. You just upload a video in any one of more than a dozen different formats and anyone with any device can view the video. Facebook is clearly the leader for hosting all your creations.

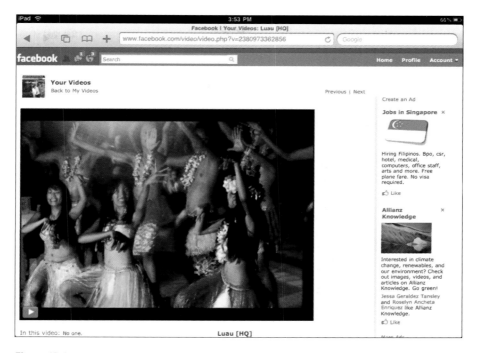

Figure 15-1: Video on Facebook is shown here on an Apple iPad.

- **Flickr.** Whereas Facebook provides you with near limitless opportunity, Flickr (operated by Yahoo!) is much more restrictive. Flickr assesses maximum storage per user according to bandwidth. You can only upload so many times, then you have to wait until the next month to upload additional photos. It's much more limiting than other services and video files are restricted to small sizes. You can upgrade to a premium account for a fee, but why bother when you can get it all free with a much better user interface on Facebook?

- **MySpace.** MySpace (operated by Google) is great until you want to share videos with iPhone/iPod/iPad users. All their videos are transcoded to Adobe Flash and the Apple devices can't see them.

- **Photoshop.com.** The entire user interface for Photoshop.com (operated by Adobe) is Adobe Flash. If you want to share videos with iPhone/iPod/iPad users, they can't get into the site let alone view any photos or videos.

✔ **What types of creations can I share?** Obviously, you can upload individual photos to any one of the online services. You can use the Share panel and click the More Options button in the panel, then choose from one of the listed services. If you want to share with Facebook or MySpace, save your edited photos to a folder on your hard drive, then open the service URL in your Web browser and follow the guidelines for the service to upload photos and create albums. In addition to uploading single photos to a service, some of the creations you might want to share include

- **Slide shows.** On Windows, you can create a slide show and choose to export the slide show as a movie file (.wmv) or a PDF. On the Macintosh you are limited to PDF only. If you work on Windows, export to .wmv and upload your file to an online host. If you use Facebook, all devices show your creations. Slide shows have an additional benefit in supporting audio files. You can add audio to the creations and the audio plays on all devices when uploading to Facebook. If you try to upload the same file to Flickr, more often than not the file size will be too large to host.

- **Flipbooks.** Flipbooks are Windows-only creations. Flipbooks are similar to slide shows without transition effects and audio support. You can easily upload Flipbooks to both Facebook and Flickr. Unless you have a huge number of photos, you aren't likely to run into a file size constraint when uploading to Flickr.

- **Webhosting.** If you want to host videos on your own Web site and make the videos available to iPhone/iPod/iPad users as well as computer users, you need a little help from Adobe Premiere Elements. In Premiere Elements you can export video for mobile devices and the resultant file can be viewed on iPhone/iPod/iPad as well as computers. Also, Premiere Elements supports some of the services on the Macintosh that you don't have available in Photoshop Elements such as slide shows exported as movie files and Flipbooks.

Understanding some common setup attributes

The Create and Share panels are available in both Edit Full and Edit Quick modes. Options available to you in the panels are identical in each editing space. You also have the same options available in the Organizer. When you open the Organizer and look at the Panels Bin, you see two tabs on the right side at the top of the bin for Create and Share. There are some differences for Create and Share options available on Windows and the Macintosh. In Figure 15-2 you can see the various choices you have in both panels as it appears for Windows users. In Figure 15-3 you see the choices available for Elements running on a Macintosh.

✔ **Create:** The Create tab contains options for making different kinds of projects, such as photo books, photo calendars, greeting cards, photo prints, photo collages, slide shows, instant movies, and photo stamps.

✔ **Share:** The Share tab provides a number of different options for sharing photos. On this tab, you find options for developing online photo albums, e-mailing photos, sending photo mails, writing files to CD/DVDs, sharing online videos, and exporting photos to mobile phones.

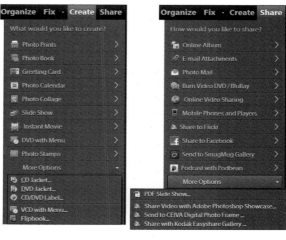

Figure 15-2: The Create and Share options are available on Windows.

Note that each panel contains a More Options button. Click the button to find more creation and sharing options.

In Chapter 14, we talk about ordering online prints by using the Order Prints option on the Share panel. In this chapter and in Chapter 16, we cover various commands on the Create panel and other options on the Share panel.

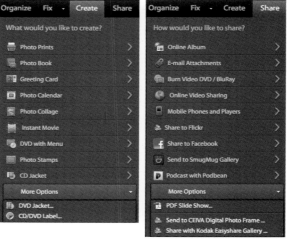

Figure 15-3: The Create and Share options are available on the Macintosh.

Creating a Slide Show (Windows only)

This *Million Dollar Baby* is no *Mystic River* — it's simply *Absolute Power!* Well, maybe you won't travel the same path from Rowdy Yates to multiple Academy Award–winning director and filmmaker Clint Eastwood, but even Mr. Eastwood might be impressed with the options for movie making with the Photoshop Elements slide show creations. When he's not rolling out his Panaflex camera, he may just want to take photos of the grandkids and do the directing and producing, as well as the editing, right in Photoshop Elements.

The rest of us can channel our own Clint Eastwood by using the powerful features of the Photoshop Elements Slide Show Editor to create PDF slide shows and movie files. It's so easy that Elements promises you won't be *Unforgiven.*

Creating a project

You create a project file in the Slide Show Editor and then export it for a number of different uses. In this section, you can find out how to create and save your project. In the following section, you dive into exporting.

A Photoshop Elements Project has an advantage over a PDF document in regard to revising the content. You can simply open your project, make revisions, and produce the slide show — something you cannot do with a PDF file.

Here's how you go about creating a slide show project that you can edit and export later:

1. **Open the Organizer and select the pictures you want to use in your slide show.**

2. **Click the Create button in the Panels Bin and click Slide Show.**

   The Slide Show Preferences dialog box opens. Just about everything in the dialog box can be adjusted in the Slide Show Editor, so don't worry about making choices here. If you want to keep the Slide Show Preferences dialog box from reappearing when you make slide show creations, deselect the Show This Dialog Each Time a New Slide Show Is Created check box.

3. **Click OK in the Slide Show Preferences dialog box.**

   The Slide Show Editor opens, as shown in Figure 15-4.

4. **If your Slide Show Editor doesn't show a screen similar to the one in Figure 15-4, click the Maximize button in the upper-right corner of the window.**

   This way, you can see the Storyboard at the bottom of the screen and the Panels Bin on the right side of the editor.

Figure 15-4: The Slide Show Editor is where you create slide shows.

5. **(Optional) Create a Pan & Zoom view.**

   When slides are shown, you can zoom and pan a slide. Click the Enable Pan & Zoom check box and click the Start thumbnail. A rectangle appears in the preview area. Move any one of the four corner handles in or out to resize the rectangle. Moving the cursor inside the rectangle and clicking the mouse button enables you to move the rectangle around the preview.

   For the end zoom position, click the End thumbnail and size the rectangle to a zoomed view or a view that you want to stop the zoom. Notice in Figure 15-4 that the End thumbnail is selected and the rectangle is sized down to the zoom area on a portion of the photo.

6. **(Optional) Add a graphic.**

   A library of graphics appears on the Extras pane in the Panels Bin. Drag a graphic to a slide. If you want a blank slide to appear first and then add text and graphics to the blank slide, click Add Blank Slide on the Shortcuts bar at the top of the Editor.

7. **(Optional) Add text.**

Click the Text tool on the Extras pane in the Panels Bin, and drag a text style to the blank slide or the opening slide in the slide show. After you drag text to a slide, the Properties pane opens in the Panels Bin. The text you drag to the slide is a placeholder. To edit the text, click Edit Text in the Properties pane. You can also select a font, style, size, color, and alignment. After setting the type attributes, click inside the text and move it to the position you want.

8. **(Optional) Set transitions.**

   The icons between the slides in the Storyboard (at the bottom of the Slide Show Editor) indicate a default transition. You can change transition effects for each slide independently or to all the slides in the show. Click the right-pointing arrow on the right side of a transition icon to open a pop-up menu containing a number of different transitions, as shown in Figure 15-5. If you want to apply the same transition to all slides, choose Apply to All at the top of the menu commands.

Figure 15-5: Click a right-pointing arrow on a transition to open the Transitions pop-up menu.

Be conservative with the transition effects. Too many transitions of different types can make the slide show appear amateurish and be distracting to the viewers.

9. **(Optional) Add audio and media.**

   You can add audio to the slide show by choosing Add Media⇨Audio from Organizer (or from Folder). Select an audio file and click OK.

   You can also add movie files to your slide show. A movie file can be added on top of a slide or on a new slide. When the slide show is played, the video file plays. Choose Add Media⇨Photos and Videos from Organizer (or from Folder).

   This same set of commands can also be used to add more pictures to the slide show.

10. **(Optional) Record your own sounds.**

    If you want to add narration, click the Narration tool (represented by a microphone icon to the right of the Text tool) in the Panels Bin, and the Extras panel changes to provide you with tools to record a sound or import a sound file. Note that this option requires you to have a microphone properly configured on your computer.

11. **(Optional) Fit slides to the audio.**

If you have 3 minutes of audio and the slide duration is 2 minutes 30 seconds, you can, with a single mouse click, fit the slide duration uniformly to fit the 3-minute audio time. Just click the Fit Slides to Audio tool below the preview image.

If you want to manually adjust time for slide durations, click the down arrow on the time readout below the slide thumbnails in the Storyboard.

12. **Click Save Project on the Shortcuts bar and then, in the dialog box that opens, type a name and click Save.**

Your project is added to the Organizer and is available for further editing later. Or, you can open the project to save in a number of different output formats, as we explain in the following section.

13. **Preview the slide show.**

Before exporting the slide show, you can see a preview by clicking the buttons directly below the image preview area. If you want a full-screen preview, click the Preview button on the Shortcuts bar and click the Play button.

This section does export the slides yet to a file. It simply saves the project that you can reopen and edit. To create the slide show file, follow directions in the next section, "Exporting to slides and video."

If you don't like the order of the slides when you open the Slide Show Editor, you can easily reorder the slides by dragging back and forth along the timeline.

Exporting to slides and video

After creating a project, you have a number of output options. You can write a project to disc for archival purposes and include slide shows on a VideoCD (videodisc) or DVD. You can e-mail a slide show to another user, share a project online, write a project compatible for display on a TV, or save to either a PDF slide show or Windows movie file.

To write a PDF slide show or a movie file, follow these steps:

1. **In the Organizer window, double-click the project thumbnail.**

The project opens in the Adobe Photoshop Elements Slide Show Editor.

2. **Click the Output tool on the Shortcuts bar.**

   The Slide Show Output Wizard opens, as shown in Figure 15-6 on Windows.

Figure 15-6: Select Output in the Photoshop Elements Slide Show Editor to open the Slide Show Output Wizard.

3. **Select the type of file you want to export.**

   • *Movie File (.wmv):* Select this option to export a Windows media video file. Your exported video can be viewed in Elements or in the Windows Media Player. You can import the video in all programs that support .wmv files.

   • *PDF File (.pdf):* Select this option if you want to create a PDF slide show. If you create a PDF slide show, some of the animation features, such as zooming slides and transition effects, aren't shown in the resultant PDF document. Users can view the slide show using the free Adobe Reader software.

 To read how to convert video for viewing on iPhone and iPad and viewing PDF documents on these devices, see Chapter 4.

4. **In the dialog box that opens, which prompts you to add your output file to the Organizer, click Yes.**

   You can now easily view the file by double-clicking it in the Organizer window.

 If you use an iPhone, iPod, or iPad, and have Adobe Premiere Elements installed you can choose the last option in the Slide Show Output Wizard and choose Edit with Premiere Elements. In Premiere Elements you can export directly to iPod/iPhone format that is readable on all your iHardware devices. (See the next section, "Creating an Instant Video," for more on Adobe Premiere Elements.)

Creating an Instant Video

Photoshop Elements is not a video editor. You can create some video files and import video in the Organizer. However, when it comes to editing video, you need another application. The application that works very well in tandem with Elements is Adobe Premiere Elements. Macintosh users can use Apple's iMovie, but you also have support for Premiere Elements running on the Macintosh.

On the Create panel, you find a selection for Instant Movie. When you click this button, the Ready to Edit dialog box shown in Figure 15-7 opens. It describes how to acquire a trial version of Adobe Premiere Elements.

Figure 15-7: When you click Instant Movie an option for downloading a trial version of Adobe Premiere Elements is made available.

Click the Download Trial button, and the trial version of Adobe Premiere Elements commences a download. You can use the program for a 30-day trial period. If you're interested in turning your photos into movie files, Adobe Premiere Elements has all the tools you need to edit videos.

Writing Creations to CDs and DVDs

You can output creations — such as slide shows and images you optimize for TV — to a CD or DVD by using the Slide Show Output Wizard. If you have a movie but don't have a DVD burner, most DVD players sold today enable you to view videodiscs written to CDs. The CDs just don't hold as much content as DVDs do.

VCDs display at lower resolutions than DVDs. (VCD is an 1150 Kbps video stream with a 352 x 240 resolution for NTSC, and DVD is 720 x 480 at variable bitrates between about 3000 and 9800 Kbps.) You can get 80 minutes of VCD on a 700MB CD (74 minutes on a 650MB).

Writing options to external media vary between the platform you use and those services supported by Elements. On Windows, you have options for writing videodiscs. On both platforms you have support for writing DVDs. If you want to create a DVD on the Macintosh, you need to use a program like Apple's iDVD.

Notice in the Create panel on both platforms you have an option for DVD with Menu. Using this option requires Adobe Premiere Elements.

VCDs are limited to Windows users. When you want to export to a VCD, you first need to create a slide show. After saving the slide show project you can choose to export to a VCD format.

To write to a VCD on Windows, follow these steps:

1. **Open a project in the Slide Show Output Wizard by double-clicking a project in the Organizer.**

2. **Click Output in the Slide Show Editor.**

3. **Click Burn to Disc in the Slide Show Output Wizard.**

4. **Click OK in the first screen in the Slide Show Output Wizard.**

   If you want to burn additional slide shows to the same disc, click the Add Slide Shows button and select additional slide shows to add to the CD/DVD. Otherwise, just click OK to burn a single slide show to a disc.

5. **Choose a video option.**

   Click either NTSC or PAL for the video format you use, as shown in Figure 15-8. NTSC is commonly used in the U.S. and Japan, whereas PAL is commonly used in Europe and other countries. Be certain to check the format used by your video players and TV before making a choice here.

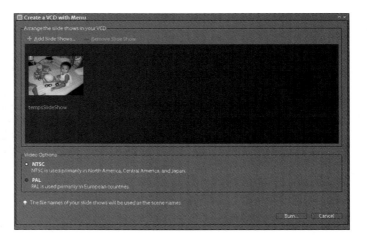

Figure 15-8: Choose a video option.

6. **Click OK.**

   The Burn dialog box opens, and the CD drive door on your computer opens.

7. **Insert a CD and click OK.**

   The status bar shows the writing progress.

After the CD or DVD finishes writing, pop open your CD/DVD drive and remove the disc. Place the disc in your DVD player and press Play. The movie automatically starts playing, like any commercial videodisc.

Creating an Online Photo Album

When you click Share in either the Organizer or Edit Full mode and open the Share panel, you find Online Album at the top of the list. The term *Online* is a bit misleading here because you can use this sharing option for both online and local file creations.

The process for creating an album is the same regardless of the destination you want for your file. When you select photos in the Organizer and click Online Album, the Share panel displays three options for your output. These include

- ✓ **Photoshop.com.** Choose this item if you want to upload an album to your space on Photoshop.com.

- ✓ **Export to CD/DVD.** Use this option to write an album to a CD/DVD that can be viewed on your DVD player.

- ✓ **Export to Hard Disk.** Choose this item to export files to a folder. Once the files are exported, you can view the album locally on your hard drive by using your Web browser or upload the files to a Web site so any visitor can view the album.

In this chapter we talk about more local file saves so we stick with creating an album and exporting it to your hard drive.

If you want to share files on Photoshop.com or write a CD/DVD, follow the same steps but be certain to choose the appropriate option in the Share panel when you start the creation (see Figure 15-8).

Creating a beautiful album with an attractive layout and transitions between the photos is one of many great things you can do with Photoshop Elements with just a few mouse clicks. To see how easy it is to create an album showing off your photos, follow these steps:

1. **Open the Organizer and select the photos you want to use for your album.**

2. **Click Share in the Panels Bin and choose Online Album from the panel options.** See Figure 15-9.

   The panel displays several output options. You can choose to send an album to Photoshop.com, export an album to a CD/DVD,

Figure 15-9: Choose an option for exporting files in the Share panel.

or export to your hard disk as you see in Figure 15-9. In our example we use the Export to Hard Disk option so files can be later uploaded to a Web site or written to a CD/DVD.

3. **Click Export to Hard Disk and click Next at the bottom of the panel.**

If you created an album, as we explain in Chapter 6, you can open the Organizer, click the Organize button in the Panels Bin, and click the album you created for showing photos online. This option frees you from having to sort through the Organizer window to find photos you want to add to the online gallery. Notice in Figure 15-9, we use an existing album.

You can first select photos in the Organizer, then click Share➪Online Album. All the selected photos are added to a new album.

4. **Type a name for your album.**

If you create a new album instead of using an existing album type a name in the Album Name text box shown in Figure 15-10.

5. **Click the Sharing tab.**

Notice the two tabs in the Share panel. We've been working in the Content tab where selected photos were displayed, and we named the album. When you click the Sharing tab, the panel options change to what you see in Figure 15-10.

6. **Choose a template.**

At the top of the window you find a number of different template choices. Click a template and preview your photos in the template view.

7. **Preview the album.**

At the top-right corner of the image window you see a tiny right-pointing arrow as shown in Figure 15-11. Click the arrow and your slides are previewed.

8. **Click Browse.**

In the Browse dialog box locate a target destination on your hard drive and click OK.

If you want to create a new folder, click Make New Folder and click OK.

9. **Click Done.**

Your files are saved to your hard drive.

Figure 15-10: Type a name for your album.

If you want to preview the album, you can open your default Web browser and open the `index.html` document on your hard drive.

Figure 15-11: Click the tiny arrow to preview the slide show.

Flip 'Em Over with Flipbooks

Below the Create and Share buttons (on both the Create and Share panels), you can find a More Options button. Click More Options to open a menu where additional create and share items are found. With regard to the Create panel, the More Options menu contains a number of items, such as CD/DVD jackets and labels, VCD with a menu, and a flipbook.

At the bottom of the More Options menu in the Create panel, you can find a Flipbook option. If you want to create a quick little video that shows off your photos by flashing stills on your screen or your TV set, you can quickly create a flipbook. Here's how you do it:

1. **Open the Organizer and select the files you want to use.**

   Note that you must select at least two files in order to create the flipbook.

2. **Click the Create tab in the Panels Bin and choose More Options⇨ Flipbook.**

   The Elements Organizer Flipbook opens, as shown in Figure 15-12.

3. **Set the playback speed by typing a value in the Speed text box or moving the slider to the desired speed.**

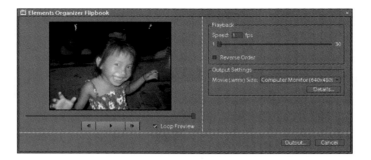

Figure 15-12: The Photoshop Elements Video Flipbook dialog box permits you to select a speed and movie file size.

Note that flipping through photos looks best at low speeds, such as 1 or 2 frames per second (fps). Also, you can select the size for your video file from options on the Movie (.wmv) Size drop-down menu.

4. **Click Output.**

   The Save Video Flipbook dialog box opens.

5. **Type a filename and click Save.**

Your file is written as a .wmv (Windows) or QuickTime (Macintosh) file. You can use Windows Movie Maker to write the file to a CD or DVD or iDVD on the Macintosh to write the file to a DVD.

Making Creations and Sharing

*A*dobe Photoshop Elements offers you a number of creations that can be shared onscreen or in print. From both the Create and Share panels in the Panels Bin in the Organizer and both editing modes, you have a number of menu choices for making creations designed for sharing.

In Chapter 15, we look at creating files for screen and Web viewing. In this chapter, we talk about creations designed for print and sharing. It's all here in Elements 9 for both Windows and Macintosh users.

Grasping Creation-Assembly Basics

In Chapter 15, we talk about slide shows, videodiscs, online galleries, and video flipbooks and sending creations to various sources. These creations are completely focused at sharing photos and videos on a computer, tablet, or mobile phone.

Creations such as Photo Books, Photo Collages, Photo Calendars, Greeting Cards, and PhotoStamps (most of which we talk about in this chapter) are intended for either output to print or screen sharing.

When you make a creation that will ultimately be sent to an online service for printing or shared with other users, keep in mind that you first must select the photos you want in your creation. For example, creating a Photo Book by clicking the Photo Book button on the Create panel first requires you to select photos. If you happen to click a button and nothing happens, more than likely you haven't selected any photos.

Many creation options follow a similar set of steps to produce a file that is shared with other users or sent to an online printing service. In the Panels Bin, you can find all you need to make a new project by choosing layouts and producing a creation. Among the common tasks you'll find when making a choice from both the Create and Share panels are

🖛 **Select Photos:** In the Organizer, select the photos you want to use for your creation. Sort photos (as we explain in Chapter 5) or use keyword tags (as we explain in Chapter 6) to simplify finding and selecting photos you want to use for a creation. In Figure 16-1, we catalogue a keyword tag containing 12 images.

Figure 16-1: Images containing a keyword tag were used for slecting photos for a Photo Book.

✔ **Click a choice in the Create tab:** Click the Create tab, and the Create panel in the Panel Bin opens. Click an option for the type of creation you want — Photo Book, Photo Calendar (Windows only), Greeting Card, Photo Collage, and so on.

✔ **Choose a Theme/Layout:** Many of the creation options provide you with a selection of templates you can use for creations. When you click a creation option on the Create panel, the panel changes to display choices for various themes, backgrounds, and borders. You make choices by clicking the theme or background.

✔ **Number of Pages:** Elements automatically creates the number of pages to accommodate the number of photos you selected in the Organizer or have open in Edit Full mode. Note that some creations require a minimum number of photos to produce a project. Photo Book, for example, requires a minimum of 18 pages.

After assembling your creation, click the Done button. Elements then adds the selected photos to the layout and the theme you specified in the panel. Be patient and wait for Elements to complete the task.

After a creation has been made, the document appears like any other image you open in Elements. You can crop, modify images, print, and more. After editing, choose File⇨Save to open the Save As dialog box. Type a name and click Save.

Creating a Photo Book

Elements provides some fancy ways to create pages for a photo album. With the Photo Book creation panel, you have many different options for choosing page templates, adding artwork and type, printing your album pages, or sending the files to an online service for professional printing.

Follow these steps to create a Photo Book:

1. **Select files in the Organizer and click the Create tab.**

   The procedure for all creations is the same. You first select files in the Organizer (or an editing mode) and then click the Create tab in the Panels Bin. Ideally, it's best to create an album, as we explain in Chapter 6, and click the album to display the album photos in the Organizer window. But remember, after you display an album in the Organizer, you still need to select all the photos.

   To select all photos shown in an Organizer window, press Ctrl+A (⌘+A on the Macintosh).

2. Click Photo Book in the Create panel.

Regardless of whether you're working in the Organizer or an editing mode, the Photo Book option is available in the same Create panel. When you click Photo Book, the Photo Book Wizard opens, and you make a choice for using the Kodak EasyShare service, the Shuttefly service, or print your Photo Book to your desktop printer. (For more on using the Kodak EasyShare and Shutterfly online services, see Chapter 14.)

3. Choose an output source in the Photo Book Wizard.

In the left panel of the wizard, click an option, as shown in Figure 16-2.

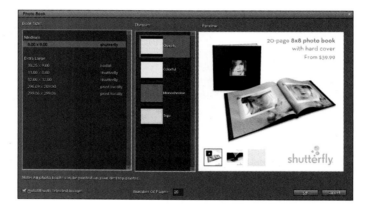

Figure 16-2: Click an output option in the PhotoBook Wizard.

4. Select a theme.

Click a theme in the center panel.

5. Click OK and Elements prepares your Photo Book.

6. Choose Photo Book attributes.

After the Photo Book is prepared, you see the cover page containing the first photo. In the Create panel, you find tabs for Pages, Layouts, Artwork, and Text, as shown in Figure 16-3. Explore each panel and look over various items you can add to your photo book such as a different layout, artwork that you can add to the pages, and a font choice.

7. Select the output.

Click Print to pring the photo book to your local printer. Click Order if you want to place an online order. The order source is derived from the choice you make in Step 3.

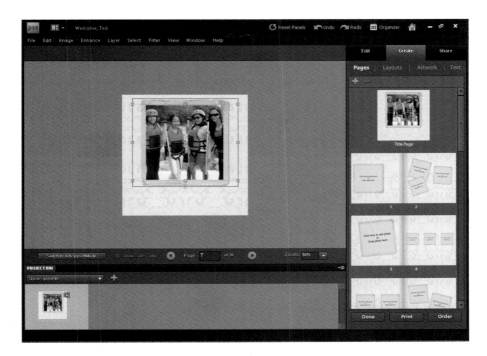

Figure 16-3: Set attributes and click the output source.

Greetings!

Creating greeting cards provides you with options for printing greeting cards to your desktop printer or ordering cards using an online service.

To demonstrate using options for themes and content, the following steps explain how to create a greeting card for output to your desktop printer:

1. **Open the Organizer or Edit Full mode and select a photo.**

2. **Click the Create tab to open the Create panel, and click Greeting Card.**

   The Greeting Card Wizard opens, as shown in Figure 16-4.

3. **Choose a size and output source in the left pane and make a choice for the theme in the center pane.**

   The options you have for greeting cards are similar to the choices you have for Photo Books.

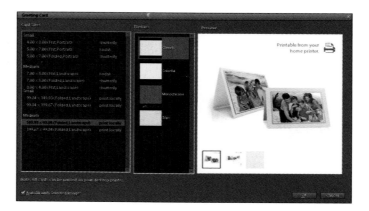

Figure 16-4: The Greeting Card Wizard.

4. **Click OK.**

   A preview of your greeting card is displayed.

5. **Make choices for artwork and text.**

   The Preview window contains a panel similar to the preview you find with Photo Books. Make choices for the attributes and add text and artwork as you desire.

6. **Choose an output option.**

   Click Print or Order at the bottom of the Preview window to print to a desktop printer or place an online order.

7. **Save the file.**

Creating CD and DVD Labels

Another creation option in Elements is the simple, easy way to create CD and DVD labels. From the Create panel, click More Options and choose a menu item for CD Jacket, DVD Jacket, or CD/DVD Label. From templates provided in the panel, Elements offers you an easy method for printing your own, personal labels and jackets for CDs and DVDs.

This feature for printing CD/DVD labels is a bit weak in Elements. You may need to fiddle around quite a bit to get the images to fit a label. Using templates provided by the label developers is often a much better method for printing labels.

Spreading the Love through Sharing

Several methods of sharing your creations are available in Elements. You can use various resources, such as Photoshop Showcase, Shutterfly, Kodak EasyShare, and more.

Creating a calendar online

Are you ready to design a personal calendar using your favorite photos? Elements helps you design an attractive calendar of the kids, the girl's soccer team, the bullhead moose fraternity, or any other type of activity or event you want to work with. Elements makes it easy to create professional-looking calendars.

Here's how you create a calendar that can be professionally printed and ordered via an online service:

1. **Select photos in the Organizer.**

   For calendars, you might want to select 13 photos — 1 photo for the calendar cover and 12 for each month. You can also choose 12 photos and use one of the calendar months for the cover photo.

2. **Open the Create panel and click Photo Calendar.**

   The Photo Calendar Wizard opens. This wizard is virtually the same as you have available with Photo Books and Greeting Cards, as shown in Figure 16-5.

Figure 16-5: Click a theme in the scrollable window.

3. **Sign up or enter your account info.**

   If you don't have an account, sign up on the opening page in the Kodak EasyShare Wizard. If you have an account, supply your logon and password.

4. **Make choices for the starting month and year in the left pane and a theme in the center pane.**

5. **Click OK.**

   Follow online instructions for ordering your calendar from Kodak EasyShare services.

E-mailing creations

After you put together a creation with the Creation Wizard, you can e-mail the creation to your whomever you want by choosing a simple menu command. (We introduce this method and other ways to share creations in the section "Grasping Creation-Assembly Basics," earlier in this chapter.) Additionally, you can e-mail photos to mobile phones. The options are all located in the Share panel.

Rather than save your file from Elements and then open your e-mail client and select the photo to attach to an e-mail message, you can use Elements to easily share photos via e-mail with one click.

When you want to e-mail a creation, follow these steps:

1. **In the Organizer, select the photos you want to e-mail to a friend.**

2. **Open the Share panel and select E-Mail Attachments.**

3. **Choose a quality setting for the attachment and click Next.**

   Drag the slider where you see Quality and observe the file size below the slider, as shown in Figure 16-6. If the file is large, you may need to resize in the Image Size dialog box before e-mailing the photo.

Figure 16-6: Set Quality to a medium setting for faster uploads to your mail server.

4. **Add recipients or bypass this option.**

   You can add recipients from your Address Book. If you want to add a new recipient, click the icon in the top-right corner of the Select Recipients tab. Check each recipient listed in the Select Recipients pane.

   You can bypass adding recipients to your Address Book. If no recipients are listed in the Select Recipients panel, you can add recipient e-mail addresses in the new message window in your e-mail client, as shown in Figure 16-7.

5. **Click Next and the photo(s) is attached to a new e-mail message in your default e-mail client.**

6. **Review the To, Subject, and Attach fields to be certain the information is correct and then click the Send button.**

   By default, Elements uses your primary e-mail client application, which may or may not be the e-mail program you use. You can change the default e-mail client by pressing Ctrl+K (⌘+K on the Macintosh) to open the Preferences dialog box when you're in the Organizer and then clicking Sharing on the left pane. From a drop-down list in the Sharing preferences, select the e-mail client application that you want Elements to use.

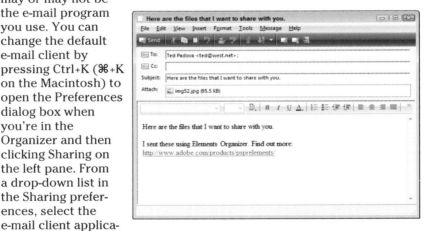

Figure 16-7: Your attachment appears in an e-mail window, where you can also add recipients.

Showcasing Your Photos

Almost all the creation and sharing options we discuss in Chapter 15 and this chapter, other than those creations you assemble for printing to a desktop printer, require you to make purchases. Wouldn't it be nice if you could share your photos without paying an online service fee or paying for a Web address? Well, your answer lies in the Photoshop Showcase services that are easily accessible in Elements.

Open the Share panel and click Online Album. Elements provides you with a number of sharing options for distributing photo albums, as shown in Figure 16-8. For more information on creating albums, look over Chapter 6.

Your choices for sharing albums follow:

- **Share Existing Album:** If you have an album assembled, the album(s) appears in the Albums list.

- **Create New Album:** If you don't have an album in the list, or you want to create a new album, select this option.

- **Photoshop.com:** This free online hosting service lets you share photos and albums and invite family and friends to see your images free of charge.

- **Export to CD/DVD (Windows only):** This option enables you to export albums to CDs and DVDs.

- **Export to Hard Disk:** Use this option to export an album to your hard drive. The export is an HTML file that you can view in a Web browser.

Figure 16-8: Sharing albums online provides several different choices.

To share your photos on the free Photoshop Showcase service, follow these steps:

1. **Click the Photoshop Showcase radio button on the Share panel.**

   The panel changes to display two tabs. One tab is denoted as Content and the other tab is denoted as Sharing. By default, the Content panel is in view and displays all selected photos in the Organizer as thumbnail images.

2. **Select the photos you want to share and then click the Sharing tab.**

   The panel changes with a preview display of the showcase in the image window, as shown in Figure 16-9.

3. **Make sure Photoshop Showcase is selected and click Done on the Share panel.**

   The Adobe Photoshop Services Wizard opens.

4. **If you do not have an account, you can sign up on the opening wizard page. If you do have an account, supply your logon information and click Next.**

Figure 16-9: Click the Sharing tab on the Share panel, and a preview of the showcase appears in the image window.

The Welcome screen you see is shown in Figure 16-10. The Welcome screen informs you of the amount of space you have remaining on your account and the current usage. If it's your first effort in using the service, you'll find 0 percent used.

5. **Click Next, and you can add recipients, set viewing options, and upload your photos.**

   You can restrict viewing to invited participants only or make your showcase public where anyone can view the photos.

6. **When you're finished uploading, click Done.**

   Your default Web browser loads the Web page where your album resides on Photoshop Services, as shown in Figure 16-11.

The URL listed in the Location bar in your Web browser can be copied and pasted into an e-mail message. If you elect to display your showcase to all viewers, anyone visiting the URL can see your photos.

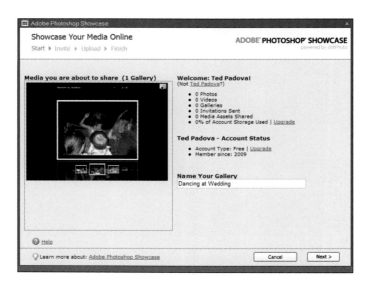

Figure 16-10: This is the first screen you see after logging on to the Adobe Photoshop Services.

Figure 16-11: You can copy the URL in the Location bar and paste it into e-mail messages you send to family and friends.

Part VI
The Part of Tens

The 5th Wave   By Rich Tennant

COSMETIC SURGERY

"This time, just for fun, let's see what you'd look like with bat ears and squash for a nose."

In this part . . .

The Part of Tens offers a couple of fun chapters to help you take your photography and Elements skills a little further. In Chapter 17, you can find our top ten tips for composing better photos. Find out about the rule of thirds, framing, and other simple tricks that can make your photos look better than ever. Also, in Part V, we introduce the creations that Elements helps you make, but why stop there? Chapter 18 offers even more ideas for projects you can create for your home or work, such as flyers, posters, inventories, and more.

17

Ten Tips for Composing Better Photos

In This Chapter

▶ Finding a focal point and using the rule of thirds

▶ Cutting the clutter and framing your shot

▶ Employing contrast, leading lines, and viewpoints

▶ Using light and giving direction

▶ Considering direction of movement

A few things have to come together to make a great photograph. One is being in the right place at the right time. Another is the ability to tell a story. Yet another is excellent composition. Unfortunately, we can't help with your schedule or storytelling, but we can give you several easy tips on how to take photographs that are interesting and well composed. Some of these tips overlap and contain common concepts. But they're all free; they don't require any extra money or equipment. They require only an open mind and an eye that's willing to be trained over time.

Find a Focal Point

One of the most important tools for properly composing a photo is establishing a *focal point* — a main point of interest. If too many elements are competing for attention, a photo probably doesn't have a clearly defined focal point. Your eye, therefore, doesn't know where to look. Too many images without a focal point cause the viewer to tire quickly or lose interest. The eye wants to be drawn to a subject.

Excessive background elements, such as furniture, walls, tables, fences, buildings, and even random bystanders don't add much to the compositional or emotional value of your shot. What you really want to capture are the smiles and expressions of your family and friends.

Keep these tips in mind to help find your focal point:

- **Pick your subject and then get close to it.**

- **Include a point of interest in scenic shots.** Sunrises and sunsets are pretty, but after you've seen a few, you've seen them all. Try to capture an early morning fisherman casting his line off the pier or a child checking out a rogue hermit crab at dusk. That potentially ho-hum scenic shot now has some visual punch.

- **When it's appropriate, try to include an element in the foreground, middle ground, or background to add depth and a sense of scale, as shown in Figure 17-1.** Just make sure that it's a meaningful element and not random clutter.

Brand X Pictures

Figure 17-1: Including elements in the foreground adds depth to a photo.

Use the Rule of Thirds

After you find a focal point for your shot, the next step is to try to put that focal point, or subject, in a prime location within your viewfinder or LCD display. Those prime locations are based on the photographic principle called the *rule of thirds*. If you divide an image into a grid of nine equal segments, as shown in Figure 17-2, the elements most appealing to the eye and most likely to be noticed first are those that fall close to one of the four intersections of the dividing lines.

Corbis Digital Stock

Figure 17-2: Position your subject at one of the intersecting points on the rule-of-thirds grid.

When you're composing your shot, try to mentally divide your frame into vertical and horizontal thirds and position your most important visual element at any intersecting point. When you're shooting landscapes, remember that a low horizon creates a dreamy and spacious feeling and that a high horizon gives an earthy and intimate feeling. For close-up portraits, try putting the face or eyes of a person at one of those points.

If the rule of thirds is too hard for you to remember or employ, when you look through the viewfinder, just repeat the mantra, "Move from center." We all have a natural tendency to want to center everything. Get it nice and orderly. But centered subjects are often static and boring. Asymmetry often gives you more dynamic and interesting images.

If you have an autofocus camera, you need to lock the focus when you're moving from center because the autofocus sensor locks on to whatever's in the center of the viewfinder — not on your point of interest. Autofocus can also be problematic when you're trying to do something as simple as photographing two people (in this case, you may want the two people in the center) and your camera keeps focusing on the space in the distance between them. Center your subject in the viewfinder and apply slight pressure to your shutter-release button to lock the focus. Then, reposition your subject at an intersecting point on the rule-of-thirds grid and press down all the way to snap the photo.

Cut the Clutter

Contrary to what you see on supermarket tabloid covers, those telephone poles, branches, car antennas, and other everyday objects don't naturally grow out of people's heads. Although these *mergers,* as photographers call them, are good for a laugh, they're not good enough to make it into picture frames and scrapbooks.

Here are some ways you can cut the clutter from your background:

- ✔ **Get up close and personal. Many amateur photographers worry that they'll take a photo that accidentally leaves all or a portion of a subject's head outside the frame.** But more often than not, photographers tend to capture too much boring or distracting background. Fill your viewfinder frame with your subject. Although you can always crop your image later, you should try to fill the frame with your subject when you take the photo.

- ✔ **Shoot at a different angle.** Yes, you can turn your camera! Most photos are horizontal merely because it's easier to hold the camera that way. That's fine for a lot of shots (such as the requisite group photo and some landscape shots), but other subjects (buildings, trees, waterfalls, mountain peaks, giraffes, Shaquille O'Neal) lend themselves to a vertical format (referred to as portrait orientation).

- ✔ **Move around your subject.** Moving around may help eliminate unwanted clutter. Shoot from below or above your subject, if necessary.

- ✔ **Move your subject, if possible, to get the optimum background.** Although there are exceptions, an ideal background is usually free from distracting elements, such as tree branches, poles, wires, chain-link fences, signs, bright lights, a lot of loud colors, busy wallpaper, and so on. Include only what complements your subject.

✔ **Use background elements to enhance, not distract.** On the other hand, if your background is interesting and can make your photo stronger, include it. You can use famous landmarks, props, and even decorations in the background to give context to images, as shown in Figure 17-3.

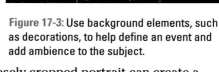

Figure 17-3: Use background elements, such as decorations, to help define an event and add ambience to the subject.

✔ **Use space around a subject to evoke a certain mood.** A lot of space around a person can give a sense of loneliness, just as a closely cropped portrait can create a feeling of intimacy. Just make sure that the space is intentionally used in the shot.

✔ **If you're stuck with a distracting background, you can try blurring it by using a wider aperture (such as f/4, rather than f/11 or f/16) on your camera.** This makes the *depth of field* (areas of sharpness in relation to your focal point) shallower so that your subject is in focus but the background isn't.

Because consumer digital cameras use image sensors that are typically one-third the size of a 35mm frame, the lens is very close to the sensor, which really increases the depth of field. This deep depth of field can make blurring the background difficult. Not a problem — you can also blur the background by making a selection and using the Blur filter in Elements. See Chapters 7 and 10 for more on selections and the Blur filter, respectively.

Frame Your Shot

When it's appropriate, use foreground elements to frame your subject. Frames lead you into a photograph. You can use elements, such as tree branches, windows, archways, and doorways, to frame a wide or long shot, add a feeling of depth, and create a point of reference, as shown in Figure 17-4. You don't have to reserve the use of framing for wide and long shots, however. Close-ups can also be framed. Your framing elements don't always have to be sharply focused. Sometimes, if they're too sharp, they distract from the focal point. And remember to avoid mergers!

Employ Contrast

Just remember "Light on dark, dark on light."

A light subject has more impact and emphasis if it's shot against a dark background, and vice versa, as shown in Figure 17-5. When people view an image, their eyes go first to the area of the most contrast. Obviously, finding contrast in the environment is sometimes beyond your control. But when you're setting up a shot, you can certainly try to incorporate this technique. Keep in mind, however, that contrast needs to be used carefully. Sometimes, it can be distracting, especially if the high-contrast elements aren't your main point of interest.

ImageState

Figure 17-4: Use elements that frame your subject.

PhotoDisc, Inc./Getty Images

Figure 17-5: High-contrast shots demand attention.

Use Leading Lines

Leading lines are lines that, by either the actual elements in the image or the composition of those elements, lead the eye into the picture and, hopefully, to a point of interest. These lines add dimension, depth, and perspective by carrying the eye through the photo:

- ✔ **Diagonal lines** are dynamic and evoke movement.
- ✔ **Curves** are graceful and harmonious.
- ✔ **Horizontal lines** are peaceful and give a feeling of balance.
- ✔ **Vertical lines** are direct and active.

The best leading lines are those that enter the image from the lower-left corner. Many elements — such as roads, walls, fences, rivers, shadows, skyscrapers, and bridges — provide natural leading lines, especially in scenic or landscape photos. The photo shown in Figure 17-6 of the Great Wall of China is an example of curved leading lines.

Experiment with Viewpoints

Not much in the world looks fascinating photographed from a height of 5 to 6 feet off the ground. Unfortunately, this is the viewpoint of "Snapshotville." Try to break out of this mode by taking photos from another vantage point. Experiment with taking a photo from above the subject *(bird's-eye view)* or below it *(worm's-eye view)*. A different angle may provide a more interesting image:

Flat Earth

Figure 17-6: You don't have to trek to China to find leading lines, although you may not find a longer unbroken curve than the Great Wall.

✔ **Unexpected angles can exaggerate the size of the subject.** The subject may appear either larger (see Figure 17-7) or smaller than normal. Try extreme angles with scenic shots, which otherwise can tend to be rather static or boring.

✔ **Changing your viewpoint can change the mood of the image.** If the photo in Figure 17-7 had been taken from a front angle, it would've been pretty dull. Taken from below, looking up, exaggerates the height and makes for a stronger and more exciting composition, making the cactus seem like nature's skyscraper.

✔ **Use direct eye contact when you're photographing people.** It provides a sense of realism and makes the image more intimate and warm, pulling you into the photo. But remember that children are not at the same eye level as adults. We often shoot down at them, making them appear smaller than they really are. Try kneeling or sitting on the floor and getting down to their level. You'll also find that you get a less distracting background in the frame, and the lighting from your flash more evenly covers the face. Do the same for pets and other short-stature sub-jects, such as flowers.

Use Light

When we think of light in regard to photography, the first thing that comes to mind is all those photos we took in the past that are either *over-exposed* (too light) or *underexposed* (too dark). With lighting, you have to consider not only whether you have the right amount of lighting, but also these factors:

Corbis Digital Stock

Figure 17-7: Shooting subjects from extreme angles can exaggerate size, resulting in a more interesting shot.

- ✔ The direction of the light
- ✔ The intensity of the light
- ✔ The color of the light
- ✔ Natural light (outdoors) or artificial light (indoors)
- ✔ Creative use of lighting to lead the eye and create a certain mood

If the light isn't right for your shot, you have quite a few choices: Hurry up and wait, move yourself, move the subject, add more light with a flash, or diffuse the light. Of course, which one you choose depends on the circum-stances of the shot and what's convenient or most productive.

Here are a few tips about light:

- ✔ **The best light for photographs is in the early morning and later after-noon.** The light is warmer and softer, and the shadows are longer and less harsh.

- **Avoid taking portraits at midday.** The overhead sun causes ugly shadows and makes people squint. If you must shoot then, use a reflector to block some of the sunlight or fill in the shadow areas. Or you can use a *scrim* (white translucent fabric stretched across a frame) to diffuse the light.

- **Cloudy or overcast days can be great for photographing, especially portraits.** The light is soft and diffused and flatters the face.

- **Shooting subjects with** *backlighting* **(where the lighting comes from behind the subject) can produce dramatic results.** Figure 17-8 shows an example. If you want to see the details of the subject, and not just a silhouette, use a fill flash to lighten the shadow areas.

- **Ensure that the brightest light source isn't directed right into the lens.** This causes *lens flare,* those strange light circles that appear in the photo.

- **Take into account the color of the light.** The light at noon is white, the light at sunset is orange, and the light at twilight is blue. The color of the light can make an image feel warm or cool.

- **Use a flash when necessary.** Use a flash in low-light conditions. If your built-in flash isn't cutting the mustard, you may want to invest in an accessory flash.

Corbis Digital Stock

Figure 17-8: Backlighting can yield dramatic images.

✔ **Get creative with light.** Look for those unique compositions created by the interplay between light and shadow areas, or how the light illuminates a particular subject. Lighting by itself can make or break a certain mood or emotion. Think of a simple beam of light coming through the roof of an old barn. Even in the lousiest weather, the most beautifully lit images can emerge. When wet objects are lit, they seem to shimmer, as shown in Figure 17-9.

Corbis Digital Stock

Figure 17-9: Lighting can create drama from the simplest objects.

Give Direction

When you look at magazines that feature the year's best photos, they all appear as instances of pure serendipity. Sometimes that's the case, but more often than not, the photographer arranged the shot or waited for the right light or a special moment.

As a photographer, you also shouldn't be afraid to play photo stylist:

✔ **Give directions about where you want people to stand, how to stand, and so on.** For example, tell people to touch each other, bring their heads toward each other, or put their arms around each other, as shown in Figure 17-10.

✔ **Designate the location.**

✔ **Arrange people around props, such as trees or cars.**

✔ **Use a variety of poses.** Have some people sit and others stand.

IT Stock Free

Figure 17-10: Provide direction to the people you're photographing while also trying to capture their personalities.

✔ **If you're dealing with a large group of people, rambunctious kids, or excited pets, get someone to help direct.** Just make sure that the parties being photographed pay attention and look at the camera.

✔ **Try to get people to relax.** Although spontaneity can yield great images, you can still get good photos from posed subjects if they aren't hating the experience.

Consider Direction of Movement

When the subject is capable of movement, such as a car, person, or animal, make sure that you leave more space in front of the subject than behind it, as shown in Figure 17-11. Otherwise, the viewer may subconsciously experience a feeling of departure or discomfort. You want to try to give the person or object room to move into the frame. Likewise, if a person is looking out onto a vista, make sure that you include that vista so that the person is given a point of view and the scene is given context.

Brand X Pictures

Figure 17-11: Always include room for your subject to move into the frame.

18

Ten More Project Ideas

*Y*ou posted all your holiday and vacation photos in an online gallery and made enough photo books, slide shows, flipbooks, and greeting cards to keep your family and friends content for months to come? Sounds like you may be ready to take a crack at some other projects. In this chapter, you find ideas for using your inventory of digital images to make your life more productive, more organized, and more fun. This chapter just scratches the surface. With a little imagination, before you know it, there won't be anything left in your life that doesn't include your photos.

Wallpaper and Screen Savers

If you like an image so much that you want to gaze at it while you're toiling away at your computer, why not use that image for the background of your computer, better known as the *desktop wallpaper?* If you can't choose just one favorite image, you can use several to create a multi-image screen saver.

If you're serious about image editing, you really should have a neutral gray background. But as long as your wallpaper isn't showing while you do your color corrections, feel free to decorate your desktop with your favorite colorful photo. Follow these two easy steps to turn a photo into wallpaper:

1. **From the Organizer, select the photo you want to use.**

2. **Choose Edit➪Set as Desktop Wallpaper.**

   That's all there is to it! Your photo has now been transformed into desktop wallpaper.

If you have two or more photos you want to use, you can create a Windows screen saver. Follow these steps in Windows 7:

1. **Select the desired photos from the Organizer.**

2. **Choose File➪Export As New File(s). In the Export New Files dialog box that appears, choose JPEG as the file type.**

3. **Select your photo size and choose a quality setting, as shown in Figure 18-1.**

   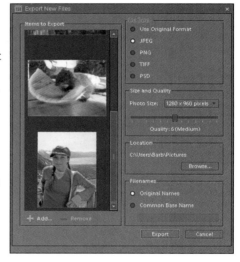

   We recommend using a size that matches the resolution setting you're using for your monitor. Use a quality setting of 12 for maximum quality.

4. **Click the Browse button.**

5. **Click the Make New Folder button, save the photos as JPEGs to that folder, and name the folder something appropriate, such as _Screen Saver._ Click OK.**

6. **Choose whether to use the original names of your files or a common base name, such as screen 1, screen 2, and so on.**

   Figure 18-1: Specify your screen saver photo size and quality.

7. **Click Export.**

   If all goes well, Elements informs you that it has executed the command.

8. **Click OK.**

9. **In Windows 7, choose Start➪Control Panel.**

10. **Click Appearance and Personalization in the Control Panel window. Under Personalization, click Change Desktop Theme. Then, click Screen Saver in the bottom-right corner.**

11. **In the Screen Saver Settings window, choose Photos from the Screen Saver drop-down list. Click Settings.**

12. In the Photos Screen Saver Settings window, select Use Pictures and Videos From. Click Browse and navigate to the folder containing your desired images.

13. Click OK and Save.

14. Specify your other options, such as wait time, power settings, and so on.

15. Click Apply and then OK to close the window. Close the Control Panel window as well.

Mac users can create custom screen savers even more easily:

1. Choose System Preferences from the Apple menu.

2. Click Desktop & Screen Saver and then click the Screen Saver tab.

3. The list of possible screen savers is on the left. To choose one of your photos, click the plus sign and choose Add Folder of Pictures. Locate the folder with your images and choose your desired image(s).

4. Specify your options, such as Display Style, if you want the clock to show with the screen saver. Click the Options button for even more options, such as cross fading between slides.

5. Click Test to see a preview. If you're happy, click the Close button in the top left.

Flyers, Ads, and Online Auctions

Everyone knows that a picture is worth a thousand words. Whether you're selling puppies or advertising an open house, adding a photo to an ad or flyer really helps to drive home your message.

Here are the abbreviated steps to quickly create an ad or flyer:

1. In Edit Full mode, choose File➪New➪Blank File.

2. In the New dialog box, enter your desired document specifications and then click OK.

   Note that you can choose a preset size, such as U.S. Paper, from the Preset drop-down menu.

We recommend entering the final dimensions and resolution for your desired output. If you want to print your ad or flyer on your desktop printer or at a service bureau, a good guideline for resolution is 300 pixels per inch (ppi). For more on resolution and sizing images, be sure to check out Chapter 3. Leave the color mode as RGB and the Background Contents as White.

If you want to fill your background with color, as we did in Figure 18-2, choose Edit⇨Fill Layer and choose Color from the Contents pop-up menu. Choose your desired color in the Color Picker and then click OK.

3. **Open your photos and then drag and drop them onto your new canvas with the Move tool. Make sure to choose Window⇨Images⇨Cascade to view all your canvases at the same time.**

Your image is automatically put on a separate layer. For more on layers, see Chapter 8. If you want to use only a portion of the image, as we did with the puppy in Figure 18-2, use your favorite selection method to pluck out your element. For more on selections, see Chapter 7.

PhotoDisc, Inc./Getty Images

Figure 18-2: Quickly put together ads and flyers.

4. **Select the Type tool, click the canvas, add your desired text, and then position your type with the Move tool.**

Note that your type will also reside on its own layer.

5. **When you're done, choose File⇨Save.**

6. **Name your file and choose Photoshop (.PSD) from the Format drop-down menu and make sure that the Layers and Color check boxes are selected.**

If you want to take your document to a service bureau or copy shop, such as FedEx Kinko's, you should save your document as a Photoshop PDF (.pdf) file. That way, you don't have to worry about fonts, compatibility issues, or printing snafus.

7. **If you want to save a copy of your ad or flyer in the Organizer, select the Include in Elements Organizer check box. In addition, select Layers, ICC Profile (Embed Color Profile on the Mac), and Use Lower Case Extension (Windows only) options.**

8. **Click Save.**

If you're preparing photos for online auction sites, such as eBay or Yahoo! Auctions, keep your images at a low resolution — 72 ppi, to be exact — and at 100-percent scale. Save the file as a JPEG to ensure that your file stays lean and mean while preserving colors. Be sure to check the image specifications posted on your online auction site.

Clothes, Hats, and More

Many local copy shops, retail stores, and Web sites (such as Zazzle.com or Cafepress.com) enable you to add photos to T-shirts, hats, tennis shoes, tote bags, ties, mouse pads, and many other items. If you can produce it, they can put a photo on it. But it's easy, and less expensive, to tackle this project yourself.

Buy plain white T-shirts at your local discount store or plain aprons and tote bags at a craft or fabric store. Then, buy special transfer paper at your office supply or computer store. Print your photos on the transfer paper (be sure to flip the images horizontally first), iron the print onto the fabric, and you've got yourself a personalized gift for very little cash.

What do you get for the person who has everything? How about a blanket of memories? You can transfer photos onto patches of fabric and create unique memory quilts. What grandmother wouldn't love to have a quilt with photos of her children and grandchildren?

 Costco, the bastion of everything from A to Z, now sells 54 x 70 inch woven photo blankets for a mere $60, as well as hardback photo books, mugs, calendars, and other ephemera.

Posters

For special events, important announcements, or maybe just your favorite family photos, you can get posters and large-size prints at many copy shops and service bureaus. Call and talk to a knowledgeable rep so you know exactly how to prepare your file. Here are a few questions to ask:

- What file format and resolution should the file be?
- What print sizes do you offer?
- Do you provide mounting and lamination services?

In addition to printing large prints, many service bureaus mount prints on foam core or the sturdier *gator board.* These service bureaus also can laminate prints to protect them from scratches and UV rays.

Again, at Costco, 20 x 30 inch posters sell for $10, while 20 x 24 inch prints on canvas (think wedding gift) sell for around $70.

Household and Business Inventories

Don't wait for a natural disaster or theft to motivate you to prepare an inventory of your household or business assets. Take your digital camera and shoot pictures of your items. Double-click your selected image and add text to describe the items in the caption section of the Organizer. You can also select the image and choose Edit⇨Add Caption. Be sure to include makes, models, purchase dates, and dollar values of each piece.

Then, create a single PDF document from those multiple files by creating a slide show, as shown in Figure 18-3. Chapter 15 explains how to create the slide show PDF.

After the PDF is finished, you can upload the PDF file to a Web storage site, such as www. barracudanetworks. com or www.mediafire. com, or burn a CD or DVD and place it off site in a safety deposit box or other secure location. If the need arises, your insurance agent can view the PDF by using the free Adobe Reader software. For more on outputting to slide shows and writing to CD and DVD, see Chapter 15.

Camera Lenses Purchased 10-08
SN 1246329

PhotoSpin

Figure 18-3: Create an inventory of your assets.

Project Documentation

Nothing helps to document a process like images. The spoken word and the written word are great, but showing how something comes together is even more effective. Consider using your photographs to help document your projects from beginning to end. Whether it's a project involving home improvement, furniture building, crafts, or cooking, take photos at each stage to record the project. If you're taking a class or workshop and the instructors don't mind, take your camera to class. Documenting the positions or steps of that new yoga, pottery, or gardening class can help you practice or re-create it on your own later, either for yourself or to explain to someone else.

Import your desired photos into the Organizer and create notes on each step of the project in the caption area. You can also insert text on the image itself by using the Type tool in the Editor. Output the images to a PDF (described in Chapter 15), as shown in Figure 18-4.

Step 5

Garnish with bell, ivy, ribbon and fresh flowers.

PhotoDisc, Inc./Getty Images

Not into killing trees? Not to worry. You don't have to print every project you make. Any file you create can be left as a purely digital file and e-mailed to other users. For details on sharing files, see Chapter 16.

Figure 18-4: Document your favorite projects for easier re-creation later.

School Reports and Projects

There's nothing like some interesting photos to jazz up the obligatory school report. Doing a botany report? Include some close-ups of a flower with text labels on the parts of the flower. Have to write a paper on the habits of the lemurs of Madagascar? Trek down to your local zoo and have a photo shoot. Create a simple collage of lemurs eating, sleeping, and doing the other things that lemurs do.

You can use the PhotoCollage command on the Create panel. (See details about this command in Chapter 16.) Or you can create your own custom collage by making selections (see Chapter 7) and dragging and dropping them onto a blank canvas. In fact, buying your children their own inexpensive point-and-shoot cameras may give them a little more enthusiasm for school work.

Create a Blog

If you haven't take the blog plunge yet, what are you waiting for? We know people who have created blogs not only about themselves, but about their newborn babies, as well as the family dog! Now that you have the software to polish up your images, creating a simple blog is a great way to share not only your latest and greatest photos (which you can do on sites like Flickr, SmugMug, and Kodak Easy Share Gallery), but also recent *news* about family and friends. A great way to get started with blogging is to create it around a vacation. Rather than sending postcards, create blog entries about your trip and share them with your personal network. Some great blog sites are Google's `http://blogger.com`, `http://wordpress.com`, `http://livejournal.com`, `http://squarespace.com`, `http://blogsome.com`, and Microsoft's Spaces at `http://home.spaces.live.com`.

Wait — There's More

Before you start taking your photos to the next dimension, here are a few extra ideas: Make fun place cards for dinner party guests; create your own business cards or letterhead if you need only a few; design your own bookmarks, bookplates, and notepads; or label storage boxes with photos of their contents. Check out `www.kodak.com` for a slew of projects, such as party kits (from invites to gift tags), kids' mobiles and door hangers, photo recipe cards, and magnets. The possibilities are endless.

Index

• E •

• *S* •